# The Public Career of Cully A. Cobb

Cully A. Cobb in 1973, at age 89.

# The Public Career of
# CULLY A. COBB

A STUDY IN AGRICULTURAL LEADERSHIP

ROY V. SCOTT
and
J. G. SHOALMIRE

UNIVERSITY AND COLLEGE PRESS OF MISSISSIPPI

JACKSON

ISBN 0–87805–020–5
Library of Congress Catalog Card Number: 72–76850
Copyright © 1973 by
University and College Press of Mississippi
Manufactured in the United States of America

*Designed by J. Barney McKee*

# Contents

# Preface

WE first came into contact with the subject of this brief study several years ago during one of his periodic visits to our campus. After talking with Cully A. Cobb at some length, we decided that his career, touching as it did so many aspects of twentieth century agricultural history, warranted examination and that it was a suitable topic for a doctoral dissertation. When the student who was assigned the task failed to make satisfactory progress, we resolved to complete the project ourselves. This book is the result.

Since we have concerned ourselves primarily with Cobb's career in agriculture, we have given only brief attention to his activities after 1937 and to his personal life. Nor have we tried to write a history of the Cotton Section of the Agricultural Adjustment Administration, although there is considerable justification for such a study. The reasons for these self-imposed limitations would seem to be obvious. The focus of the book is on agricultural leadership in a period of dramatic change, a topic which we hope is illuminated by an examination of the activities of one individual.

In writing this study, we have incurred all of the debts common to authors. Heading the list of those who made substantial contributions are the subject of the book and his wife, Lois Dowdle Cobb. Both were unsparing of their time and energy in helping us locate information. In no case did they exercise any control over our writing; our judgments are ours alone. A special note of gratitude is owed to two of Cobb's long-time associates, Wofford B. (Bill) Camp of Bakersfield, California, and H. H. Williamson of Bryan, Texas. Camp, Cobb's closest associate in Washington, is an extensive and successful farmer and one of the nation's more influential citizens. Williamson is an elder statesman of agricultural extension. Both of them invited us into their homes and granted lengthy interviews. Several members of the administrative staff at Mississippi State University gave us all the support we could have wanted. Professor John K. Bettersworth, Academic Vice-President, and Lyle C. Behr, Dean of the College of Arts and Sciences, made outstanding efforts to satisfy our research needs. Professors Harold S. Snellgrove and Glover Moore of the Department of History read all or parts of the manuscript and made valuable suggestions.

Librarians at Mississippi State University, the University of North Carolina, the National Archives, Hyde Park, and the University of Iowa were helpful as always. Mississippi State's Judith Kirkpatrick, Marilyn Boyd, and Willie D. Halsell deserve special mention. Helen Finneran of the National Archives and Gladys Baker of the United States Department of Agriculture Library were generous with their aid and advice. Patricia Jones typed part of the manuscript. Finally, we owe a tremendous debt to Gloria Jean Cummings, a lovely and talented young lady from Mississippi's Pontotoc County who worked for us the full time that the study was in progress. As typist, note taker, and general Girl Friday, she was superb, but her greatest contribution was in her good humor and good sense which in innumerable ways lightened our burdens. We, of course, are solely responsible for any errors in fact or interpretation that may remain.

R. V. S.
J. G. S.

*Mississippi State University*
*January, 1973*

# The Public Career of Cully A. Cobb

# CHAPTER I

# Grit and Determination: The Formative Years, 1884–1908

AS he waited for the chairman to finish his introductory remarks Cully A. Cobb became anxious. He sorted through his address once again, hurriedly glancing over his first few lines. Always one who enjoyed public speaking, Cobb was now ready to begin. He had returned, thirty-three years after he first enrolled, to Mississippi State College (now Mississippi State University). In 1904 the presence of a poor and bewildered but determined Tennessee farm boy went unnoticed. Now, in 1936 as the director of the Southern Division of the Agricultural Adjustment Administration, he was the featured speaker at a conference of rural ministers.[1] *

The remarks of the chairman droned on; Cobb relaxed. As he stared pensively through the window to the campus scene, poignant memories entered his mind. The façade of the campus was changed, yet there was a spirit, an essence, prevalent now that was much the same as that which he had found on that cold February day when he had taken the first giant step and enrolled at Mississippi Agricultural and Mechanical College. In the ensuing years, this school and the many opportunities it had afforded him had had perhaps the most profound effect of any influence in the life of Cully Cobb.

Opportunity. Cobb was suddenly captivated by the word. Here at this place he had been given opportunity, many opportunities. It seemed to him that those opportunities, those chances for growth and success, had been the key to his life. Indeed, opportunity had been a dominating factor in the lives of his forebears. It must have been that chance for a better life that had driven Cobb's ancestors,

* Notes appear at end of each chapter.

3

who were landowners in England and then in Virginia, to seek a new life in the undeveloped country of Middle Tennessee. It had been a lack of opportunity for his children that had driven Cully Cobb's father to abandon a poor hill farm and move into a community which offered better educational advantages.[2] Yes, it seemed to Cobb as he sat savoring these recollections that the chance to succeed had been peculiarly important for him.

Cully Cobb had often heard his great-grandfather Beasley Cobb relate how his great-great-grandfather, Ambrose Cobb, had made the trek from Virginia to Tennessee. Ambrose had apparently felt that opportunities in Virginia had been limited. He had a wife and a growing family to support, and the prospect for improving his lot in Virginia looked bleak. A new tract of Tennessee lands opened in 1805, and this seemed to be just the chance he needed.[3]

The Cobb ancestors settled in Giles County, Tennessee. Life was hard in the new territory. The Cobbs operated small farms and apparently none of them attained material affluence. Religion was the center of their lives and probably received more of their attention than their farms. Many of them were Baptist preachers who devoted their time to the progress of churches in the area. The original Tennessee migrant, Ambrose Cobb, helped establish the first churches in Giles County.[4] His son Jesse Bradley Cobb, Cobb's grandfather, was a preacher at several churches in four states; and Jesse's son Napoleon Bonaparte Cobb, Cully's father, was a part-time preacher as well as a farmer.[5]

Napoleon Bonaparte Cobb was born near Muscle Shoals, Alabama, on July 10, 1849. He was the third child of Jesse Bradley and Judith Johnston Cobb. Like his father, Napoleon became a Baptist minister. Unlike his father, however, Napoleon lived most of his life in Giles County, Tennessee. A gentle and perhaps subdued man of unswerving principles, he had little formal education and no specialized religious training. He was keenly aware, however, of the value of education and conscious of his lack of it. To compensate, Napoleon became an avid reader. He used the Bible, an assortment of books, and subscriptions to national magazines, farm journals, and major newspapers as sources of his education. He refused to limit his world to the affairs of Giles County.[6]

Napoleon Bonaparte Cobb family portrait. Front row, left to right, Napoleon Bonaparte Cobb, Mary Agnes Woodward Cobb, Mary A. Cobb, the youngest daughter. Top row, left to right, Cully A. Cobb, aged twelve, Jesse M. Cobb, the oldest of the Cobb children, and his wife. The two small children are Jesse Cobb's sons.

On February 2, 1872, Napoleon Bonaparte Cobb married Mary Agnes Woodward, his second cousin. The young couple endured many difficulties during the early years of marriage. Preventive medicine was unknown, and only one of their first five children lived to maturity. The pastorates which Napoleon served boasted of good solid people but were generally so poor that financial rewards were few. Because of a deep religious faith, these hardships served only to strengthen and mature the young couple, endearing them more to each other.[7]

Napoleon and Mary Cobb's sixth child, Cully Alton Cobb, was

born in a small log cabin on his grandfather's farm near Prospect, Tennessee, on February 25, 1884. The boy grew up at Chambers Mill on Richland Creek, the family having moved there in 1886. Their farm was a poor one; the land was not suitable for efficient grain farming, and the property was too small for livestock raising. To supplement his meager income from his farm and from the ministry, Napoleon Cobb dealt in livestock. He freely admitted that he often used his time to help his neighbors rather than work his own property. As a result, the family's financial status was poor, even by the standards of that time and place, but in the opinion of the father matters could not be otherwise.[8]

As a youngster living on his father's small farm, Cully was assigned his share of chores. He helped tend the livestock, worked in the fields, and assisted with the general farm work. When the necessary chores on the Cobb farm were completed and work was temporarily finished, the youngster labored for wages on neighbors' farms. More often than not, the small income Cully Cobb earned from these jobs was contributed to the assets of the family. This early work developed in him a sense of satisfaction from working with his hands. He also came to appreciate the fact that no task that contributed to the general welfare of people should be considered demeaning and that the individual who performed any such jobs should be respected for his labor and his contribution, no matter how small.

Cobb's relationship with his parents was one of quiet and reserved respect, admiration, and love. His father tried to impress upon the boy the value of a life based on never-yielding principles such as honesty, fairness, and consideration for others. Later, Cobb was to recall how he had commanded the respect of his most scrutinizing critics, his neighbors.[9]

Mary Agnes Woodward Cobb was a warm, good-humored, and level-headed woman who expected much from her children. Her manner, like that of her husband, was quiet and gracious. She encouraged her children to excel at whatever they did. While she was always there to counsel and comfort after small failures, she made certain that the children understood that they bore the responsibility for their own mistakes and shortcomings.

Mary Cobb was a proud woman—proud of her ancestry, her husband and his profession, her friends, and even the family farm. But like many frontier mothers, Mary Cobb's children were the real source of her energy and vitality. Although she accepted the financial hardships of Napoleon's ministry, Mary Cobb was especially pleased when her children used their initiative and talents to experiment in business. She was immeasurably pleased when Cully sold a large consignment of bluing in the neighborhood and received a pocket watch for his effort. Later, she was touched in a special way when Cully sold a shipment of tea, spice, and soap and presented his mother with a number of household items, including a set of English bone china.

By the time young Cully was of high school age, Napoleon Cobb, being especially sensitive about the education of his children because of his own limitations in this area, decided to move from the Chambers Mill community. Aside from the economic limitation of this area, the community also lacked high school facilities. After carefully evaluating the neighboring towns, their schools, and his own financial situation, Napoleon Cobb gave up farming and moved his family to the small town of Elkton. He took a house in the town, held preaching positions at several churches near Elkton, and continued his business of selling livestock.

In 1895 Elkton was a busy little town of three hundred. Located on the Elk River in southeast Giles County, the town depended upon local agriculture and the Pulaski Turnpike, a regional highway, for its business.[10] The high school at Elkton was its greatest asset in the mind of Napoleon Cobb. The school had good teachers, including some who had college training, a rarity in rural Tennessee during the period. In addition to good physical facilities, the school had a fine baseball team, an asset of interest to young Cully Cobb in particular.

Cully Cobb soon found that he must adjust to his new surroundings. He was accustomed to the freedom of the open country and freshness of the farm; the activity of town life was completely different. The most difficult adjustment, and one Cobb was never able to make completely, was adapting to the town's social structure and what he considered the lack of incentive among its citizens.

Other members of the Cobb family experienced some degree of rejection, though they may have felt it less than young Cully. Napoleon Cobb was able to break some of the barriers because of his religious work. His reputation for honor and fairness soon gave the residents little choice but to accept him. Within a short time he was given nominal acceptance in the local social structure.

Cully Cobb quickly learned that as the son of a poor back-country preacher he was not totally accepted by his new associates. Many of the young people his age in Elkton were the children of local merchants and doctors who saw themselves as civilized and genteel and who felt that Cobb's open and honest nature was proof of his being a country bumpkin. Having worked closely with Negroes, Cobb accepted them as fellow laborers and was friendly toward them. The young people of Elkton were open in their discrimination against the Negro and criticized Cobb for his views.

Probably the greatest source of friction between Cobb and his peers in Elkton was their differences concerning life goals. Admittedly, Cobb had not yet experienced life outside Giles County, and he had no idea where his future might lie. Nonetheless, he was grimly determined to set his goals high and to become successful. It greatly disturbed him that the young people of Elkton were quite content to remain there and take life as it came, with no concern for the future and little incentive to change and improve and with no discoverable ambition. His awakening to and awareness of these differences provided Cobb with a lifelong drive.

Cully found one means to improve his social standing—baseball. A robust lad with exceptional physical strength, above average in height, Cully had little trouble making the school team. An eager player, he quickly became the outstanding pitcher. Since the Elkton community was enthusiastic about the team, its winning record scored in Cobb's favor in his struggle for acceptance.

In spite of his partial acceptance by his classmates, young Cobb's disenchantment with Elkton grew. A closer relationship with the other young people served only to emphasize to Cobb that his own future certainly lay beyond the boundaries of Giles County. His dissatisfaction and frustration led to disgust, which in turn led him to feel that the school work that had once offered such a challenge

8

Elkton, Tennessee, baseball team, c. 1900. Cobb, who pitched for the team, is seated in the front at the far left.

was now elementary and limited. A feeling persisted that he should break away and search beyond, but at that time he was not sure how to sever the ties with the family and the town. Napoleon Cobb, himself so aware of Elkton's limitations and of his son's impatience, could do little more than encourage the boy to persevere and not to compromise his ambitions.

Cobb finally found counsel with one of his teachers, M. L. Caneer. Caneer was not a typical country schoolteacher. A product of Peabody College in Nashville, he had been exposed to a more varied life than Elkton offered. When young Cobb's dilemma was brought to his attention, Caneer offered the straightforward advice that was needed. He told Cobb to break, suddenly and completely, away from Elkton; he advised that he find a relative, a friend, anyone who would take him in and then leave Elkton. With this advice went a warning: if he were to leave his home for good, if he planned to follow the dream of success, vague and nebulous as it was at this time, he would have to receive an education.

Caneer's direct suggestions seemed to be the only push Cobb

needed to take his first steps. He easily persuaded his parents that he should leave school since he had already outgrown it. Convincing them that he should be allowed to leave home required more effort. He seemed too young, too inexperienced, to be away from the guidance and security of his parents. However, he convinced them that he could never know fulfillment until he made an effort to find his future, that the experience would be of much benefit to him, and that he wanted their approval and sanction to leave. The Reverend and Mrs. Cobb suggested that Cully contact his half-uncle, Marcellus Woodward, in Decatur, Alabama.[11] Marcellus Edward Woodward was a family enigma. He had moved from Giles County to Decatur in the early 1890s. Woodward was a warm-hearted man who often asked his kinsmen to visit him in Alabama. Not many came. Living apart from the tightly knit religious clan, Woodward became involved in a saloon business—an obvious rejection of his background. Napoleon Cobb must have felt confident that his son's early religious training would serve him in good stead and that perhaps a firsthand experience with alcohol would help mature him.

After he had made the decision to go to Decatur, Cobb's immediate concern became the money needed for transportation to Alabama and for a small emergency reserve. Some months earlier Cobb had noticed that one of the local builders in Elkton, Alex Austin, was in the process of wrecking an old store building, salvaging the materials for later use. One of the most time-consuming tasks involved cleaning mortar from the old bricks. Cully studied the project and, after making agreements with several small Negro boys, persuaded Austin to give him a contract for cleaning the bricks. Austin agreed and the work commenced. Cobb's net income amounted to about one dollar a day. Upon completion of the job, Cobb invested his profits in pigs, hoping to feed and sell them as his father often did. The profits from the sale of the pigs provided Cobb with enough money to buy his railroad ticket to Decatur, with a few dollars left over for other expenses.[12]

Cobb moved to Alabama in late summer of 1902. With enthusiasm and perhaps a little naivete, the young adventurer set out to find a job. He was determined to be self-supporting as soon as possible. He learned that Decatur, a small town that drew its economic blood from the Tennessee River and the Louisville and Nashville Railroad, had many of the employment problems that he had seen in Elkton.[13] Cobb accepted the situation as merely another challenge. Within a few days he had secured a job as cook at the Brown Hotel for ten dollars a month, with room and board, despite the fact that he had no training or experience for such work. It just seemed natural for him to seize what opportunity he could find, observe closely, and do the best he could.

The job at the hotel left little free time, but Cobb tried to make good use of what he did have. He attended a local church and was soon an accepted member of the young peoples' Sunday School group. He became acquainted with several of the young bank clerks in town and spent many of his leisure hours with them. He played the guitar with a small group which played for its own entertainment. Perhaps seeking more assurance that he was truly independent, Cully Cobb began to smoke. He became a popular spectator at the traditional center of small southern towns—the "spit and whittle" group at the local store.

In the middle of what was obviously a busy schedule, Cobb found time to contemplate his future and the life about him. He never completely understood why his uncle engaged in a business that involved alcohol. Eventually, however, he came to accept alcohol as a problem beyond his ability to solve. He never used intoxicants himself and believed in prohibition; but in Decatur, Cobb found that he could accept life as it was, rather than as he would have it.

Of more concern was his life's work. The hotel business did not interest him, nor was a well-regarded men's clothing store which his uncle had bought after leaving the saloon business any more appealing. The financial aspect of any business aroused some interest, but he discovered that the outlook of his bank clerk friends was appallingly narrow. Although largely uninformed of the difficulties involved, Cobb set his goal on the medical profession.

The serenity of the Tennessee River created an atmosphere for such contemplation on long Sunday afternoon walks. Cobb reached many of his decisions in this setting. Alone he could turn his thoughts to Giles County and measure his progress against what he had set out to accomplish when he left home. Some of his decisions were affirmations of his earlier ideas. Other decisions, such as his idea to experiment with tobacco, resulted in reexamination which caused him to give up smoking.

One thought was always with him. It cropped up everywhere, on his walks, in discussions with friends, even during the sessions at the general store: he must get an education. Cobb knew how his poorly educated father had seeded and nurtured that idea in his mind. His mother had reinforced it, and Caneer had proven its value to him. Cobb also knew that he was floundering in his crude attempts to achieve formal education. He was obtaining valuable experience in Decatur, but this was not an education. The Decatur public schools were little better than those of Elkton; thus there was little reason to complete his high school training there. Since the town did have a small business school, Cobb decided to try it. This, too, was a disappointment; and after his short experience there, Cobb was more certain than ever that he must begin a college education as soon as possible.

After reaching the decision that going to college was his immediate goal, the young man's next step was to select the college he would attend. His contact with the University of Tennessee was limited, but he had no desire to go there. He knew that Tulane University had a fine medical school, but he soon learned that the expenses at Tulane were extremely high. He gained what information he could concerning the state colleges and other medical schools in the South, but the data seemed merely to add to his bewilderment.

The topic of Cully Cobb's college education and his plans for the future were discussed many times at sessions around the pot-bellied stove in E. B. Ferris' grocery store where Cully worked for a short time. Cobb was popular with the men there and he wanted their views on his problem. They enthusiastically encouraged him to get an education. None of this group had college training, but they all saw it as the best means to improve one's situation.

During one cold December evening, the question arose as to which school was best suited for Cobb. Most of the men had a favorite school and they each urged him to go there. Cobb told them that he was giving serious consideration to the agricultural college at Auburn, Alabama. His uncle had advised him to look into that possibility before making a final decision. All but Ferris agreed that this would be a good choice. Ferris reminded Cobb that his son, E. B. Ferris, Jr., had graduated from Mississippi Agricultural and Mechanical College and had supported himself for the entire four years through work on the campus. Ferris pointed out to Cobb that for his particular situation, with no financial support coming from his family, the Mississippi college might be his best choice.[14] This was what Cobb wanted to hear. Mississippi Agricultural and Mechanical College was a school that would give a poor boy a chance.

In 1904 Mississippi Agricultural and Mechanical College was entering the second era of its history. Founded in 1878 with the ex-Confederate general, Stephen D. Lee, as the first president, the school began a struggle to achieve a respectable reputation in the South. Lee had personally pulled the institution through a most trying period, succeeding remarkably. Always a soft-spoken moderate who was willing to compromise with a reluctant legislature, the first president had developed public faith and confidence in the school. He made every effort to make the school serve the needs of the people, to make it become the "People's College." [15]

Within a year after Lee's retirement, a second exceptional educator, John C. Hardy, was named president. Hardy was young, vigorous, and controversial. He assumed the position with the conviction that he should seize the principles of Lee's earlier work and faithfully push on as fast as possible. Hardy's administration began in 1900 and ended when he was appointed president of Mary Hardin-Baylor College in 1912.[16] During his twelve years at Mississippi Agricultural and Mechanical College Hardy was directly responsible for major changes. The physical plant almost tripled. Enrollment increased from three hundred to twelve hundred, an increase that may be credited to Hardy's active recruiting of students and his concern for the school's public image.[17] Hardy expanded the original curriculum and substantially enlarged the faculty. He spent much time meeting with the state legislature in Jackson, pleading and pushing for more funds. In addition to adding new physical facilities, Hardy, a devout Baptist, was determined to use his position to enrich the spiritual life of his charges. He generally gave the morning devotional at the early chapel service on campus, and he required that all students attend. At the chapel services and in most of his speeches to the student body Hardy constantly emphasized religion and a belief in God as essential to success. Although he made a sincere effort to be fair and unbiased in dealing with the students, Hardy had little patience with those who were negligent in their religious activities. He was a dynamic administrator, one capable of drawing enthusiasm or provoking bitter criticism with his hard-sell tactics. According to his public supporters he was an educator who strived to make the school serve

Buildings on the campus of Mississippi Agricultural and Mechanical College, c. 1904. Above, from left to right, Science Hall (later Montgomery Hall), Old Main Dormitory, Chapel, Chemistry Building. Below, Textile Building.

the people's needs. His critics claimed, however, that Hardy was only interested in enhancing his own reputation and that he probably had political aspirations. The students considered him friendly, ardently defensive of the school, and progressive. On matters of discipline, Hardy was tough but fair. Perhaps his most controversial characteristic was his absolute loyalty to his principles. The students felt that after Hardy had reduced an issue to a stand on principle, his mind simply could not be changed, regardless of the consequences.[18]

Cully Cobb arrived in Starkville, Mississippi, on Saturday, February 6, 1904. He had $2.10 in his pocket and a vague idea that he wanted to become a medical doctor. He did not know anyone associated with the school or anything about the courses the institution offered. Indeed, all he knew was that Mississippi Agricultural and Mechanical College offered courses in agriculture and provided some form of work assistance for poor boys. Although he had asked E. B. Ferris to write a letter of recommendation for him, Cobb had not informed the college officials of his intentions to enroll immediately and had no idea of the proper enrollment procedure. The situation might have bewildered a less resourceful youth. Whether blinded by youthful idealism or possessed by supreme confidence, Cobb was not discouraged. He found an inexpensive room in Starkville and began to explore his new surroundings.[19]

As he walked about Starkville, Cobb decided on a course of action: he would seek the advice of the local Baptist minister. He attended the First Baptist Church on Sunday morning and approached the minister, Dr. Duke Thornton, after the services. Cobb explained his situation to Thornton. Obviously impressed with the boy's resourcefulness and confidence, the minister advised Cobb to go to the college on Monday morning and talk with Professor W. H. Magruder, the vice-president. Thornton instructed Cobb to follow the tracks of the Mobile and Ohio Railroad to the college, which was located about two miles southeast of town. Professor Magruder's home was one of the first houses on the campus.

Cobb had seen the college as his train approached Starkville. He was impressed by the pastoral setting. As he walked onto the campus Monday morning he was immediately aware of the size of the school. It was the largest institution he had ever seen. There was a large classroom building, a dormitory, a large combination chapel-classroom building, and a chemistry building. In addition, the college had recently added a textile building and a dairy building on the edge of the campus. These, with a large number of outlying agricultural structures, made a great impression on the prospective student.

Cobb found Magruder, the senior member of the faculty, and told the elderly gentleman of his situation. Magruder listened patiently as Cobb explained that he had no money and no support from home but that he had a burning desire to obtain a college education. The professor questioned Cobb concerning his high school training and his prospective major. Magruder was surprised that a boy who had not finished high school and who had not selected an area of study would be interested in attending college. He sympathized with Cobb's plans but warned him that his introduction to the school was quite unorthodox. This was not the ideal time of the year to enter school, and the fact that Cobb did not know this indicated something of his general lack of awareness of colleges in general. Nonetheless, Magruder tentatively accepted Cobb as one of the working students until a more definite arrangement could be determined.

Magruder told Cobb that he could sleep for the present in the Kline home, an abandoned house located in the college pasture. The old structure served as a barn for the livestock and the upstairs as a dormitory for the working boys. Magruder, a stern, no-nonsense administrator, told Cobb that he frankly doubted that he could take the rigors of such an environment.[20]

Magruder's remarks touched a sensitive spot. Cobb took the professor's tough warning as a challenge. As he walked toward the Kline house, he made up his mind that he would make it. This might be his only chance, and he could not afford to let it slip away.

The next morning Cobb was put to work with the other working boys clearing away brush and weeds in the pastures. Cobb knew that he must prove himself here. He went at his task with a spirit. His farm experience in Tennessee and his belief in honest work served him well.

The freshman class at Mississippi Agricultural and Mechanical College, 1904. Cobb is in the sixth row from the front, fourth from the left.

Cobb's enthusiasm was not unnoticed. After being on campus a week, he was called to the office of President Hardy. The president had seen favorable reports of his work and had investigated his background. He gave Cobb a rather thorough oral examination to establish the depth of his scholastic training and quizzed him regarding his goals and personal life. Apparently satisfied with his findings, Hardy assigned Cobb to a job with the Horticulture Department under Dr. A. B. McKay. Cobb was to be the foreman of the working boys in the department and would receive ten cents per hour for his labor.[21]

Of all the programs Hardy pushed, he seemed particularly proud of his efforts to keep the school within the reach of students of meager means. General Lee had made this one of his primary goals and Hardy vigorously continued the work. No tuition was required of these students, and necessary expenditures, including meals and laundry, were kept at a minimum, easily within the reach of working boys. Expenses for books, matriculation, laundry, and other items were generally less than a hundred dollars per year. For those boys who could not raise that small sum, the school offered the Practical Working Boys' Course. This made it possible for a boy to come to school, and "without a dollar and by grit and determination finally get an education." [22] Boys who entered school in this manner were considered only prospective students until they proved their ability. They were employed on the school farm every day and given classes in the evenings. Since most students in the course had come from rural areas with poor schools, their evening classes were usually refresher courses in high school subjects. Once the student had proved that he could master the combined work load of classes and labor in the fields, he was enrolled fulltime and given a campus job. If the student was willing to sacrifice, he could cut the financial burden on his parents to a bare minimum.[23]

For the present, Cobb was enrolled in the Preparatory Department in order to fulfill the academic requirements for full admission as a freshman in September. He attended evening classes after each day's work in the Horticulture Department. Since Mississippi students were given priority in assignment to the Old Main dormitory, Cobb was temporarily given quarters in the horticulture greenhouse. The privacy and convenience of the greenhouse were so satisfactory that Cobb remained there until his graduation.

From the beginning, Cobb assumed responsibility for the task at hand. He was diligent and cooperative under all conditions. Because of his poor educational background and the work load of his campus jobs, Cobb was never an outstanding scholar. Indeed, he had trouble with his studies. But conquering troubles had become ordinary for the young man. If the school work required additional time, Cobb was willing to put forth the effort. Consequently, though he struggled at times there was never any doubt in his mind, at least, that he would graduate in the shortest possible time.

The faculty of Mississippi Agricultural and Mechanical College was small but not without some distinction. Cully Cobb came to know three of his professors better than most students. They were W. H. Magruder, the vice-president of the college and professor of English whom Cobb had met on his first day on campus; Dr. W. F. Hand, professor of chemistry; and A. B. McKay of the Horticulture Department. Cobb worked directly under McKay's supervision during the four and a half years he was at the college. Cobb thought McKay was an understanding employer and a good teacher. Professor Hand had already become an institution at the school by 1904. He was a perfectionist who expected as much from students in his chemistry classes. A Chesterfield in manner and appearance, Hand had a reputation for making life difficult for the students. Cobb was no exception; he worked hard for his marks under Hand.[24] Magruder was Cobb's favorite professor. An elderly gentleman, Magruder was deliberate and often dramatic, constantly lacing his lectures with scripture and references to the Almighty. Like most great teachers, Magruder tried to instill in his students as many lessons in life as in English literature.[25]

The quarters in the greenhouse were ideal for Cobb. The building was convenient to his work with the Horticulture Department and it afforded Cobb a good deal of time alone. Cobb was older than most of the other students and he was aware of the differences between them and himself. Alone in the greenhouse Cobb had time to indulge in self-examination and appraisal. His goals had been set so high that he had constantly to remind himself of where he was going.

Cobb took seriously his responsibilities to the Horticulture Department. Living in the greenhouse allowed him to study his work closely. Cobb often transplanted plants late into the night. On at least one occasion most of the college's young tomato plants were saved because Cobb literally slept with them. During one bitterly cold night a malfunction in one of the heating flues caused a rapid loss of heat in the hot houses. Cobb knew that there was no time to awaken anyone. The plants would be dead in a short time. He quickly reasoned that the beds themselves held enough heat to save the plants if he could contain it. Working feverishly, he covered the plants with heavy canvases, then set up a regular schedule to check the plants for the first signs of wilt.

Professor C. T. Ames, the superintendent of the greenhouse, was also concerned about the young plants that night. Aware of the falling temperatures and their possible effect, Professor Ames came to check the situation. He found Cobb at two o'clock in the morning, just as he finished covering the plants. At once Ames knew that the plants would survive the severe temperatures. Ames also realized that Cobb's sense of responsibility was a rarity. But he said nothing to Cobb that night. Instead, he reported the incident to President Hardy the next morning. Although Hardy later complimented Cobb for his work, Cobb did not realize the full significance of his efforts until several years later.[26]

Cobb had completely adjusted to the school, his surroundings, and his new classmates by the middle of his freshman year. He was friendly and had no trouble attracting a wide circle of associates. His novel quarters in the college greenhouse became a popular gathering place. During the cold months, Cobb and his friends treated themselves to college sweet potatoes roasted in the ashes in the greenhouse furnace. They were a typical group of college students, but most knew the importance of giving their courses the attention necessary.

At least by reputation, Mississippi Agricultural and Mechanical College was a school with more poor students enrolled than the somewhat more prestigious University of Mississippi at Oxford. Although Cobb later claimed that there was little noticeable distinction between the poor and wealthy students, there were several clubs and activities which directly or indirectly were limited to the elite. Cobb seemingly did not let such distinctions bother him. The atmosphere was so superior to that in Elkton that Cobb felt fortunate to have the change. He was friendly with the more affluent students, and they generally responded favorably. All of the students who knew Cobb were aware of his financial hardships and respected his drive to succeed. They also understood his enthusiasm for Hardy. Cobb felt obligated to the president and was often heard praising Hardy's actions.[27]

Cobb's schedule was undeniably a busy one, but he did participate in a number of activities. He was a member of the YMCA and a stalwart in the debating society. He was an enthusiastic sports fan and generally scraped up the funds to go to some of the off-campus games, especially the Mississippi A & M–Ole Miss football contest.[28]

Cobb returned to Tennessee only once during his years in college, in the summer of 1906. Quite apprehensive on this occasion, he wondered how Elkton would react to the triumphal return of the preacher's son. Would it be jealous of his success in breaking away? His misgivings were ill-founded. When he donned his crisp cadet's uniform and went into town with his father, his old friends gave him a warm welcome. Cobb was a little puzzled by the reaction. Had he misjudged these people? As he thought about it, Cobb decided that his success had left them no other choice. But it really was of no concern. The important thing was that the complacency and discrimination had made him become independent, a quality of which he was proud.[29]

In addition to the income from his designated tasks, Cobb was able to find other work and income from time to time. In fact, he quickly developed a talent for discovering and exploiting potential sources of money. For example, he sought the furniture concession authorized by the college and granted to selected students each year. Residents of the dormitory bought their room furnishings each fall and sold them as they were leaving in the spring. The furniture concession was established to meet the needs and to extend to the more enterprising students an opportunity to learn the basic fundamentals of business.

According to the arrangements of the concession four students were selected, divided into two teams, and authorized to buy and sell the furniture on the campus. On one occasion Cobb and another working student, W. G. Johnston, were selected as one of the teams. They decided to inject a new practice into the procedure. Cobb contacted a mattress firm in Meridian, Mississippi, and made arrangements to buy two boxcar loads of new mattresses, borrowing the money to finance his team's bold venture from Professor P. P. Garner of the Preparatory Department. When the shipment arrived, Cobb and Johnston sold one of the car loads to the other team for enough money to repay the loan. They were then free to sell the other load for their profits.

Perhaps Cobb's most lucrative enterprise was a soda fountain that he and his friend Johnston operated during a summer institute for teachers. Cobb and Johnston pooled their meager resources to rent equipment from local merchants in Starkville and to buy supplies from a Memphis dealer. Johnston did most of the work in the

The soda fountain at Mississippi Agricultural and Mechanical College, c. 1907. While a student at the College, Cobb developed several money making propositions. This soda fountain was one of them.

fountain since Cobb was employed fulltime by the Horticulture Department. After meeting their debts the partners divided their income according to investments of time and money. Cobb and Johnston's profits came to almost $1,500 each, a tidy profit for an undergraduate.[30]

Most campus financial ventures were controlled by the college and Cobb was granted permission to participate in them because of his close relationship with President Hardy. Cobb felt that Hardy was his friend and he worked hard to maintain that relationship. Hardy was almost Cobb's ideal; he saw Hardy as a driving, progressive man who never sacrificed his religious beliefs or backed away from a struggle. Cobb felt that the president was a man of principle and of worthwhile goals, both of which he admired.

Cobb's loyalty to Hardy was tested under fire in the student strike of 1907–1908. The strike directly involved Cobb's class and was the most serious disturbance at the school during Cobb's years there. The episode started when two apparently isolated incidents became confusingly connected in the minds of the students. Before the smoke of the incident cleared, most of the senior class had resigned and been reinstated, two staff members had been discharged, and Cobb had taken the most difficult stand in his young life—one against his colleagues and classmates and in support of his friend President Hardy.

Hardy had worried for some time that the Army officers in charge of the college military program were usurping his authority. He was particularly uneasy about Captain Ira C. Welborn, the commandant. Welborn, a Medal of Honor veteran of the Boxer Rebellion, was popular among the elite members of the student military. Members of the group spent a good deal of time at Welborn's home, listening to his tales of foreign combat and courting his attractive daughter. Apparently Welborn was critical of what he considered interference by the school officials in military affairs, and he voiced his opinions to the visiting students.[31]

A comparison of Welborn and Hardy is an interesting study. Welborn's character was classically military. He was brash and swashbuckling. He prided himself on his independence, on never yielding to the easy course. He obviously relished the thought of

Faculty at Mississippi Agricultural and Mechanical College, c. 1908. President John C. Hardy is seated in the second row, sixth from the left. Next to him, on his right, is Professor W. H. Magruder. The army officer is Captain Ira C. Welborn. On his right is Professor A. B. McKay. Peter P. Garner is seated directly above President Hardy. Professor W. P. Hand is in the second row, third from the left.

irritating Hardy. He called parades on Sunday afternoons because this practice would conflict with Hardy's religious views. He made no attempt to conceal his drinking habits, and he delighted in telling the students that the "damned missionaries" were the real cause of problems in the Far East.[32]

The Cadet Captain at the time was E. R. Blanton, the most popular student on the campus and apparently one of the frequent visitors in Welborn's home. Blanton was a perennial college politician. He was regularly elected to one of the class offices and held positions in most of the important clubs. He served on the student newspaper and on the staff of the college annual. Whether prompted by selfish motives or guided by his conscience, Blanton was always ready to listen to the complaints of his fellow students and could be counted on to point out problems to the authorities.[33]

The situation was delicately balanced and any small pressure could have tipped the scale. The initial clash came when Blanton, probably with Welborn's sanction, refused to grant permission to a fellow cadet to go into Starkville to get a perishable express package. Since Hardy was out of town, the student appealed the order to Professor Magruder. Magruder granted the request and immediately received the condemnation of Welborn and the military element. Upon his return, Hardy supported Magruder's decision and suspended Blanton for overstepping his authority. Welborn protested the suspension, and when he refused to accept the president's view Hardy dismissed him. As one event began triggering another Dr. L. W. Crigler, the college physician, sided with Welborn. Without so much as a hearing, Hardy fired the doctor.[34]

Hardy was clearly within his rights to suspend Blanton although he had allowed a student's problem to become involved in what was essentially a staff conflict. However, the reason for Blanton's suspension became muddled by the campus grapevine. The students came to believe that Blanton's sentence had been imposed on him because of his involvement in a student petition concerning the quality of food served in the mess hall. Since several students had signed the petition, Blanton's classmates were angered that he should be singled out for punishment. Hardy refused to clarify the real issues and Blanton naturally did nothing to avoid what appeared to be instant martyrdom.[35]

In a rapid series of events the students began venting their grievances. Rallying behind Blanton, they demanded that he be reinstated. Hardy finally agreed to meet with the senior students the day before the Christmas holidays began. At the meeting Hardy avoided the Blanton case as much as possible and attempted to pacify the malcontents by assuring the students that the food situation would improve.[36] Hardy was counting heavily on the holidays serving as a cooling off period.

The students were not in a forgive-and-forget mood when they returned in January. Before leaving the campus for the holidays they had vowed to resign unless Blanton was allowed to return. Many of the students were so certain that Hardy would continue his hard line that they did not return to the college at all. Those who did made sure that Hardy understood their determination. The senior class called a meeting on January 10, 1908, to voice their complaints.[37] They decided to go directly to Hardy with an ultimatum—if Blanton was not reinstated the class would resign as a unit.

Harold McGeorge and Ernest C. McInnis were elected to call on Hardy. McGeorge was a member of an old and distinguished Columbus, Mississippi, family and was the star quarterback on the football team.[38] He and Hardy were on friendly terms despite the fact that McGeorge was a close member of Welborn's group. Still thinking that Hardy had based the suspension on the food petition, McGeorge and McInnis prepared evidence proving the charges of poor food service.[39]

McGeorge and McInnis felt they would have a fruitful meeting with Hardy. They were confident that their complaint was valid and reasonable and that they could defend their requests. But Hardy quickly eliminated such high hopes. He stubbornly refused to alter his decision—Blanton had to go. When the senior representatives threatened wholesale resignations, Hardy did not flinch. The two students explained, pleaded, and talked with the president for more than an hour. Hardy listened patiently, accepted some of their arguments, and even conceded minor points. But he remained immovable on the subject of the cadet captain. Defeated in their attempt to compromise, McGeorge and McInnis left to report to the class. Hardy did not mention Blanton's usurpation of authority during the entire meeting.[40]

McGeorge and McInnis talked on their way back to the meeting and decided that they had gone too far to turn back. Neither wanted to risk losing his diploma, but there seemed to be no other choice. When they reported to their companions that the president would not relent, McGeorge and McInnis said that they were going to resign. The room was instantly alive with cries to rally behind the representatives and resign as a unit. Visiting representatives from the other classes shouted that they would support the seniors.

In the midst of chaos in the student meeting, Cully Cobb asked for the floor. Since the Tennessean was older and had a reputation for maturity, his classmates quieted to hear what he had to say. Cobb told them that although he sympathized with most of their views, he could not simply walk away. He had worked too hard and had made too many sacrifices to take such a step. He would not turn his back on his diploma. He said that he would not attempt to change their minds or try to convince them to join him. Rather, Cobb pointed out that each student should make up his own mind since he would have to live with his decision. Cobb had complete trust that Hardy would make the right decision and Cobb, like Hardy, would not be swayed.[41]

Cobb's decision was the most difficult in his young life. He felt that Blanton could not always be trusted and he was aware of the connection between Blanton and Welborn. But he somehow felt that suspension of a senior a few months before graduation was indeed a serious sentence to be imposed so quickly. He thought Blanton's case had its merits. On the other hand, Cobb thought Welborn was a despicable person. Welborn was the personification of many of the things Cobb had grown to hate. Welborn's cocky arrogance and disdain for religious principles enraged Cobb. He and the commandant had clashed several times.[42] The issue that upset Cobb most of all was Welborn's disloyalty to Hardy. When he reduced his dilemma to a fight between the personalities involved, Cobb had no choice but to support Hardy against Welborn.

McGeorge and his friends were adamant. They resolved to resign. Leaving Cobb with only a half a dozen or so sympathizers, the rest of the seniors left the meeting and made plans to leave campus.

The college grounds became a madhouse. The lower classes began holding rump meetings and planning their own resignations. Hardy had forced the students' hands and they had revolted. He called on the faculty to meet in his home to discuss the problem. Little was accomplished because Hardy again refused to change his mind. Finally, the executive committee of the board of trustees of the institution met and began to deal directly with the problem.[43]

State newspapers had always given Hardy attention. He was good copy because of his busy schedule and his dynamic approach. Some papers were less friendly to Hardy than others. These had been waiting for the students when they returned from the holidays, and when the protest became a revolt the hostile papers immediately took up the story.[44] The wide attention it received necessitated the quick action by the board.

The executive committee made a restoration of order its first item of business. It agreed at the January 10 meeting to make a temporary concession to the students, hoping to keep some of them on campus. The following morning the committee met with the students at the breakfast hour and offered a proposal. All students, regardless of their roles in the affair, were invited to resume their normal duties. Any student who failed to support the trustees was considered dismissed. The scheme succeeded and a majority of the students, about five hundred by some estimates, agreed to drop the insurrection. The remaining belligerents, mostly seniors, awaited the meeting of the full board of January 14.[45]

Governor James K. Vardaman presided over that meeting. The board seemed determined to clear away the confusion and get to the cause of the unrest. The representatives of the senior class opened the meeting with a clarifying statement. The seniors maintained that they had not meant to criticize Hardy or his administration. Still, they insisted that they were within their rights to voice their opinions and insisted that all students, including Blanton, should be reinstated. The board then began to sift through the events leading to the wholesale resignations. It learned of Welborn's clash with Hardy. Students testified that Dr. Crigler had helped the students write the food petition and that he had a reputation for supporting anti-Hardy schemes. Concerning the food situation, the board listened as students described the rotten, half-cooked cabbage, pastelike rice, and decaying meat.[46]

After listening to many witnesses and much conflicting evidence, the board was ready to make its judgment. All students, including Blanton, were reinstated with no apparent penalty. The dismissal of Welborn and Crigler was upheld. Although the board sternly condemned Crigler's conniving with the students, its members noted that Hardy had perhaps been too quick in firing the doctor. Since most students agreed that the food service was inexcusably poor, the board directed that immediate action be taken to remedy the situation. Hardy was instructed to hire a new steward in the mess hall and to provide him with an adequate staff.[47]

Hardy was pleased with the board's decisions. Most of his actions had been upheld and he was rid of two troublesome staff members. Although he did not admit it publicly, the infamous food petition had obviously played an important part in the incident. Hardy knew that Welborn and Crigler were involved, and he saw the petition as a defiant step. Also, the petition had been sent to the newspapers and, as one who was concerned with his public image, Hardy had reacted.

Welborn and Crigler were less willing to accept the board's decision. The pair immediately began to protest the injustice that had been done them. They petitioned the new governor, Edmund Noel, to call for an investigation by the legislature. Noel refused.[48] Welborn began to cry that the faculty did not support Hardy and that the professors had no confidence in the president. When the board of trustees held its annual June meeting, Welborn was there to voice his new and more serious charge. By now he had enlisted the support of Professor R. H. Leavell, who also charged that the faculty had no confidence in Hardy. Determined to be rid of the Welborn-Hardy controversy once and for all, the board directed that a public investigation be held on the college campus on June 11.[49]

The June investigation was even more serious than the January affair. The charge of lack of confidence in the president was a grave matter. Almost all the members of the faculty were called on to testify as to their attitudes toward Hardy. Charges and counter-charges fired back and forth between Hardy and Welborn and their supporters. Hardy's productive but irritating tactics were exposed and examined. Among other things, the president was accused of running an inefficient administration, and Welborn claimed that Hardy had waged a vicious personal war against him.[50] It was soon obvious that Hardy's reputation would not escape unscathed and the decisions of the board would determine his future.

In order to evaluate Hardy properly, the board called in a number of students to state their views.[51] Fortunately for Hardy, most of the seniors involved in the January trouble had graduated and left campus. Furthermore, several of the students called to testify were working students and perhaps felt indebted to Hardy for his assistance.

Cully Cobb was one of the group of students and former students called before the board to give testimony. Cobb was indebted to Hardy for many favors, and he was glad to have the chance to speak favorably for his friend. He explained to the panel that, in his mind, Hardy's programs made it possible for poor boys such as himself to go to college. According to Cobb, Hardy served as a guiding symbol for the poor boys. They admired him, trusted him. Certainly the working boys had the utmost confidence in the president.

Cobb had never liked Welborn, a sentiment probably resulting from his earlier denunciation of missionary activity in China. Consequently, it was with an almost revengeful spirit that Cobb cited examples of how Welborn deliberately worked against Hardy. Cobb had seen the empty whiskey jugs stored under Welborn's quarters and he had heard students discussing Welborn's criticism of the president. Governor Noel was obviously shocked when Cobb told of Welborn's remarks concerning the missionaries in the Pacific.[52]

The June hearings aired a variety of criticisms of Hardy. Although the item under examination concerned confidence in the man, all the malcontents came forward to voice their pet complaints.[53] Observing immediately that the educator had aroused many people, the board realized that its decision in the matter would not be easy. After more than a month's deliberation, it finally cleared Hardy of all charges.

The continuing Welborn-Hardy controversy did not disrupt the campus again after the January hearings. After quiet had been restored the seniors settled down to finish their last semester. Like his classmates, Cobb tried to put the incident out of his mind and concentrate on his studies. He had to finish several uncompleted courses accumulated during previous years and survive a rather rigorous schedule of senior classes. With so many sources of distraction—concern over prospective jobs, the mutual indifference in the wake of Cobb's refusal to join his classmates in the strike, and his recent appointment to a fulltime position as assistant horticulturist—the

Cobb as a senior at Mississippi Agricultural and Mechanical College, 1908. He is wearing the military dress uniform required by the College at that time.

semester was probably Cobb's most difficult one. His grades declined sharply.[54] Cobb apparently treated the academic responsibilities in a businesslike manner and simply allocated his time according to the necessity and priority of the task. Some work must be done at the moment and therefore other assignments must be postponed. Nonetheless, Cobb's indomitable self-confidence assured the marks necessary to graduate.

Undaunted by his difficulty with some technical courses, Cobb still planned to go to medical school at Tulane after he received his degree. Even the high cost of medical training did not discourage him since he had worked out a long-range plan to save the necessary funds. Based on the anticipated income from a teaching job in September and his determination to live frugally, Cobb hoped that within a year or so he could set aside enough money to enter Tulane. He felt sure that he could find additional resources after he reached New Orleans.[55]

Even before he graduated or had a firm commitment for a job in September, Cobb began to look for a summer position. As a matter of pride and principle, he could not and would not return to Tennessee and overtax his family. It was not long before President Hardy became aware of Cobb's predicament and, as on so many previous occasions, Cobb's friend offered a solution. The Horticulture Department had a temporary position available for the summer, and since Cobb's work had been so satisfactory he was the logical choice. Hardy's offer amazed Cobb. Becoming even a temporary member of the faculty was quite an accomplishment.[56]

Cobb's graduation on June 2, 1908, ended one of the most difficult but most rewarding experiences in his life. Cobb had enjoyed his undergraduate career. The obstacles had been many and the struggle was often uphill, but Cobb's experiences had proven beyond any doubt that given an opportunity a poor boy worth his salt could overcome handicaps and succeed. This lesson became part of Cobb's philosophy—provide the poor with the opportunity and let the cream rise to the top.

Cobb's last summer at Mississippi Agricultural and Mechanical College was an enjoyable one. As assistant horticulturist, his duties were similar to those that he had performed for four years. There was, however, a great difference in compensation. As a working boy he had received ten cents per hour. His salary as a fulltime employee was seventy-five dollars per month.[57] Cobb was able to save much of his salary because he continued to live in the college greenhouse and his expenses were no greater than they had been.

As the last days of August approached, Cobb made preparations to leave the college community that had become almost a second home. The thought of a move was traumatic, but Cobb was not one to live in the past. He had accepted a job that was much to his liking. Agricultural high schools represented a new concept in rural education and, as principal of the first of such schools in Mississippi, Cobb would be "clearing new ground." So with his belongings stuffed in a newly acquired Reo automobile, Cobb drove the fifty miles to Chickasaw County, Mississippi, where he would undertake his first task in agricultural education.

## NOTES TO CHAPTER I

1. C. A. Cobb, "The South's Farm Tenancy Problem, An Address before the Conference of Rural Ministers, State College, Mississippi, June 26, 1936," United States Agricultural Adjustment Administration, *Southern Region Series*, Item 1 (Washington, 1936).

2. *The Cobbs of Tennessee, Descendants of John Cobb of Cobbs Court, County Kent, England, 1325–1968* (Atlanta, 1968), 41; hereinafter cited as *Cobbs of Tennessee*. Cully A. Cobb and Lois D. Cobb interviews. Mr. and Mrs. Cobb were interviewed by the authors on perhaps a dozen occasions. Typescripts of some of these interviews are available in Mississippi State University Library.

3. *Cobbs of Tennessee*, 44.

4. David Benedict, *A General History of the Baptist Denomination in America* (2 vols.; Boston, 1813), II, 225; *Cobbs of Tennessee*, 41; Cushing B. Hassell, *History of the Church of God, From the Creation to A.D. 1885* (Middleton, N.Y., 1886), 912.

5. *Cobbs of Tennessee*, 55.

6. *Ibid.*, 55–56; Cobb interviews; C. A. Cobb Papers (Mississippi State University Library). A general and unclassified assortment of Cobb's father's newspapers and magazines may be found in the Cobb Papers.

7. *Cobbs of Tennessee*, 50, 55, 56; Cobb interviews.

8. *Ibid.* Cobb's father never seemed to be able to turn down a request to visit sick neighbors or preach a funeral anywhere in the county. Later Cobb remembered his father spending many of his evenings instructing local Negro preachers in the Bible.

9. *Ibid.*

10. James McCallum, *A Brief Sketch of the Settlement and Early History of Giles County, Tennessee* (Pulaski, Tenn., 1876), 20, 41–43.

11. Cobb interviews; *Class of 1908* (Atlanta, 1963), 37.

12. Cobb interviews.

13. Stanley J. Folmsbee, Robert E. Corlew, and Enoch L. Mitchell, *Tennessee, A Short History* (Knoxville, 1969), 298; McCallum, *Giles County*, 100–101, 109.

14. Cobb interviews; *Class of 1908*, 37; *Cobbs of Tennessee*, 63–64.

15. John K. Bettersworth, *People's College: A History of Mississippi State* (Tuscaloosa, 1953), 55–56, 111–14, 170.

16. *Ibid.*, 179–80. John M. Stone, a former governor of Mississippi, was named interim president upon Lee's retirement and served until March, 1900.

17. Bettersworth, *People's College*, 183–85; Mississippi Agricultural and Mechanical College, *Biennial Report*, 1906–1907 (Nashville, 1908), 5; *ibid.*, 1908–1909, 5; unidentified newspaper clipping in John C. Hardy Papers (Mississippi State University Library).

18. Starkville *News*, January 31, February 7, 1908; assorted newspaper clippings in Hardy Papers; *The Mary Hardin-Baylor College Bells*, April 20, 1937.

19. Cobb interviews; *Class of 1908*, 38.

20. Cobb interviews.

21. *Ibid.*

22. Mississippi Agricultural and Mechanical College, *Bulletin*, 1904–1905 (Agricultural College, 1905), 129.

23. *Ibid.*, 11–13, 129. The working time for the students under the working boys' program was generally four to six hours per day. An enterprising student could usually find additional work if he desired. All on-campus jobs of this nature were controlled by the president.

24. Cobb interviews; interview with Harold McGeorge, October 16, 1971; Ben Hilbun, *William Flowers Hand: The Life and Philosophy of a Mississippi Scientist and Educator* (State College, Mississippi, 1952), *passim*; Memphis *Commercial Appeal*, June 25, 1933.

25. Cobb interviews; assorted clippings and notes in W. H. Magruder Papers (Mississippi State University Library).

26. Cobb interviews.

27. *Ibid.*; interview with Harold McGeorge, October 16, 1971. McGeorge, a fellow student and a member of the prestigious James Z. George Rifles, a social club, remembered that Cobb's financial status was well known and the Tennessean was generally accepted by all students. McGeorge reasoned also that Cobb was naturally excluded from activities of private clubs because of his lack of money.

28. Cobb interviews; Mississippi Agricultural and Mechanical College, *College Reveille*, 1908 (n.p., n.d.), 44. Cobb was a member of the Cosmopolitan Club, Tennessee Club, and Agricultural Club in addition to the YMCA and debating society.

29. Cobb interviews.

30. Cobb interviews; *Class of 1908*, 40; *Cobbs of Tennessee*, 64.

31. Bettersworth, *People's College*, 227; interview with Harold McGeorge, October 16, 1971; Dwight D. Eisenhower, *At Ease, Stories I Tell to Friends* (Garden City, N.Y., 1967), 138.

32. Cobb interviews; interview with Harold McGeorge, October 16, 1971. McGeorge remembered Welborn as a well-disciplined officer who did not make his liquor available to the students but who made no secret of his differences with Hardy. Evidently Welborn's criticism of Hardy's puritanical manner made him very popular with the more liberal students.

33. Cobb interviews; interview with Harold McGeorge, October 16, 1971; *Class of 1908*, 39.

34. Bettersworth, *People's College*, 228.

35. Interview with Harold McGeorge, October 16, 1971. McGeorge, who was

intimately involved in the whole affair, did not learn of the military-related charges for some time.

36. J. W. Sargent to his father, January 19, 1908, Hardy Papers; interview with Harold McGeorge, October 16, 1971.

37. *Ibid.*; Starkville *East Mississippi Times*, January 10, 1908; Starkville *News*, January 17, 1908.

38. *Class of 1908*, 131–33.

39. Interview with Harold McGeorge, October 16, 1971.

40. *Ibid.*

41. Cobb interviews; interview with Harold McGeorge, October 16, 1971; interview with Guy H. Palmes, October 16, 1971.

42. Cobb interviews. Cobb had serious difficulty with his courses in military science. Some of the difficulty may well have resulted from Welborn's opposition to Hardy's policy of excusing working boys from military duties.

43. Bettersworth, *People's College*, 229.

44. Assorted clippings in Hardy Papers.

45. Mississippi Agricultural and Mechanical College, Minutes of the Board of Trustees, January 14, 1908, Mississippi State University Library.

46. *Ibid.*; Cobb interviews; interview with Harold McGeorge, October 16, 1971; interview with Guy H. Palmes, October 16, 1971; Bettersworth, *People's College*, 230.

47. Mississippi Agricultural and Mechanical College, Minutes of the Board of Trustees, January 14, 1908.

48. Starkville *East Mississippi Times*, January 24, 31, February 7, 1908.

49. Mississippi Agricultural and Mechanical College, Minutes of the Board of Trustees, June 13, 1908.

50. *Ibid.*, July 18, 1908; Bettersworth, *People's College*, 231–32.

51. Cobb interviews; *Southern Farm Gazette*, Vol. 13 (June 27, 1908), 9; *ibid.*, Vol. 13 (July 11, 1908), 9.

52. Cobb interviews.

53. Hardy apparently had a long-standing feud with the Starkville *Southern Farm Gazette* and its editor, E. A. Scherer. Scherer threw the full force of his paper against Hardy, accusing the president of saving his job by making political alliances. Scherer observed that working boys had testified in Hardy's behalf, a clear case of academic patronage. Scherer's charges so enraged Cully Cobb that he wrote a stinging rebuttal. *Southern Farm Gazette*, Vol. 13 (June 27, 1908), 9; *ibid.*, Vol. 13 (July 11, 1908), 9. For Cobb's statement see Starkville *News*, July 31, 1908.

54. An examination of Cobb's transcript in the Registrar's Files at Mississippi State University shows a decline from an average of C plus to D grades during the senior year.

55. Mississippi Agricultural and Mechanical College, *College Reveille*, 1908, 44; Cobb interviews.

56. *Ibid.*

57. C. A. Cobb to Mary A. Cobb, February 12, 1908, Cobb Papers.

# CHAPTER II

# A First Task in Agricultural Education: The Buena Vista Years, 1908–1910

WHEN in 1908 Cully A. Cobb elected to take a job in agricultural education, he could hardly have chosen a more dynamic, challenging, and important field. It is accurate to say that the three decades between 1890 and 1920 saw the establishment of the modern American system of agricultural education. That system would play a major role in the unparalleled productivity of American farming in the twentieth century. It would also become a model for much of the world as underdeveloped nations sought to strengthen their rural economies. By agreeing to go to Chickasaw County, Cobb became part of one of the more important developments in American history.

The skeleton of the American system of agricultural education was largely completed by 1908, but the body still lacked a great deal of flesh. The land-grant colleges had been important centers for resident instruction in agriculture for no more than twenty years; their research programs were of even more recent origin. Agricultural extension was still in its infancy. Practically all of the colleges were engaged to some degree in farmers' institutes, the first extension technique that reached large numbers of actual agriculturists; many of the schools were developing other extension methods that leaders hoped would be more effective in influencing the thinking and practices of the nation's farmers. Seaman A. Knapp's demonstration work had been in existence less than half a dozen years, and much remained to be done.

While some agricultural educators were perfecting their resident instruction and experiment station programs and were searching for an effective extension technique, others were thinking in terms of education for the children of farmers. Cornell University's Liberty Hyde Bailey launched his nature study project for elementary school children in the 1890s, and by 1904 the first steps had been taken toward the establishment of rural youth clubs in Illinois, Ohio, and elsewhere.[1] *

Given this ferment of activity, it was inevitable that men would begin to think in terms of formal agricultural education at the secondary level. The high school was becoming a widely accepted part of the public school system, not only in cities but also in rural towns and villages. Enrollments were soaring. With agricultural education in the high school, or the creation of high schools for the teaching of agriculture, it became possible to reach many of those rural youth who could not be expected in the foreseeable future to spend four years on the campuses of the agricultural colleges.[2]

Accordingly, the 1890s, and even more the next decade, witnessed a flowering of agricultural education on the high school level. At least three types of secondary schools appeared. First in order of establishment were schools connected with the agricultural colleges. The pioneer was the Minnesota School of Agriculture, established in 1888 on the University of Minnesota's agricultural college campus in St. Paul. By 1912 there were thirty-seven such schools. Using the facilities and to some degree the faculties of colleges, these schools offered two- or three-year "practical" courses designed to train young men and women for the farm without requiring them to take large doses of the usual academic fare. Generally, students were admitted directly from the common schools of the state.[3]

In terms of numbers of students taught, these institutions were soon overshadowed by the growing number of public high schools. The expansion of the teaching of agriculture in these schools was especially dramatic. According to the United States Department of Agriculture, not one public high school in the nation offered such instruction in 1897. But sixteen years later, more than two thousand did so. In fact, they accounted for about 80 percent of all institutions giving training in agriculture, not counting the one-room elementary schools for which no records were available.[4]

Finally, there appeared a variety of types of separate agricultural

* Notes appear at end of each chapter.

high schools. All of these sought to train boys and girls for the farm; they differed in amount and source of support, facilities and enrollments, and the extent of the geographical areas from which they drew sustenance, both in terms of finances and students.

Some were maintained by states and were expected to draw students from the entire state. Such was the California Polytechnic School that opened at San Luis Obispo in October, 1903. To students at least fifteen years old who had completed grammar school it offered a three-year course of "training in the arts and sciences which deal peculiarly with country life. . . ." Four years later, California established a similar institution at Davis; and by 1911 Minnesota had two schools, located at Morris and Crookston, that were roughly comparable.[5]

Other states placed separate agricultural high schools in various political or other subdivisions. Alabama led in establishing such schools in congressional districts. By 1911, there were nine of these institutions in that state. They offered a four-year course, comparable in grade to that of ordinary public high school. Each institution received $4,500 annually from the state. Each had an experimental farm and a variety of buildings, animals, and machinery which were used in the instruction and which also contributed to meeting operating and maintenance costs.

In June, 1906, the Georgia legislature provided for the establishment of agricultural high schools in that state's congressional districts. Five years later, there were eleven such schools. These institutions offered a four-year course, only two years of which were on the high school level; and each of the schools had at least two hundred acres of land for instructional and other purposes. They were supported by the state oil and fertilizer taxes and by local contributions. Virginia was another state that established agricultural high schools in congressional districts.

Oklahoma used the judicial district as the geographical unit for its separate agricultural high schools. The state's first legislature provided for one school in each of five districts plus a sixth institution in the Panhandle. In Arkansas the legislature simply divided the state into four approximately equal districts and appropriated funds to establish schools at Jonesboro, Magnolia, Monticello, and Russellville.[6]

Finally, some states authorized and aided the establishment of county agricultural high schools. By 1911, at least one county agricultural high school existed in Michigan; and Maryland, North Carolina, and Mississippi had moved toward the creation of such schools. But Wisconsin was the first state to do so, when schools opened in Marathon and Dunn counties in October, 1902. These pioneers were soon followed by others in Marinette, Winnebago, and La Crosse counties.[7]

Fairly typical of the institutions in Wisconsin was the Dunn County School of Agriculture and Domestic Economy. Located in the town of Menomonie, the county seat, the campus of the school occupied only a half block but a mile distant on the county fairgrounds was a six-acre tract used for instructional purposes. The main building was three storied, of brick construction, and there were three smaller structures. The county provided these facilities and equipped them. The school had no dormitory, and students from out of town were required to live in nearby private homes. There was no tuition. Attendance during the first years averaged seventy. The school was coeducational, and students were admitted who had completed the eighth grade. The regular course covered two eight-month sessions, each beginning in October. Instructional methods included the use of both textbooks and laboratory, but in every case the object was to offer training that would be most useful to boys and girls "when they take charge of the home farm or the farm home." Total operating costs amounted to about six thousand dollars a year; of that amount the state contributed four thousand.

In addition to the regular instructional work the Dunn County school engaged in various kinds of extension activity among neighborhood farmers. The school issued a quarterly bulletin and placed exhibits at the county fair. Faculty members wrote articles for local newspapers and participated in farmers' institutes and other rural gatherings in the county. Finally, the school operated each year a twelve-week winter short course for adult farmers.[8]

The establishment of special agricultural high schools presented educators with a multitude of problems and generated vigorous debates at any number of professional meetings and elsewhere. In many instances, the arguments raised against the agricultural high schools were similar to those voiced a quarter of a century earlier in opposition to the land-grant colleges. Some educators criticized the whole concept of special high schools for agriculture and concluded that there was no need or place for them. Indeed, Dean Eugene Davenport of the Illinois College of Agriculture considered the establishment of separate agricultural high schools not only unnecessary and wasteful but also dangerous to secondary education and to society as a whole. "Combine the vocational and the non-vocational in our high schools . . . and each will be the better for the other," he claimed. To do otherwise would tend to produce a large number of specialized but weak schools that would train but not educate their students, retard severely the existing secondary schools, and constitute a danger to democratic institutions by producing a rigid stratification of society.[9]

On the other hand, the United States Department of Agriculture saw no such dangers and actively encouraged the establishment of agricultural high schools. Dick J. Crosby, a leading spokesman in the Department on these matters, sought to refute such arguments as those put forth by Davenport and others who contended that "the place of the agricultural high school is within, not without, our system of public education." [10] Separate schools, Crosby said, would not take the place of or compete with either the public high schools or the agricultural colleges. Instead, they would "occupy an intermediate field which neither had fully occupied—much less cultivated." More specifically, he argued that agricultural high schools would stimulate and set the pace for the teaching of agriculture elsewhere, aid in the preparation of suitable teachers for the rural schools, relieve the agricultural colleges of much secondary and short-course instruction, and take up better than any other agency the management of many of the forms of extension work then emerging.

At the same time, the United States Department of Agriculture offered suggestions concerning the proper management of agricultural high schools. Because some students would use the schools as a step toward college, the institutions should not be excessively narrow but should give instruction in such subjects as English, history, mathematics, and chemistry; and the course of study in these areas should conform in a general way to that of the ordinary public high schools. Courses in agriculture should include basic information but they should be organized in such a way as to focus attention on the particular types of farming prevailing in the area. Finally, the Department of Agriculture was convinced that the number of agricultural high schools should be limited so that individual schools would serve relatively large districts, possibly ten to fifteen counties, depending upon population, value of farm land, and other factors. One county, the department felt, was too small a unit to support adequately a school, either in terms of financial resources or students.[11]

Despite the Department of Agriculture's injunction against establishing agricultural high schools in counties, Mississippi used that political unit in setting up her system. Justification for that decision, in part, could be found in the distressing status of secondary education in the rural areas of the state. Writing in 1903, Henry L. Whitfield, the state superintendent of public instruction, stated that one "of the greatest needs of the State . . . is a number of well distributed free rural high schools. Under our present laws," he continued, "public high schools can be maintained only in the towns . . . but . . . less than 10 per cent of the children live within the bounds of these districts . . . and it becomes manifest that some provision should be made whereby the rural youth may have similar advantages." [12]

That state official was pointing to the general need for a secondary school system in the rural areas of Mississippi; he was not concerned specifically with agricultural education. But the overwhelming preponderance of farmers in the state's population, combined with knowledge of developments elsewhere, turned the attention of many of the state's educational and political leaders to the idea of the agricultural high school. In November, 1906, the United States Department of Agriculture's Dick J. Crosby spoke on the topic at the Conference on Secondary Education in the South, held at the University of Virginia. Later his paper was published in the widely read *Southern Educational Review*. Crosby discussed specifically the county agricultural high schools of Wisconsin. Meanwhile, the Farmers' Union, an organization with growing strength in the state, gave its support to the movement; and in 1906 a convention of county superintendents unanimously adopted a resolution supporting the establishment in each county of "at least one agricultural high school . . . supported by local taxation, with State aid and under State supervision." [13]

Reacting to these pressures, the Mississippi legislature moved in the spring of 1908. A law approved March 21 authorized each county school board to establish one agricultural high school for the instruction of white youths in "high school branches, theoretical and practical agriculture, and . . . other branches of study." Funds for establishing and maintaining the schools were to come from three sources. Communities within a county desiring an agricultural high school were to bid for the institution, the school going to the highest bidder. A successful bid had to include the offer of twenty or more acres of land, a suitable school building, and dormitory and dining facilities for at least forty boarders, as well as a cash contribution. If such funds were inadequate for the support of the school, the county board of supervisors was permitted to levy a special tax of not more than two mills. Finally, when satisfied that local and county support was sufficient, the state was to provide a thousand dollars annually. To the state board of education fell the task of determining whether counties had met the requirements; that agency was also empowered to approve the course of study offered in the schools. Local control rested in a five-member board of trustees, made up of the county superintendent of education and four others elected by the board of education and the board of supervisors.[14]

The law left much to interpretation by the state board of education. After studying the matter, that agency concluded that the new institutions were to admit any girl or boy who had completed the eighth grade. A committee was appointed to formulate a course of study for the high school work. Since the new schools were to be established for the education of country youth, the state board decided that it should discourage the location of schools in the larger towns where they might be combined with existing separate district, public high schools.[15]

In framing the 1908 law, Mississippi's legislators quite obviously failed to concern themselves with its constitutionality; in fact, the law practically invited a legal test. It came quickly. Robert Goins, a Negro from Jasper County, brought suit against the county's tax collector; and by the fall of 1909 the issue had found its way into the Mississippi Supreme Court. Justice Edward Mayes gave his decision on November 2. "If the fourteenth amendment to the Constitution . . . means anything at all, it certainly means that all citizens of the United States shall stand equal before the law," he wrote. Any law would be void that openly abridged the privileges or immunities of a certain class of citizens or denied them the equal protection of the laws. Since the Agricultural High School Act of 1908 failed to make any mention of schools for black children but provided for the taxation of all property owners, it clearly fell into that category, so Mayes struck it down.[16]

Fortunately for the schools established under the 1908 law, the legislature was scheduled to meet only two months after the adverse decision was handed down. Sentiment for agricultural high schools remained strong, so the legislators resolved to produce a new law that would pass the test of the courts. The product of their labors was approved March 16, 1910. By its terms, the school board in each county was empowered to "establish not more than two agricultural high schools . . . one for white youths exclusively and the other for colored youths exclusively. . . ." Like the earlier measure, the new law provided for a county levy of not more than two mills for each school established; but it required that taxes collected and their uses be kept separate, no doubt to discourage those who might urge the establishment of Negro schools. Requirements for state aid remained essentially as in the 1908 law, but the amount of such aid was increased to $1,500 a year. Finally, the new law permitted two counties to establish a joint school that would serve both.[17]

The 1910 legislature also passed a number of special laws to help those schools that had been created under the now unconstitutional measure of 1908. One new enactment insured continuity for them

43

by protecting their sites, property, and income. Another special law allowed the board of supervisors in Noxubee County to donate to its agricultural high school those tax revenues that had been collected under the 1908 law. Finally, the legislature authorized the state to donate a thousand dollars to each of two county schools faced with particularly difficult financial problems.[18]

The first decade of the agricultural high schools in Mississippi was a successful one, measured by the number of schools established, by increases in state aid, and by the growth in enrollments. In some counties at the outset, there was organized resistance to the levying of the special tax for the schools, but opposition seems to have weakened after 1910. Leading the fight for the schools in several counties was the Farmers' Union, and state Superintendent Joseph N. Powers missed few opportunities to argue for them as he traveled about the state. By the end of 1912, thirty schools had been established and the number had reached fifty by 1920. Joint schools at Perkinston and Wesson served the counties of Harrison and Stone and Lincoln and Copiah so that by that time fifty-two of the state's counties could claim agricultural high schools. State appropriations rose from $60,000 in 1912 to $450,000 in 1920. Meanwhile, as early as December, 1912, total enrollment was reported to be 2,843.[19]

There is some controversy concerning the location of the first agricultural high school in the state. More than a decade after the event, the Mississippi State Board of Education gave the honor to Jasper County. By that account, Jasper was followed by Yalobusha in 1908 and by Alcorn, Calhoun, Jefferson, Leake, and Madison counties in 1909. The leading historian of the teaching of agriculture in Mississippi accepted without question the state board's view of the matter.[20] But it is certain that the state board was in error. The United States Department of Agriculture labeled Noxubee County as the leader. By September, 1908, admittedly, that county had selected a site at Mashulaville and had levied a tax of one mill to support the school. But Noxubee County had to construct the necessary school buildings, and instructional work was delayed. Chickasaw County, on the other hand, was able to begin a reasonably full program during the 1908–1909 school year, and the institution there may accurately be described as the first agricultural high school in Mississippi. Its success seems to have stemmed from two factors, the availability of reasonably acceptable school buildings and the energy of the school's first principal.[21]

The agricultural high school law of 1908 had no more than cleared the governor's desk when leaders in Chickasaw County took the first steps toward establishing a school. The county superintendent was one of the first to contact state authorities seeking information, and newspapers in the county urged their communities to move promptly in making bids. After all, according to Superintendent Powers, communities that succeeded in getting the schools could expect to prosper, both financially and intellectually. A number of towns did present bids, but in July, 1908, county authorities chose Buena Vista. Important in the decision was the offer of over eight thousand dollars in cash and property. Included were facilities that previously had housed the Buena Vista Normal College, a now-defunct institution established in 1884 which numbered among its graduates several distinguished Mississippians, including George M. Hightower, prominent agricultural and educational leader.[22]

Having selected the site, the next step for the Chickasaw County authorities was the employment of a principal. They turned to the state's agricultural college; there they found Cully A. Cobb. During his senior year, the Tennessean had displayed an interest in the new type of schools, working out a model curriculum for them. Moreover, Cobb's training, work habits, and character suggested that he might well be the ideal man for the job. A strong recommendation from President John C. Hardy of Mississippi Agricultural and Mechanical College no doubt influenced the Chickasaw countians. Only a few months later, Hardy would call Cobb one "of the strongest men this college has ever turned out." [23]

Cobb was familiar in a general way with conditions in Chickasaw County; beginning in September, 1908, he was to learn much more, and quickly. The county where the young agricultural educator was to spend two years was located in northeast Mississippi, approximately 100 miles southeast of Memphis, Tennessee, and 150 miles northeast of Jackson, the state capital. Containing slightly over five hundred square miles, the county was divided into three parts by topography and soils. The eastern portion of the county was flat, black prairie with a deep and fertile soil. Farther west, running north and south, was the southern extremity of the Pontotoc Ridge. The land there tended to be hilly and sandy, with generally low fertility, and it was subject to serious erosion. The western part of Chickasaw County was in the Flatwoods, a well-timbered area with a firm clay soil of perhaps average fertility.

Before the Civil War, Chickasaw County had been plantation

Grounds and main building of the Chickasaw County Agricultural High School, Buena Vista, Mississippi, c. 1908.

country. With 9,000 slaves and some 2,000 fewer whites, it had produced over 26,000 bales of cotton in 1860. But the war and its aftermath had affected Chickasaw County as it did the rest of the state and, indeed, most of the South. Population growth was slow and the economy was depressed. In 1910 census takers counted 22,846 people in the county; about 44 percent were white. That year there were 3,474 farms in Chickasaw County. Like those in the state as a whole they tended to be small; the average was seventy acres. Tenancy was common. Only a third of all farms were tilled by their owners; the balance were equally divided between share and cash tenants. Only 53 percent of the farm land was improved. Cotton was the major crop, followed by corn, and yields were low in both cases. In 1909, 49,000 acres of cotton produced about one fourth of a bale to the acre, and 32,000 acres of corn yielded fourteen bushels to the acre. Cotton acreage was about ten times that of hay and forage, showing the lack of diversification. In short, Chickasaw was a poor county, badly in need of agricultural improvement.

By Mississippi standards, Chickasaw County in 1910 had two fair-sized towns, Okolona with a population of 2,584 and Houston with 1,400. But in the contest for the agricultural high school, these towns lost to Buena Vista. Located in the extreme southern part of Chickasaw County, some seven miles west of Okolona, Buena Vista was founded in the 1840s. It was first called Monterey for the Mexican War battle in which Chickasaw County volunteers participated, but the modern name was soon adopted. Reportedly, Buena Vista was a prosperous community in the 1850s, but in 1900 it had a population of 225 and ten years later there were only 231 people in the town.[24]

The physical facilities that Buena Vista provided for its agricultural high school could only be described as unpretentious. The main building, a two-storied wood structure located on a five-acre tract on the west edge of town, was in poor repair. Farther west, across a street and situated in the middle of a two-acre plot, was a dormitory of similar construction and in about the same condition. Adjacent to it was a small structure used as a buggy house and stable. To the northwest of the school grounds was the farm,

47

consisting of some sixty acres. It was largely unimproved and some of it was covered by a heavy growth of timber.[25]

Despite the rather unpromising appearances of his new surroundings, Cobb went to work with energy, enthusiasm, and remarkable initiative. Since the two main buildings inherited from the old normal school were in disrepair, Cobb had to oversee their remodeling. While that work was in progress, he improved the grounds and established a garden. Not until spring were the buildings ready for full use, although months earlier Cobb had begun to give instruction to a small non-resident enrollment. In March, 1909, advertisements in county newspapers announced the formal opening of facilities and described the planned operation of the school. "The Chickasaw Agricultural High School," Cobb wrote, "offers exceptional opportunities to young men and young ladies who want a practical education at nominal cost. Pupils are paid eight cents an hour for work done on the grounds, to be credited on actual cost of board. Rooms in dormitory are clean and well furnished and are free to county pupils. Scientific farming, gardening, dairying, canning, fruit and berry growing, as well as the high school course are taught. Buena Vista is noted for morals and health. Come and inspect the place for yourself."

Come they did, but not in droves. By the end of the 1908–1909 term, Cobb was able to count thirty-two pupils. Enrollment was better the next year. That session opened on September 14 with a faculty of four and a student body that numbered forty by November. Before the end of the school year, more than eighty pupils had enrolled. In the main, the student body was an accurate reflection of the white, adult population of Chickasaw County. A few of the pupils were the children of town residents but most came from the small farms that were so numerous in the area.[26]

As closely as facilities allowed, the course of study followed an outline approved during the 1908–1909 school year by the state board of education. According to that outline, the program consisted of three years of high school work, plus an option between a fourth year of high school training or a year of preparatory work. Using as a measure a standard unit (the equivalent of a continuous course of high school level work covering a period of thirty-two

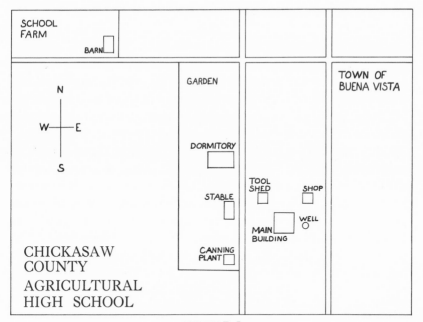

FIGURE I

weeks with forty-minute periods per week), the course of study called for two units of mathematics, three of English, two of history, two of a foreign language, one of general science, one of electives, and two units each of agriculture and industrial training. A fourth year added more training in mathematics, English, history and civil government, foreign languages, and science. In the preparatory year, students received the usual eighth grade fare. Finally, the Chickasaw County school gave some instruction in the lower grades. Cobb himself taught the agriculture and mathematics and such other subjects as circumstances dictated.[27]

Since the law under which Mississippi's agricultural high schools were established talked of practical training in agriculture, Cobb required manual labor of all of his boys. The standard work assignment was two hours a day Monday through Friday and all day Saturday at the going rate of eight cents an hour.

Under these arrangements, Cobb's pupils performed ordinary chores around the school and farm and during the formative period undertook a number of major projects. For example, they cut oak timber for barn framing and posts and built a barn and a canning house and installed enough woven and barbed wire fence to enclose the entire property. Since Cobb and the boys planned and completed these tasks themselves, the boys were exposed to a variety of new ideas and practical procedures. For the first time for most of them, they heard of the basic principles of agricultural engineering, used construction tools not found on the ordinary farm of that time, and learned how to draw and read building plans.

The pupils also joined in getting the farm into production. In addition to helping with the standard field crops, the boys cleared some fifteen acres of land the first year and planted a garden that yielded substantial amounts of cabbage and tomatoes. Under Cobb's direction, the cabbage was converted to kraut and most of the tomatoes were canned. In every case, Cobb's objective was not only to accomplish the task at hand but also to teach the boys the principles of good farming and the practical application of them. In the course of the program, for example, pupils learned to identify soil types and their capabilities, studied weather and its cycles, noted the effects of fertilization, and saw the value in having some knowledge of agricultural economics and bookkeeping. They were also instructed in elementary surveying and learned how to construct terraces. In contrast to many agricultural college students required to do manual labor, Cobb's pupils were "very anxious" and worked "willingly" at those tasks laid out for them.

During the years that Cobb was at Buena Vista, only boys were housed in the dormitory. In 1909–1910 board averaged $6.32 a month, but to this expense was applied the amount that each boy earned by working on the farm. As a result, the cost of attending the school, even for boarding students, rarely exceeded $3.00 a month. Students who lived at home paid nothing.

Lack of facilities prohibited the housing of girls during Cobb's tenure in Chickasaw County. Nor was there an instruction program in home economics or practical work for girls. These Cobb planned to add later.[28]

While getting his classroom program under way, Cobb was busily developing the school's more than sixty acres of farm land so that they might be of use for instruction and demonstration purposes. Crops produced on the place were either consumed at the school or sold to help meet the institution's financial needs. During the winter of 1908–1909 Cobb had a well bored and he acquired a team, wagon, and small stock of farm equipment. A few months later, a leading farm machinery manufacturer donated six hundred dollars worth of tools and equipment. In the spring of 1909 Cobb planted almost two hundred fruit trees and a small plot of strawberries and began to develop a garden. When it produced abundantly, Cobb acquired a canning outfit, placed it in a small building constructed for the purpose, and made ready to put up vegetables for the school's tables and in the future to instruct farm girls in proper canning techniques.

Most of the farm was planted to corn and peas. Since that "post-oak" land was low in fertility, Cobb applied acid phosphate and cottonseed meal, leaving a few rows unfertilized to serve as a demonstration for both pupils and visiting farmers. Cobb also started a small flock of high grade chickens, some of which he later distributed among neighborhood farmers in an effort to start a poultry industry in Chickasaw County.[29]

The primary purpose of the Chickasaw County agricultural high school was the instruction of boys and girls, but Cobb and the school's board of trustees believed that the institution should play a role in adult education. Accordingly, in the summer of 1909, Cobb held a school for rural teachers in the county. A major effort was made to interest them in elementary scientific agriculture with the hope that they would introduce it in their one-room schools. Concluding ceremonies on August 13–14 featured talks by professors from Mississippi Agricultural and Mechanical College, the president of the Industrial Institute and College, and the state superintendent of education. A barbecue the final day contributed to the festivities and induced a county newspaper to observe that the "Agricultural High School is now fully launched upon its great career."

An added attraction during the summer school for teachers was a farmers' institute, similar to those so common throughout the United States in the two or three decades before 1914. To the farmers who attended, Cobb showed his fertilizer demonstrations and other features of the school, seeking always to induce the visitors to take new ideas home with them.[30]

Later in the year, in November, Mississippi Agricultural and Mechanical College held a short course of a week's duration at the school. Practical lectures and demonstrations were used to instruct the farmers who attended. College officials pronounced the affair such a success that they planned to hold similar affairs at other agricultural high schools in the state.[31]

In addition to these types of adult education and extension work on the campus, Cobb found time to aid directly any farmer who asked for help. Convinced that if the school were to prosper, it had to have friendly relations with its rural neighbors, Cobb functioned much like a county agent, visiting farms, answering questions, and otherwise making himself useful in the area. He also did what he could to encourage the corn club movement. The organization in November, 1908, of what was reported to be the largest club in the state resulted in part from these efforts.[32]

Many sided though Cobb's work was, he was far from satisfied that he and the school were doing enough. His farm girls should have practical training in home economics, he knew, and the school needed facilities for systematic instruction in manual training. To make possible those programs he drew up plans for a new building to be located near the main structure and in close proximity to the school's water supply. Projected also was a farm machinery display shed. The willingness of manufacturers to donate or lend modern farm implements for Cobb's use pointed to the need for that building and at the same time presented a new opportunity for the school to be of service. Certainly the school should set an example by providing proper housing for the machinery, but in addition Cobb thought the institution should have a display building where the implements might be examined by farmers. Such an arrangement would in effect give the institution yet another useful role in the neighborhood. That sort of thinking typified Cobb's concept of the proper function of the agricultural high school. As he viewed it, the school should not simply provide agricultural education, narrowly defined, but rather it should seek to meet in a practical way the educational needs of the entire rural community.[33]

The character and extent of Cobb's work at Buena Vista compared well with that at the other agricultural high schools in the state, although it appears that Cobb had less with which to work. In Pearl River County, for example, the school that opened there in September, 1909, with sixty-five pupils had buildings worth sixteen thousand dollars. Authorities planned to construct another structure costing twenty thousand dollars and including an auditorium seating one thousand. That county was unusually generous, having voted a full two-mill levy for the school's support. Meanwhile, the school in Yalobusha County had a two-storied brick building worth eleven thousand dollars, but the farm contained only twenty-six acres of land.[34] In Alcorn County enrollment of boarding students in 1909–1910 exceeded the forty-bed capacity of that school's dormitory, and some pupils had to find quarters in private homes. Like Cobb's school, the one in Alcorn County operated on the cooperative plan. Boys worked at various tasks and were paid for their labor. That school, however, was able to provide similar opportunities for girls. The actual cost of attending the school ranged from $3.40 to $4.85 a month. The farm was reported to be "one of the poorest in the county," but the principal was determined to make a demonstration farm out of it and to "show what can be done with scientific methods."[35]

A study made in June, 1909, by a faculty member at Millsaps College in Jackson brought out in some detail the condition of five schools whose principals replied to questionnaires. Attendance at these institutions averaged eighty-seven, including an undisclosed number of elementary pupils. Each of the schools received $1,500 a year from the state, and income from county tax levies averaged $3,795. The local communities had contributed an average of $5,350. Annual operating expenses ranged from $5,000 to $6,000. Agricultural instructors received from $900 to $1,500 a year.[36]

Despite the promising beginnings that had taken place at Buena Vista and elsewhere in the state during the first years, it was apparent that the agricultural high schools and their principals faced a multitude of serious problems. The biggest, no doubt, was the one of finances. The United States Department of Agriculture had been correct when it advised against establishing agricultural high schools in counties; that political unit was simply too small to support adequately the institutions, especially in a poor state. As a result, Mississippi's agricultural high schools compared poorly with those in neighboring Alabama and Georgia. Nor did Mississippi's schools equal those in Wisconsin, though admittedly, the Wisconsin schools had a much easier task since they were expected to provide only two years of instruction.[37]

In Chickasaw County during Cobb's tenure the problem of money was a continual one. No figures are available for operating expenses during the school's first year, but the needs seem to have been met through local contributions. Not until September, 1909, did the board of supervisors vote a one-half mill levy, and because of the adverse decision of the Supreme Court in November, that tax produced little immediately in the way of revenue for the school. In the spring of 1910 the state agreed to "donate" $1,000 to Chickasaw County to help the agricultural high school meet its most pressing needs. That amount failed by $200 to equal Cobb's salary.[38] Total income for the 1910–1911 term, the year after Cobb left Buena Vista, was $5,184. Of that sum, $1,500 was the state contribution, $177 came from the sale of farm produce, and the balance was revenue from the county's one-half mill levy.[39]

Another difficulty stemmed from the new and experimental character of the schools and from controversy concerning their purposes and methods. Some in the state felt the schools should be purely agricultural in character, giving little attention to academic subjects. Others saw the schools as college preparatory institutions for rural youth. Reacting to the poor conditions in education generally in country areas, still other people wanted the agricultural high schools to take elementary pupils and to function at least in part as an improved grade school. Admittedly, there was a need for all of these types of institutions, but the conflicting demands, combined with the lack of adequate funds, placed almost impossible burdens on the schools and their principals. The state board of education, which was charged with the task of formulating a uniform program, wrestled with the problem throughout the first decade that the schools existed but generally failed to satisfy all interests. In practice, the schools tended to fall between the stools as the principals, including Cully A. Cobb, sought some reasonable compromise between the diverse needs and their abilities to meet those needs.[40]

The agricultural high schools also suffered from a lack of trained agriculturists. This was a nationwide problem as the expanding programs at the land-grant colleges in resident instruction, experimentation, and extension drained off the supply of the needed type of men. The Chickasaw County school was fortunate in this regard; Cobb was the ideal man for the task. But his successor was a principal of the "traditional" type under whose leadership the Buena Vista school tended to become "merely a high school in which Agriculture is taught." [41]

Nor did the farm attached to the agricultural high schools prove to be as useful for demonstration and teaching as had been supposed. In a great many instances, the land that had been given the schools was of the poorest type, often sharply below the average in the county. With land of such low quality and without a trained agriculturist in charge, the results were predictable.[42]

Finally, the agricultural high schools were affected adversely by the rapid increase, especially after 1920, in the numbers of consolidated schools in the rural areas. The state board of education had been pushing their development since the early years of the century, and in the 1920s, with better roads and the automobile, rural consolidated schools flowered. Students attending such schools could take the agricultural courses they offered, often aided by Smith-Hughes money, and avoid paying board. In addition, by living at home, high school age youths could help in the operation of their home farms, thereby reducing the resistance of some farmers to secondary education for their sons.[43]

It was this complex of factors that explained the failure of the agricultural high school movement in Mississippi to cover the entire state and its ultimate disappearance as a significant force in rural education. In 1920 there were fifty agricultural high schools in the state, but even at that high-water mark thirty counties had not established such institutions, nor would they do so in the future. In fact, the system began to contract in the 1920s, and the decline continued in subsequent decades. By the 1929–1930 year, three schools had ceased operations. The Buena Vista institution closed in 1936. Thirty years later, there were only five of the schools in existence. That number included the only Negro agricultural high school established in Mississippi, in Coahoma County. Enrollment had fallen to 2,700, of which number about a third were black pupils.[44]

Although the significance of Mississippi's agricultural high schools dwindled after 1920, the institutions did make some important contributions to the state's educational system. They were Mississippi's first high schools for rural children. In many ways experimental, they helped to convince doubters that it was possible and feasible to teach at least the rudiments of scientific agriculture to adolescents. Consequently, they helped to develop an undeniable demand among the state's citizens for a comprehensive system of secondary education for their children. In fact, by encouraging the development of consolidated rural schools, the agricultural institutions did much to create one of the forces that would ultimately eliminate any real need for them. Finally, the agricultural high schools played a role in the rise of Mississippi's junior college system. A few of the schools that were advantageously located started offering junior college work in the 1920s, and an enactment of the legislature in 1928 gave formal approval to such programs. In the 1950s twelve of the state's junior colleges could trace their origins to the agricultural high schools.[45]

That Cobb did a good job at Buena Vista was obvious. According to John C. Hardy, Cobb was "the best fitted man in the state" for the job.[46] Others shared that view. In a speech at Houston late in 1909, Superintendent Powers paid high tribute to the Chickasaw County school and to its principal. Cobb's school, said Powers, had the lowest board rate in the state, indicating the efficiency and economy of its operation. Moreover, the Buena Vista school was outstanding in instruction and discipline. The next year Cobb was invited to describe his school at the annual meeting of the Conference for Education in the South, certainly a signal honor for the young educator. In the summer of 1910 at the invitation of authorities at

Mississippi Agricultural and Mechanical College, Cobb spent a week on the campus, lecturing at a short course for men interested in agricultural high school work. Cobb's lectures, which earned him $25, dealt with such practical matters as the organization of the new institutions, arranging the farms connected with them, getting the boys to work, and convincing the public that the schools deserved their support. Finally, for a time, Cobb served as state inspector of agricultural high schools, charged with the responsibility of examining them to ascertain that they met state standards.[47]

Still, Cobb was not eager to make Buena Vista his permanent home. Early in 1910 he was considering taking a position in an agricultural college in São Paulo, Brazil.[48] A better opportunity came in the summer of 1910. The new job would be much more challenging and the opportunity for service much greater. But beyond these factors, Cobb was influenced by the conviction that the future, both for himself if he stayed at Buena Vista and for the school, was severely limited. Given prevailing circumstances, Cobb could see that the agricultural high schools in Mississippi would soon reach a plateau of usefulness and then decline. If he stayed in Buena Vista, his career almost certainly would follow a similar path.

## NOTES TO CHAPTER II

1. For a fuller discussion of these developments see Roy V. Scott, *The Reluctant Farmer: The Rise of Agricultural Extension to 1914* (Urbana, 1970).

2. A. M. Soule, "The Work of the Agricultural School in the Scheme of State Education," Southern Education Association, *Journal*, 1907 (Chattanooga, n.d.), 181–91.

3. Alfred C. True and Dick J. Crosby, "The American System of Agricultural Education," U.S. Office of Experiment Stations, *Circular* 106 (Washington, 1911), 21. The Minnesota School of Agriculture is discussed in *Hoard's Dairyman*, Vol. 84 (August 25, 1939), 456, 469.

4. Dick J. Crosby, "Agriculture in Public High Schools," U.S. Department of Agriculture, *Yearbook*, 1912 (Washington, 1913), 471.

5. True and Crosby, "American System of Agricultural Education," 22–24.

6. *Ibid.*, 21–22, 24–25. The Georgia schools are discussed in J. H. Reynolds, "Agricultural High Schools," Southern Educational Association, *Journal*, 1908 (Chattanooga, n.d.), 519–20. For the Alabama schools see Stuart G. Noble, "The Alabama System of Agricultural High Schools," *Educational Exchange*, Vol. 26 (January, 1911), 10–13.

7. True and Crosby, "American System of Agricultural Education," 22; Crosby, "Agriculture in Public High Schools," 472.

8. A. A. Johnson, "County Schools of Agriculture and Domestic Economy in

Wisconsin," U.S. Office of Experiment Stations, *Bulletin* 242 (Washington, 1911); Kary C, Davis, "County Schools of Agriculture in Wisconsin," U.S. Office of Experiment Stations, *Annual Report*, 1904 (Washington, 1905), 677–86.

9. Eugene Davenport, "Industrial Education: A Phase of the Problem of Universal Education," National Education Association, *Journal*, 1909 (Winona, Minn., 1909), 282.

10. Dick J. Crosby, "Special Agricultural High Schools," National Education Association, *Journal*, 1909 (Winona, Minn., 1909), 974–76.

11. Dick J. Crosby, "The Place of the Agricultural High School in the System of Public Education," National Education Association, *Journal*, 1910 (Winona, Minn., 1910), 1103–1107.

12. Mississippi State Superintendent of Public Education, *Biennial Report*, 1901–1903 (Nashville, 1904), 10.

13. *Ibid.*, 1905–1907, p. 13; George L. Robson, Jr., "The Farmers' Union in Mississippi" (M.A. thesis, Mississippi State University, 1963), 70–75.

14. Mississippi, *Laws*, 1908, pp. 92–93; Houston *Advocate*, May 22, 1908; *Southern Farm Gazette*, Vol. 13 (September 19, 1908), 3.

15. *Mississippi School Journal*, Vol. 12 (May, 1908), 36–37; *ibid.*, Vol. 13 (January, 1909), 1–2.

16. *Southern Reporter*, Vol. 50 (St. Paul, 1910), 493–94; Jackson *Daily Clarion-Ledger*, November 3, 1909, p. 8.

17. Mississippi, *Laws*, 1910, pp. 110–113; *Mississippi Educational Advance*, Vol. 2 (December, 1912), 25.

18. Mississippi, *Laws*, 1910, pp. 35, 115, 266.

19. Ronald J. Slay, *The Development of the Teaching of Agriculture in Mississippi* (New York, 1928), 98–99, 100–101; *Mississippi Educational Advance*, Vol. 2 (December, 1912), 22; *Mississippi School Journal*, Vol. 14 (October, 1909), 6–11; *Progressive Farmer and Southern Farm Gazette*, Vol. 15 (June 25, 1910), 449.

20. "Regulations and Suggestions concerning County Agricultural High Schools in Mississippi," Mississippi State Board of Education, *Bulletin* 12 (Jackson, 1919), 45–46; Slay, *Teaching of Agriculture in Mississippi*, 100–101.

21. U.S. Office of Experiment Stations, *Annual Report*, 1909 (Washington, 1910), 315; *Mississippi School Journal*, Vol. 13 (September, 1908), 20–21; *Okolona Messenger*, November 3, 1909; C. A. Cobb to George L. Robson, Jr., June 21, 1963, Cobb Papers.

22. Houston *Advocate*, April 3, 10, May 22, July 10, 1908; Houston *Times-Post*, *History of Chickasaw County, Mississippi* (Houston, 1936).

23. Mississippi Agricultural and Mechanical College, *Biennial Report*, 1908–1909, pp. 6–7; *Mississippi Club Boy*, Vol. 2 (May, 1919), 2; C. A. Cobb to George L. Robson, Jr., June 21, 1963, Cobb Papers.

24. James R. Atkinson, "A History of Chickasaw County, Mississippi, to the Civil War," *Northeast Mississippi Historical Journal*, Vol. 2 (December, 1968), 4, 27, 38–40; *Official and Statistical Register of the State of Mississippi*, 1912 (Nashville, 1912), 145; U.S. *Thirteenth Census: Population*, Vol. II, 1044; *ibid.*, *Agriculture*, Vol. VI, 865, 873, 881.

25. Inspection of grounds by authors; Cobb interviews. See Fig. 1.

26. C. A. Cobb, "What One Southern County Agricultural High School Has Done and Is Doing," Conference for Education in the South, *Proceedings*, 1910 (Washington, n.d.), 64–65, 67; *Mississippi School Journal*, Vol. 14 (September, 1909), 18; *Okolona Messenger*, November 3, 1909. The quotation is from Houston *Advocate*, March 5, 1909.

27. *Mississippi School Journal*, Vol. 13 (January, 1909), 1–12; Cobb interviews.

28. Cobb, "What One Southern County Agricultural High School Has Done," 67–68.

29. *Ibid.*, 65–66, 68; *Mississippi School Journal*, Vol. 14 (September, 1909), 15.

30. Cobb, "What One Southern County Agricultural High School Has Done," 66; *Okolona Messenger*, August 25, 1909; Cobb interviews.

31. Mississippi Agricultural and Mechanical College, *Catalogue*, 1909–1910 (Nashville, n.d.), 74; Houston *Advocate*, November 5, 1909.

32. Cobb, "What One Southern County Agricultural High School Has Done," 67; Houston *Post*, November 26, 1909.

33. Cobb interviews. See Fig. 1.

34. *Mississippi School Journal*, Vol. 14 (September, 1909), 13–14; *Progressive Farmer and Southern Farm Gazette*, Vol. 15 (June 25, 1910), 449.

35. *Mississippi Educational Advance*, Vol. 1 (June, 1911), 12–14.

36. Stuart G. Noble, "The Agricultural High School in Mississippi," *Mississippi School Journal*, Vol. 15 (January, 1911), 3–6. The Chickasaw County school was not included in this group.

37. Stuart G. Noble, "The Curriculum of the Agricultural High School, *Mississippi School Journal*, Vol. 15 (March, 1911), 7–11; Cobb interviews.

38. *Okolona Messenger*, December 15, 1909; Mississippi, *Laws*, 1910, p. 35; Mississippi State Superintendent of Public Education, *Biennial Report*, 1909–1911, p. 80.

40. *Mississippi Educational Advance*, Vol. 2 (November, 1912), 17; *ibid.*, Vol. 2 (December, 1912), 25; *ibid.*, Vol. 3 (October, 1913), 5–6; Mississippi State Superintendent of Public Education, *Biennial Report*, 1909–1911, p. 8; *Mississippi Agricultural Student*, Vol. 1 (March 1, 1913), 6; Mississippi Survey Commission, *Public Education in Mississippi: A Report* (Jackson, 1926), 44–45, 57.

41. *Ibid.*, 43–44; Cobb interviews; Mississippi State Superintendent of Public Education, *Biennial Report*, 1909–1911, p. 8.

42. Mississippi Survey Commission, *Public Education in Mississippi*, 44.

43. *Ibid.*, 45; Slay, *Teaching of Agriculture in Mississippi*, 100–105.

44. Dorothy Dickens, "Agricultural High School Dormitories in Mississippi," Mississippi Agricultural Experiment Station, *Bulletin* 293 (A and M College, 1931), 4; Mississippi Survey Commission, *Public Education in Mississippi*, 30–31, 46; Mississippi State Superintendent of Public Education, *Biennial Report*, 1935–1937, p. 46; *ibid.*, 1965–1967, pp. 40, 47–50.

45. Knox M. Broom, *History of Mississippi Public Junior Colleges, 1928–1953* (n.p., 1954), 8, 38.

46. J. C. Hardy to C. A. Cobb, July 19, 1909, Hardy Papers.

47. Houston *Post*, December 24, 1909; Jackson *Daily Clarion-Ledger*, April 8, 1910, p. 2; J. C. Hardy to C. A. Cobb, June 17, 1910; Cobb to Hardy, July 4, 1910, President's Correspondence (Mississippi State University Library); Mississippi State Superintendent of Public Education, *Biennial Report*, 1909–1911, p. 61.

48. C. A. Cobb to J. C. Hardy, January 24, 1910; Hardy to Cobb, January 28, 1910, President's Correspondence.

# CHAPTER III

# Corn Clubs:
# The First Stage,
## 1910-1914

CULLY A. COBB has "made the best success of the agricultural high school of any man in the state," President John C. Hardy of Mississippi Agricultural and Mechanical College wrote in the summer of 1910. "He is certainly a young man of ability and unbounded enthusiasm. I believe he will get hold of the boys in this state even better than Prof. Garner has." [1] * The new position for which Hardy was recommending Cobb was that of head of the corn clubs in Mississippi. These clubs, an early form of the modern 4-H, had only recently come under the general supervision of Seaman A. Knapp, originator of Farmers' Cooperative Demonstration Work and the father of agricultural extension in the South. In due course Knapp approved Hardy's suggestion, and on September 16, 1910, Cully A. Cobb took up his new task. That position placed him squarely in the mainstream of one of the more significant developments in American history, the rise of agricultural extension as a force for improvement of living in the country.

By 1910 the South was well on its way toward the establishment of an effective agricultural extension system. Spurred on by the threatening inroads of the boll weevil, the United States Department of Agriculture, in the first years of the century, began a series of programs designed to improve southern agriculture. Out of these efforts, almost by accident, came a teaching method which held great promise for the future. Known as the Farmers' Cooperative Demonstration Work and headed by the legendary Knapp, it rested upon the principle that farmers were more likely to adopt new ideas and procedures if they were able to see them in successful

* Notes appear at end of each chapter.

use in their own neighborhoods. The demonstration technique, as the new teaching method was called, was born in east Texas in 1903. During the next decade, aided after 1906 by substantial financial support by John D. Rockefeller's General Education Board, it spread across the South. Knapp's agents, stationed in counties or larger areas, enlisted farmers as co-operators and demonstrators, instructed them in newer farming methods, and through them reached their neighbors. Here, in fact, was the basic tool in modern agriculture extension, soon to be adopted throughout the country, and indeed abroad.

Unlike Farmers' Cooperative Demonstration Work, rural youth clubs originated in the North. Among the pioneers was Will T. Otwell in Macoupin County, Illinois. As early as 1899 he distributed seed corn to boys and staged an exhibition in the fall where some of them contended for prizes. Soon similar programs developed at numerous points elsewhere in the Middle West. O. J. Kern, superintendent of schools in Winnebago County, Illinois, organized a boys' club at Rockford in February, 1902. A month earlier in Clark County, Ohio, Albert B. Graham began work that in time would spread throughout the state. One of the leaders in Iowa was O. H. Benson, superintendent of schools in Wright County. In 1911 he went to Washington to take a post in the United States Department of Agriculture. In his baggage was the clover leaf emblem that later became the symbol of a nationwide 4-H organization.

But the South did not lag far behind the North in this phase of a developing system of agricultural education. In 1903 in Texas the Farmer Boys' and Girls' League appeared; a year later it counted 1,200 members. More successful apparently, were youth clubs in Georgia. First organized in Newton County in 1905, they became statewide after the university assumed general supervision of them.[2]

In Mississippi the pioneer was William H. Smith. Born in Alabama in 1866, Smith graduated from the Iuka, Mississippi, Normal College in 1889, and in 1903 he became superintendent of education in Holmes County. There he discovered that the rural schools were producing less than satisfactory results. The relationship between education and farm life seemed to be vague and intangible, and Smith concluded that there was something lacking in a system of

William H. "Corn Club" Smith, founder of corn clubs in Mississippi.

education that failed "to relate closely the school life of the child with the every day life of the community." Quite clearly, an agricultural people needed a school system that would bring the child into intelligent relationship with the world around him, make the home life and farm life of the child a part of his education, and in the end help to produce successful farmers. Smith had also given considerable thought to the economic development of Holmes County. The soil, he felt, was capable of producing up to a hundred bushels of corn or one to two bales of cotton per acre, but actual average yields were less than twenty bushels and about one-third of a bale. Parts of the county were ideally suited to livestock production, but except for mules farm animals were rare, and much of the pork on Holmes County tables came from the North. Was there no new teaching method, Smith wondered, that would meet the problem in the schools and at the same time contribute to a general uplifting of farming practices? By early 1907, Smith thought he had found an answer in clubs for rural school children.[3]

Inspired in part by a knowledge of developments in the North, Smith took the first step in January, 1907, when he outlined his plans to Henry E. Blakeslee, Mississippi Commissioner of Agriculture and Commerce. Blakeslee was enthusiastic, and later in the month Smith wrote to the teachers in Holmes County, asking them to discuss with their students the possibility of forming a club and to provide him with the names of those pupils willing to participate. When over 250 boys and girls indicated an interest, Smith scheduled a general meeting at Lexington, February 23. There he organized the Holmes County Corn Club with a membership of about 200 boys. To each member Smith gave enough seed to plant approximately one half an acre. A faculty member of Mississippi Agricultural and Mechanical College and a representative of the United States Department of Agriculture gave the boys some simple lessons on corn growing. During the growing season, participants received bulletins and other publications of the state and federal agricultural agencies, and Smith maintained contact with the boys through correspondence and through the teachers. In October, eighty-two of the boys exhibited the results of their work at a corn show in Lexington, and at the state fair in Jackson a month later prizes offered by local businessmen were awarded to winners.[4]

The corn club, according to Smith, served several purposes. Initially, it encouraged members to take up in a useful way the study of soils, seed selection, and approved methods of soil improvement and cultivation. But these immediate goals were transcended by others more basic in character. Smith believed that the corn club would lead to a more effective education for children and to a more prosperous and satisfying life for adults. Rural existence would become more attractive, and the countryside would cease losing its best young people to the towns and cities. Finally, he hoped that his club would prove to be a vehicle through which the agricultural college might effectively reach a greater portion of the rural population.[5]

Even as Smith was getting his Holmes County Corn Club into operation, the idea was spreading into other counties in the state. There were clubs of some sort in 1907 in Copiah, Pontotoc, Lafayette, and Panola counties, as well as in Holmes. The next year, organizations flourished in twenty-three counties and had an aggregate membership of about three thousand. Reportedly, Lee and Yalobusha counties were among the most successful, the latter having some three hundred members.[6]

Meanwhile, the scope of the work broadened. In Panola County, for example, participants grew not only corn but also cotton, potatoes, legumes, and other crops. The Mississippi farmers' institute management assumed a role in the program, publishing a corn bulletin for members and providing lecturers and judges for meetings and corn shows. The state commissioner of agriculture and commerce also encouraged the work. The state legislature authorized counties to appropriate funds for prizes, and by December, 1908, some had already done so. That autumn, in fact, boys in fifteen counties had corn exhibits at their county fairs and at the state fair; there were plans to send statewide winners to the National Corn Exposition in Omaha.[7]

An effort to systematize the work throughout the state came early in 1908. A committee consisting of Smith, the state commissioner of agriculture and commerce, the state superintendent of education, and representatives of Mississippi Agricultural and Mechanical College and the United States Department of Agriculture formulated a set of suggestions for those county superintendents wishing to launch clubs. The committee proposed that membership be open to all boys under the age of twenty-one, whether they were in school or not, and that during the first year of a club's existence members limit themselves to the growing of corn. A method for determining yield in shelled corn was worked out. All teachers were urged to inform themselves concerning corn growing so that they might more effectively encourage and aid the boys. Finally, the committee proposed that in each county a show be held in October, perhaps in conjunction with the county fair, that prizes offered by businessmen be awarded strictly on merit, and that prize-winning exhibits be entered in a statewide contest at the state fair.[8]

Certificate awarded corn club boys for excellence, 1910.

Meanwhile, other southern states were developing club work of a similar sort. In 1908 in Jack County, Texas, Thomas M. Marks organized a club that included 137 boys who exhibited their crops at a fair in the fall. V. L. Roy, superintendent of schools in Avoyelles Parish, was the leader in Louisiana, establishing a club in 1907; and in the same year A. L. Easterling took the first step in South Carolina when he organized a club in Marlboro County.[9]

From his headquarters in Lake Charles, Louisiana, and later Washington, D.C., Seaman A. Knapp watched these developments and pondered their significance and value. Almost from the outset, he was willing to encourage the work. One of Knapp's agents. A. F. Meharg of Texas, participated in Smith's organizational meeting in Lexington, and on December 11, 1907, Knapp gave Smith the title of collaborator in Farmers' Cooperative Demonstration Work, at a salary of a dollar a year in order that the Mississippian might have the franking privilege. A month later Meharg took part in the meeting at Durant, Mississippi, at which Smith and agricultural and educational officials formulated plans for spreading the clubs throughout the state. In the summer of 1908 Knapp visited Holmes County, participated in a combined teachers' and farmers' institute there, and discussed with Smith the potentialities of club work. Satisfied that organization of rural youth offered important opportunities, Knapp resolved to assume direction of the work. A major step came in March, 1909, when Oscar B. Martin, state superintendent of education in South Carolina, was appointed special agent in the United States Bureau of Plant Industry, to which Farmers' Cooperative Demonstration Work was attached. His task was to coordinate and expand the club movement under Knapp's general supervision. The work progressed rapidly. In 1909 there were 10,543 boys enrolled, and the number jumped to 46,225 the next year and to 56,840 in 1911.[10]

The decision to take control of the club movement raised a number of questions concerning the place of the land-grant colleges in the program. Knapp had a strong antipathy toward the colleges, and in the management of the Farmers' Cooperative Demonstration Work he had for all practical purposes ignored them. But some of the land-grant schools, including the one in Mississippi, were already involved in club work, so Knapp concluded that it would be possible to work with them. Discussions began in December, 1908; that month, also, the General Education Board gave its approval to cooperation with the colleges. The issues were explored further at a meeting in Atlanta, Georgia, in April, 1909. There, in fact, the basic ideas were worked out that were later implemented. The end result was the negotiation of memorandums of understanding with individual colleges covering the work to be conducted in those states. The first of these came in Alabama and was dated July 16, 1909. Before the year was out, arrangements had been concluded in North Carolina, Mississippi, Louisiana, Georgia, and Arkansas. These agreements marked the beginnings of financial and administrative cooperation in agricultural extension between the Department of Agriculture and the colleges and foreshadowed the provisions of the Smith-Lever Act.[11]

The memorandum of understanding under which club work was organized in Mississippi went into effect August 20, 1909. It provided that the "object of this cooperative work shall be to promote improved agricultural practices in the State of Mississippi. . . ."

The special agent charged with the task of conducting the program would be selected and his work planned jointly by Seaman A. Knapp and appropriate authorities at Mississippi Agricultural and Mechanical College. The Bureau of Plant Industry agreed to pay the salary of $2,000 a year and all traveling expenses of the special agent; Mississippi was required only to provide office space on the agricultural college campus and such clerical and stenographic assistance as the agent might require. Both parties to the agreement were free to use any results obtained from the work in official correspondence and publications as long as the cooperative nature of the program was clearly indicated.

The memorandum also set forth in considerable detail the character of the work to be conducted by the special agent. He was directed to institute "demonstrations in agriculture at public schools, high schools, and other educational institutions" by "correspondence, by attending superintendents' and teachers' institutes, and in such other ways as opportunity may offer. . . ." In addition, the special agent was to provide suggestions to school officials concerning instruction in agriculture and garden school work and to aid the college in its farmers' institute and short-course programs insofar

Seaman A. Knapp, the father of the cooperative agricultural extension service, with state club champions in Washington, D. C., 1909. DeWitt C. Lundy, the Mississippi winner, is second from the left.

as those programs pertained to rural youth. It was stated categorically, however, that the special agent was "under no circumstances to do regular teaching in the college." [12]

A few months later, Department of Agriculture officials concluded that the August agreement was perhaps too specific in spelling out the mode of operation and a new memorandum of understanding was signed November 15. It provided simply that "the work to be performed by and for the United States Department of Agriculture under this agreement shall consist of planning and conducting farm demonstrations in schools . . . and among organized clubs of farmers' boys on such forms as may be mutually agreed upon by the parties. . . ." [13]

To the post of special agent in charge of corn clubs, President Hardy nominated and Knapp accepted Peter P. Garner. Born in Noxubee County on October 10, 1872, Garner had studied at Peabody College, Mississippi Agricultural and Mechanical College, and at the University of Mississippi before he received a bachelor's degree at Columbia University in 1903. Returning to his native state, Garner taught mathematics at Mississippi Agricultural and Mechanical College for a year and in September, 1904, he took charge of that institution's Preparatory Department, a position that he held until August 1, 1909. In addition, he had several years experience in speaking at and managing teacher's institutes and summer normal schools in Mississippi. [14]

Circumstances dictated a change in leadership in 1910. In July, Professor David C. Hull, head of the School of Industrial Education at Mississippi Agricultural and Mechanical College, resigned to accept the presidency of Millsaps College in Jackson. Garner was appointed to fill the vacancy. [15] President Hardy proposed Cully A. Cobb as Garner's successor, pointing to his record at Buena Vista and mentioning his fine appearance in the spring in Little Rock at the meeting of the Conference for Education in the South. The salary, Hardy thought, should be the same Garner would have received. State Superintendent of Education Joseph N. Powers recommended Hugh Critz, superintendent of schools in Oktibbeha County, for the post. William H. Smith also supported Critz. But according to Hardy, Seaman A. Knapp was "governed by what I say," and he appointed Hardy's nominee, after cutting Cobb's salary to $1,800. With a "keen sense of appreciation," Cobb accepted the offer, taking his new post September 16, 1910.[16]

"I do not know of any thing I would rather have than this . . . position," Cobb wrote upon being notified of his appointment. "I have my whole heart in the work and will use [all my] energy to make it a success and to make those glad that gave it to me." [17] For nine years Cobb held the job, and there is no indication that the enthusiasm that he manifested in 1910 faded or that those who recommended him had cause to regret their support of his candidacy.

As state agents in charge of corn clubs, Garner and Cobb reported to Oscar B. Martin, Knapp's assistant in Farmers' Cooperative Demonstration Work. In addition, since their appointment was a joint one, Garner and Cobb also reported to appropriate officials at Mississippi Agricultural and Mechanical College. Garner apparently dealt directly with the president of that institution, but in 1910 Cobb's work was considered a part of the college's department of farmers' institutes and extension, and he reported to the head of that department. Cobb was given faculty status, with the title of Professor of Extension. In accordance with the memorandum of understanding by which corn clubs in Mississippi became a part of Knapp's program, the Department of Agriculture, using General Education Board funds, paid Garner's and Cobb's salaries and traveling expenses. The college contributed an office and stenographic assistance. In 1912 and 1913 the state's outlay for Cobb's work amounted to three hundred dollars a year.[18]

The bringing of corn club work under the direction of Seaman A. Knapp produced significant changes in the character of the program. The objectives of the corn clubs after 1909 came to be more than simple growing of huge yields or the production of a few ears of corn pleasing to the eye. Instead, boys learned the economics of successful farming, they were induced to see the attractions of profitable agriculture, and they were taught to respect solid achievement on the farm. Knapp and his subordinates standardized the rules for participation, established a full acre as the required unit, and formulated a criteria for choosing winners that brought into use learning and knowledge of different types. The new leadership minimized the ten-ear exhibit, long used in corn shows throughout the county, and gave it value of only 20 percent out of a possible 100 percent in the awarding of prizes. Cost of production and yield, on the other hand, were valued at 30 percent each, thereby forcing participants to maximize yield while minimizing cost. Finally, for 20 percent, Knapp's men required each boy to write a history of his crop, including such details as seed selection and soil preparation methods, planting and cultivating techniques, and significant dates of the various steps. A successful participant, in addition to being able to grow corn, needed sharp powers of observation and the ability to keep records, write acceptable English, and calculate correctly. In short, Knapp had taken the corn contest idea and had converted it into a "first-rate pedagogical" tool.[19]

Moreover, Knapp regularly emphasized the broader function of the corn clubs. When a boy produced a better crop, Knapp pointed out, it was clear proof that he had understood clearly his instructions, a prerequisite for success in any field. At the same time, the experience of producing an acre of corn would serve as an inspiration to the boy and give him confidence in his abilities, not only in agriculture but in other lines as well. Finally, the boy who succeeded in his corn club would carry his demonstration into his home, a most significant occurrence because the "home is the mightiest force in molding the race and in shaping the destiny of mankind; the farm must feed the world; the boy must ultimately preside over the home and control the land. At least we have touched in this way the very heart and soul of teaching. We have coordinated and blended the teacher, the lesson, the boy, the farm, and the home." [20]

Knapp also understood well the value of competition, recognition for achievement, and economic incentive. He insisted that club members compete against each other at every level, feeling that to do so would force them to do their best and at the same time prepare them for life. Awards, he thought, should be substantial and numerous enough to encourage all participants. But he recognized that in time such awards would lose their appeal and he demanded that every boy be allowed to keep for himself the profits of his project, after allowing a reasonable amount for rent of the land and for the use of tools and work animals.[21]

As these ideas developed in Washington, the club work retained many of the general objectives that William H. Smith had outlined years earlier in Holmes County. Writing in 1912, Bradford Knapp, who had succeeded his father as head of Farmers' Cooperative Demonstration Work, said that boys' clubs were designed to give the rural teacher a simple and easy method of teaching practical agriculture in the only way that it could be done successfully, that is, by actual work on the farm. Secondly, it sought to inspire boys with a love of the land, to show them how to get more out of it, to stimulate a friendly rivalry among them, and to help in keeping boys on the land. Finally, Knapp pointed to the relationship between boys' clubs and education of the adult farmers. Youth work, he said, was in some areas the most useful single method for breaking down the adult farmers' prejudice against new ideas in agriculture proposed by outside agencies and in promoting diversification in regions dominated by one-crop farming. In fact, according to Knapp and other officials of the Bureau of Plant Industry, the rapid expansion of Farmers' Cooperative Demonstration Work would have been impossible without the boys' corn clubs.[22]

Within this general framework, Garner for one year and Cobb for nine years conducted the corn club movement in Mississippi. In the day-by-day management of the program, the new relation with the United States Department of Agriculture produced immediately no sharp changes in the general mode of operation. The county superintendents continued to be key men in the work. Garner and Cobb contacted them and through them sought to enlist the enthusiastic aid and support of rural school teachers who encouraged boys to grow plots of corn. Quite often teachers actively supervised the work of members in their districts. Enrollment lists compiled at the county level went to the state and Washington offices. Fathers, too, had to be convinced, since they had to provide the land, work animals, and tools. One of the major tasks of the state agents was raising money from local sources for prizes. Garner and Cobb also encouraged the holding of corn shows wherever possible. Finally, through their office at Mississippi's land-grant college flowed information concerning the proper methods for growing corn and measuring the results and the prizes for those who excelled. Included in the mail that went out to members were bulletins from the Department of Agriculture and from the college. Circulars and personal letters also helped to keep the boys informed and made them feel that they were participating in a significant enterprise.[23]

In their relations with the superintendents, teachers, and boys, the special agents used persuasion as their primary tool. Cobb carried on an extensive correspondence with superintendents, urging them to push the work in their counties, announcing various prizes and awards, and beseeching them to submit promptly reports from participants. Misunderstandings were all too numerous, and patience was necessary.[24] In some instances, superintendents were reached through the pages of statewide educational periodicals and farm papers. Writing in the *Mississippi Educational Advance* in 1911, Cobb urged the superintendents to take up with their teachers the organization of clubs in the fall, rather than in the spring as had been the practice, in order that the boys might be thoroughly coached in such matters as fall preparation of soil, winter cover crops, and thorough drainage. The boys themselves were often contacted through personal correspondence and forays into the countryside. On such trips, Cobb talked to all who would listen; sincerity and clarity of thought were indispensible in dealing with those upon whom the work depended. In addition, Cobb wrote innumerable articles for the rural press in which he discussed the program, provided instructions for members, and urged them to devote their full attention to the work.[25]

Cobb found meetings at the agricultural high schools and at the college's traveling short courses to be affairs especially useful in recruiting club boys and in encouraging them to put forth their best efforts. In the fall of 1911, in response to a request from the principal of the Bolivar Agricultural High School, Cobb and William H. Smith, by then president of the state's normal college, gave a series of lectures throughout the county, speaking on behalf of the club movement. In January, 1913, Cobb appeared at a short course at Hattiesburg, where he spoke on the corn clubs, explaining their educational role, contending that cultural training and mental discipline were acquired through them, and maintaining that one's education should "hitch him up with his vocation." [26] More common, of course, were teachers' institutes and similar gatherings where Cobb would meet those in closest contact with the boys. The consolidated school movement, just then getting under way in Mississippi, also helped by providing opportunities for meeting and working with groups of boys and their parents. Commencement day often found Cobb in attendance. Newspapers serving the state made Cobb's tasks easier by giving club work extensive coverage. The Memphis *Commercial Appeal* under the editorship of C. P. J. Mooney, the New Orleans *Picayune*, and the Jackson *Daily News* were leaders in this field, but a multitude of local weeklies did their part. Country preachers, too, were always influential with country boys, and such religious leaders as Bishop Charles B. Galloway of the Methodist Church and Dr. John W. Provine, then president of Mississippi College, gave forceful and effective support to club work. In fact, so numerous were the agencies and individuals helping the program that at times Cobb felt that he was still the small boy on the farm whose task at brush-burning time was to "keep the chunks pushed together" to produce clean burning.[27]

The formulation of detailed policies and standards for the proper conduct of the program required a great deal of attention in the early days. As state club agents, Garner and Cobb participated in regular meetings in the Washington office where the general outlines of the work were determined. Other ideas were developed at the state level. In Mississippi, perhaps more than elsewhere, there was insistence that each boy cultivate a normal farm unit of land, in order to avoid "patch work," and that there be thoroughgoing cooperation with educational and rural religious forces. Everywhere there was a firm determination to "provide each club member with opportunity to demonstrate to himself the economic, educational and spiritual values inherent in successful farm life." [28]

In time, a number of more definite policies concerning the work were formulated. Membership was limited to boys between the ages of ten and eighteen. Participants within a county or district were organized into a formal club with the normal quota of offices and an executive committee. Each boy was expected to do his own work on his plot. Procedures for measuring more accurately the boys' plots and for determining yields were established.[29]

For the corn club movement to function properly, a sufficient number of prizes had to be made available to the boys. In this cause Garner and Cobb spent no small part of their time establishing contacts with businessmen, explaining the program to them, and urging them to contribute cash or other prizes. Businessmen in Mississippi were sincerely interested, as they were throughout the nation, and the contributions for awards flowed in. State, county, and town governments and county newspapers also offered prizes of various kinds. In 1910 Garner announced that the boy in each county producing the largest yield would receive a diploma signed by the governor and the commissioner of agriculture. The same year a real estate firm in Magnolia offered a bull, a colt, and a pair of pigs to the three top winners in Pike County. In 1911 the attorney general offered fifty dollars to the winner at the corn show held at the state fair. Mississippi boys that year were eligible to compete for a one thousand dollar cup offered by the American Land and Irrigation Company at a show in November in New York City. Manufacturers frequently offered one or more of their products to club winners. Among those in 1912 was the De Laval Separator Company; its prize, a cream separator.[30]

As the work progressed, the awarding of prizes became more systematic and uniform. Bankers also came to be the most important single group contributing financially to the program. The list of prizes offered in the 1914 crop year was illustrative. Individual counties had prizes ranging from fifty to two hundred dollars and many of them offered prize trips to the state fair. A seed company offered a prize of one hundred dollars, to be awarded at the state fair. At that exhibition, also, there was a twenty dollar award for the best single ear, a thirty-three dollar prize for the best ten ear exhibit, one or more scholarships to Mississippi Agricultural and Mechanical College, and a scholarship to the Knapp School for Country Life at Nashville. Finally, every boy who submitted a complete crop report at the end of the season received a corn club emblem.[31]

Meanwhile, the state sought through legislation to help in the raising of funds for premiums. As early as 1908 the legislature authorized county boards of supervisors to expend up to fifty dollars for prizes for corn club winners. Six years later, county superintendents of schools were permitted to set aside from the county school funds a similar amount for the same purpose.[32]

At least one prize was offered as an encouragement to county superintendents of schools to support club work more enthusiastically in their counties. In 1913 Cobb induced the state fair management to award a Ford automobile to the superintendent most successful in promoting corn clubs. The prize went to E. P. Clayton of Lee County. State fair authorities were sufficiently pleased to offer a similar award the next year.[33]

It also fell to Garner and Cobb to administer an award that, for a number of years, was the highest honor a club boy could win. In the spring of 1909, as a special incentive to Mississippi boys, Seaman A. Knapp announced that the club member making the best record would be treated to a trip to the nation's capital. Before the crop was harvested, others had made similar offers in South Carolina, Arkansas, and Virginia. The Mississippi winner, DeWitt C. Lundy, and his three co-winners met President Taft and Secretary of Agriculture James Wilson who awarded each of them a certificate of merit.[34]

In later years the Washington trip continued to be a highlight of the year's work. In 1910 the Mississippi representative was William Williams of Decatur who produced 147 bushels of corn on his acre at a cost of 18 cents per bushel, despite having to cope with a severe drought.[35] The 1911 winner was fourteen-year-old Bennie Beeson from Lincoln County who grew 227 bushels at a cost of $33.35 for labor and fertilizer. He had first joined the corn club in 1909 and had been a county winner in 1910. Among his methods were unusually deep plowing, heavy application of barnyard manures and commercial fertilizers, and regular weekly cultivation. Later, Beeson would be the hero of Gerrard Harris's *Joe the Book*

*Farmer*.[36] Following the 1912 season, the state bankers' association sent six boys to Washington; the next year a single winner, Jones Polk of Jefferson Davis County, received the honor. His 214.9 bushels per acre was the second highest in the United States that year. With the winners from other states, Polk met Vice President Thomas R. Marshall and appeared before the House Committee on Agriculture, presided over by Asbury F. Lever of South Carolina.[37]

At the suggestion of Bradford Knapp, the trips to Washington were terminated in 1914,[38] but club boys found no shortage of fairs, exhibitions, and shows to attend. There continued to be the local and county corn shows and the state fair remained a major target for the most successful of the boys. With its displays of corn produced by the boys as well as other exhibits both educational and entertaining, the state fair was a highlight of the season for both the club members and their state agent. In 1912, determined that the club exhibit would receive the attention it deserved, Cobb visited the fair prior to its opening, arranged for more space, and took personal charge of the exhibit. Some three hundred boys had exhibits there, and placards and other demonstration materials pointed out lessons to all who passed.[39]

In 1913 twenty of Cobb's corn club boys and Cobb himself attended the National Corn Exposition at Columbia, South Carolina. Cobb originated the idea of sending prize winners to the show, a proposal that was approved in the Washington office. Bankers throughout the state agreed to provide funds for the trip. While at the exposition, Mississippi boys participated in a demonstration school conducted by the management and competed with boys from eleven other states for national prizes. Alabama won first place, Mississippi placed third, but Cobb was certain that the boys found the trip both instructional and inspirational.[40]

The Tri-State Fair at Memphis also attracted Mississippi club boys. At its annual exhibition in 1913, the fair's management entertained two boys from each of the counties in Arkansas, Tennessee, and Mississippi that lay within a one-hundred-mile radius of the city. The communities from which the boys came were asked to raise rail fares for them, and the fair association provided tents and meals for the boys while they were on the grounds. The boys

Farmers' institute in Leflore County, Mississippi, 1910. Cobb is on the left, wearing a suit. The slight man with a beard across the table from him is Perry G. Holden, one of the pioneers in agricultural extension, then on the staff of Iowa State College.

viewed the exhibits at the fair and were given the opportunity of attending a short course conducted by personnel of the Farmers' Cooperative Demonstration Work.[41]

Closer to home, the corn club boys had the opportunity to attend an annual meeting on the agricultural college campus. In August, 1911, while the annual round-up for institute workers and farmers was being held on the campus, Cobb staged a Corn Club Day. Only a few boys attended because they had to provide their own expenses, but those who did appear were able to tour the campus and the experiment farm and to hear lectures by authorities on corn culture, including a staff member from Iowa Agricultural College. The next year, some thirty boys attended, participated in a variety of contests, and received diplomas at the end of the meeting.[42] Later, this annual meeting would grow into the Mississippi Boys' Corn Club Congress.

Quite obviously, the position of special agent in charge of corn clubs required a man of almost unlimited energy. There was little time for rest, relaxation, or reflection. During the 1912–1913 year, for example, Cobb reported that he traveled 21,309 miles by rail and over 1,000 miles by team. Among other meetings, he appeared at thirty farmers' institutes and presented his message on corn club work before almost ten thousand people.[43] But in addition to the farmers' institutes, Cobb traveled throughout the state, attending

Cobb in a Monroe County, Mississippi, corn field with club boys and others, 1911. Cobb is in the back row, sixth from the left.

local meetings of teachers, discussing the program with county superintendents, and in many cases conferring with his club members.[44]

While attending to his multitudinous duties, Cobb found time to take on other tasks. He was in considerable demand as a speaker, appearing throughout the state on behalf of general agricultural improvement. By the terms of the memorandum of understanding with the Department of Agriculture, he could perform no teaching duties in connection with the regular students on the campus, but he did speak to informal groups and campus clubs. Cobb continued a role in the agricultural high school movement and in 1913 was appointed to a committee that was given the task of formulating a uniform course of study for them. He regularly attended the meetings of the Conference for Education in the South, serving for a time as the Mississippi secretary of that group.[45] Cobb also helped to organize in August, 1913, the Mississippi Corn Improvement Association and served as its president. Two years earlier, he had been one of the main speakers at the annual meeting of the Mississippi Teachers' Association and he attended other meetings of that organization.[46]

Demanding though the work was, by 1914 Cobb felt that the task offered adequate compensation in the form of solid accomplishments. Membership in corn clubs in Mississippi had followed a pleasing if irregular growth. In 1909 Garner had reported an enrollment of 2,201. The next year it almost tripled to 6,492, but that number included many who failed to complete their projects. The discrepancy between the number enrolled and the number that actually did the prescribed work, in fact, pointed to one of the major continuing problems in the club movement. More careful management during Cobb's first full year as state agent held the enrollment to 4,642, and in 1912 it increased to only 4,825. The next year enrollment reached a new peak of 7,190.[47]

That number placed Mississippi fourth among the southern states in total club membership. Texas had the largest number, 17,825, followed by Alabama and Georgia. Geographical size and a favorable ratio of whites to Negroes in the total rural population explained in large measure the heavy enrollment in Texas. A better measure was the number of members per thousand of the rural population. On that basis, Mississippi ranked third, with a figure of 10.7, compared to 13.7 for Alabama, 12.3 for Georgia, and 7.3 for Texas.[48]

"The corn club work under the direction of Prof. C. A. Cobb is accomplishing wonderful results," wrote Richard H. Pate, head of Mississippi's Department of Farmers' Institutes and Extension, in 1913.[49] In fact, indications of significant achievement were evident throughout the state. Agricultural and educational authorities praised club work, pointing to its beneficial effects on boys and adults alike. Ordinary school work took on new meaning for participants, teachers reported a better attitude in their classrooms, and

79

Corn club boys on the campus of Mississippi Agricultural and Mechanical College, 1912.

Cobb could cite cases of boys who were inspired by their club experiences to enroll at the state's agricultural college. Equally important, perhaps, was the role that corn club work played in breaking down the idea so prevalent among some southern boys that

Boys' corn club exhibit at Mississippi State Fair, 1913.

physical labor should be left to the Negro. The General Education Board, in fact, labeled that development a "psychological revolution" and contended that it was one of the more significant contributions of the clubs.[50]

Others were impressed with more obvious and more concrete accomplishments. A boy in the clubs, said one observer, "learns that science in agriculture pays, and that to be a good farmer one has to know more than the old 'know-it-all', who will not read any paper concerning his business nor use the modern equipment and methods." Moreover, since club work affected adult farmers as well as their sons, the "corn clubs and contests are preparing for tomorrow while influencing today." The promoters of the work, he continued, were doing "more for the country's future than any statesman can ever do." [51] Less eloquently, an official of Mississippi Agricultural and Mechanical College wrote in 1913 that it "would be difficult to over-estimate the far-reaching effect of the . . . clubs. . . . The idea of an acre of corn . . . for each boy . . . will hasten the fulfillment of the meaning of Mississippi's new motto: 'Grown in Mississippi,' he proclaimed." [52]

As a matter of fact, one of the accomplishments of which Cobb was most proud was the role that the club movement presumably had in the expansion of corn production in the state. In final analysis, Seaman A. Knapp had extended his program to include the pioneer corn clubs because he recognized in them a way to reach and effectively influence adult farmers, and Cobb knew that in large measure the significance of the clubs had to be calculated in those terms. Accordingly, Cobb pointed to the increase in corn production from twenty-eight million bushels in 1909 to sixty-three million in 1913 when the state produced about 75 percent of its requirements. Admittedly, a number of factors contributed to this increase, but Cobb argued strongly that the club movement was one of the influential agencies promoting it. The fact that the average yield per acre for the state on a whole in 1912 was only 18.3 bushels while that of the club members was 66.6 bushels gave his argument a strong ring of validity.[53]

Moreover, Cobb could point to the role of corn club work in increasing the usefulness of Mississippi-grown corn. According to Cobb, club work helped to bring out the fact that corn produced in Mississippi usually had a lower moisture content than northern corn, a fact that should give it an added attraction to both exporters and feeders. The establishment of shelling stations throughout the state, a product in part of the club movement, facilitated the handling of the crop.[54]

Still, Cobb believed that figures on corn production, moisture content, and similar statistics, important though they were, gave no full measure of the impact of corn clubs. Their true value could only be calculated in more human terms. For instance, Cobb pointed to corn clubs as "one of the factors of our modern education scheme that is . . . relating education to the life our people must live," a statement that reflected the early ideas of William H. Smith. But even more important were the contributions the clubs were making to the acceptance of change by future adult Mississippians. The clubs, Cobb contended, were helping to rear a generation of men who would never be satisfied with the ways of the past, who would be able to think logically and act rationally, and who would "take a broader view of life and a more clearly defined understanding of those things that go to make up real life and success." [55]

By 1914 Cobb and others involved in managing the corn clubs knew that they were but the first step toward a comprehensive system of rural youth clubs. The corn clubs had shown the way and established the pattern. Needed especially was more adequate financial support. Since the work had begun in 1909, the Department of Agriculture, aided by General Education Board contributions, had supported the program. But funds from those sources were severely limited. In Mississippi in 1912 these amounted to only $2,300. Meanwhile, Mississippi continued to provide office facilities and clerical help, aggregating about $300 a year, an amount that was taken from the state legislature's biennial appropriation for farmers' institutes and agricultural extension. Not until 1914 did the state make an appropriation specifically for corn club work. At that time, it granted the amount of $1,500 per year for 1914 and 1915. [56]

Fortunately for the future of youth clubs in Mississippi, by 1914 there was a widespread recognition of the need for a national system of agricultural extension, financed by substantially larger federal and state appropriations and by local contributions. Arguments supporting such legislation had been heard in Congress for several years, and in 1914 the efforts of agricultural educators, businessmen, and others brought success. On May 8, 1914, President Wilson approved the historic Smith-Lever Act. Under its terms, the pioneer corn clubs would become the modern 4-H movement.

## NOTES TO CHAPTER III

1. J. C. Hardy to S. A. Knapp, July 7, 1910, President's Correspondence.
2. Scott, *Agricultural Extension*, 123–28, 206–36, 238; Oscar B. Martin, *The Demonstration Work: Dr. Knapp's Contribution to Civilization* (San Antonio,

1941), 53–54. The standard biography of Seaman A. Knapp is Joseph C. Bailey, *Seaman A. Knapp: Schoolmaster of American Agriculture* (New York, 1945).

3. W. H. Smith to J. F. Merry, October 21, 1907, James E. Tanner Papers (Mississippi State University Library); Smith to Perry G. Holden, P. G. Holden Memoirs (Michigan State University Library, East Lansing).

4. *Southern Farm Magazine*, Vol. 15 (June, 1907), 9; *ibid.*, Vol. 15 (December, 1907), 14; W. H. Smith to J. F. Merry, October 21, 1907, Tanner Papers; *Southern Farm Gazette*, Vol. 14 (December 19, 1908), 3.

5. W. H. Smith to J. F. Merry, October 21, 1907, Tanner Papers; *Southern Farm Magazine*, Vol. 15 (December, 1907), 14; Mississippi Agricultural Experiment Station, *Bulletin* 120 (Agricultural College, 1908), 67.

6. *Southern Farm Magazine*, Vol. 15 (June, 1907), 9; *Southern Farm Gazette*, Vol. 13 (September 19, 1908), 3; *ibid.*, Vol. 14 (April 24, 1909), 5; Tupelo (Miss.) *Journal*, November 13, 1908.

7. *Southern Farm Magazine*, Vol. 15 (June, 1907), 9; American Association of Farmers' Institute Workers, *Proceedings*, 1907 (Washington, 1908), 23; *Southern Farm Gazette*, Vol. 14 (December 19, 1908), 3; *ibid.*, Vol. 13 (September 19, 1908), 3.

8. *Mississippi School Journal*, Vol. 12 (March, 1908), 43–44.

9. Scott, *Agricultural Extension*, 240.

10. Franklin M. Reck, *The 4-H Story: A History of 4-H Club Work* (Ames, 1951), 50, 53–54, 60; W. H. Smith to Editor, Aberdeen *Examiner*, January 31, 1912, Tanner Papers; Martin, *Demonstration Work*, 53–54; Bradford Knapp and O. B. Martin, "Results of Boys' Demonstration Work in Corn Clubs in 1911," U.S. Bureau of Plant Industry, *Publication* 741 (Washington, 1912), 1–3.

11. S. A. Knapp to J. C. Hardy, December 4, 11, 1908, April 7, 21, 1909, President's Correspondence; Reck, *4-H Story*, 60–63; J. A. Evans, "Recollections of Extension History," North Carolina Extension Service, *Circular* 224 (Raleigh, 1938), 14, 16; Bradford Knapp to B. T. Galloway, January 24, 1912, Bureau of Plant Industry Records (National Archives, Washington). See also L. R. Harrill, *Memories of 4-H* (Raleigh, 1967), 2–7.

12. B. T. Galloway to W. H. Magruder, August 13, 1909, President's Correspondence.

13. B. T. Galloway to J. C. Hardy, December 13, 1909, enclosing memo; Knapp to Hardy, November 24, 1909, President's Correspondence.

14. Peter P. Garner, Personnel Records, Mississippi Extension Service Records (Mississippi State University Library); Hardy to Knapp, June 19, 1909, President's Correspondence. Early state agents in other states included the following: I. O. Schaub in North Carolina; L. N. Duncan in Alabama; H. S. Mobley in Arkansas; and V. L. Roy in Louisiana. See Evans, "Recollections of Extension History," 15.

15. Mississippi Agricultural and Mechanical College, *Biennial Report*, 1909–1911, pp. 47–48.

16. J. C. Hardy to S. A. Knapp, June 29, July 7, 28, 1910; Knapp to Hardy, July 26, 1910; Hardy to C. A. Cobb, July 13, 1910; Cobb to Hardy, July 21, 1910; J. N. Powers and W. H. Smith to Hardy, July 11, 1910, President's Correspondence.

17. Cobb to Hardy, July 21, 1910, President's Correspondence.

18. Mississippi Agricultural and Mechanical College, *Catalogue*, 1910–1911, p. 5; Report of the Director of Farmers' Institutes and Extension, May 1, 1911; President's Report, May 10, 1913, President's Correspondence; Bradford Knapp to B. T. Galloway, January 24, 1912, Bureau of Plant Industry Records.

19. Bailey, *Knapp*, 233; Martin, *Demonstration Work*, 28–30; Evans, "Recollections of Extension History," 14.

20. Seaman A. Knapp, "How Can the Masses be Induced to Adopt a Better Sys-

tem of Agriculture?" Conference for Education in the South, *Proceedings*, 1910 (Washington, n.d.), 257–58.

21. Martin, *Demonstration Work*, 33, 58.

22. Bradford Knapp to B. T. Galloway, January 24, 1912, Bureau of Plant Industry Records: Association of American Agricultural Colleges and Experiment Stations, *Proceedings*, 1912 (Burlington, Vt., 1913), 142; *Country Gentleman*, Vol. 77 (September 7, 1912), 10; Bradford Knapp and O. B. Martin, "Boys' Demonstration Work: The Corn Clubs," U. S. Bureau of Plant Industry, *Publication 644* (Washington, 1912), 1.

23. C. A. Cobb, "Boys' Corn Clubs," Mississippi Teachers' Association, *Proceedings*, 1911 (Jackson, n.d.), 145–47; Cobb interviews. For a discussion of similar work in North Carolina, see Association of American Agricultural Colleges and Experiment Stations, *Proceedings*, 1911, pp. 213–14. See also General Education Board, *The General Education Board: An Account of Its Activities, 1902–1914* (New York, 1915), 58–59.

24. C. A. Cobb to C. A. Neal, November 21, 1910; Cobb to J. W. Kimbrough, December 1, 1910; Cobb to W. W. Lockard, December 1, 1910; Cobb to Superintendents, December 5, 1910, President's Correspondence.

25. *Mississippi Educational Advance*, Vol. 1 (November, 1911), 19–20; A. A. McAlphin to Cobb, January 9, 1911, President's Correspondence; *Mississippi Agricultural Student*, Vol. II (March 1, 1914), 3.

26. *Mississippi School Journal*, Vol 16 (October, 1911), 16; *Mississippi Agricultural Student*, Vol. 1 (March 1, 1913), 5.

27. Cobb interviews; Cobb to R. V. Scott, April 9, 1971, Cobb Papers.

28. C. A. Cobb to J. E. Tanner, July 18, 1939, Mississippi Extension Service Records.

29. *Mississippi Agricultural Student*, Vol. 1 (March 1, 1914), 2–3.

30. *Progressive Farmer and Southern Farm Gazette*, Vol. 15 (March 19, 1910), 440; *ibid.*, Vol. 2 (October, 1912), 5; C. A. Cobb to Superintendents, June 17, 1911, President's Correspondence.

31. *Mississippi Agricultural Student*, Vol. 1 (March 1, 1914), 2.

32. Mississippi, *Laws*, 1908, p. 94; *ibid.*, 1914, pp. 258–59.

33. Annual Report of the Department of Farmers' Institutes and Extension, April 29, 1914, President's Correspondence; undated memo, Mississippi Extension Service Records.

34. *Southern Farm Gazette*, Vol. 14 (May 8, 1908), 16; *ibid.*, Vol. 14 (May 15, 1909), 16; Jackson *Daily Clarion-Ledger*, January 12, 1910, p. 8; *Outlook*, Vol. 114 (February 5, 1910), 279–80.

35. Reck, *4-H Story*, 74; *Progressive Farmer and Southern Farm Gazette*, Vol. 16 (July 8, 1911), 12.

36. *Ibid.*, Vol. 27 (February 3, 1912), 10; Club Work In Mississippi, undated memo, Tanner Papers; Mississippi State University, Extension Service, Annual Narrative and Statistical Reports, Club Work in Mississippi, 1911 (National Archives, Washington).

37. Annual Reports of the Department of Farmers' Institutes and Extension, May 15, 1913, April 29, 1914, President's Correspondence; *Mississippi Educational Advance*, Vol. 3 (February, 1914), 15–17.

38. Bradford Knapp to D. F. Houston, December 6, 1913; B. T. Galloway to Knapp, February 4, 1914, Bureau of Plant Industry Records.

39. *Mississippi Educational Advance*, Vol. 2 (October, 1912), 7–8; *ibid.*, Vol. 2 (November, 1912), 24; P. P. Garner to County Superintendents of Schools, October 13, 1909, President's Correspondence.

40. O. B. Martin to C. A. Cobb, February 21, 1912; Cobb to teachers, March 18, 1912, President's Correspondence; *Country Gentleman,* Vol. 77 (June 22, 1912), 11; *Mississippi Agricultural Student,* Vol. 1 (March 1, 1913) 3; *Mississippi Educational Advance,* Vol. 2 (March, 1913), 21; Bradford Knapp, "Results of Demonstration Work in Boys' and Girls' Clubs in 1912," U.S. Bureau of Plant Industry, *Publication* 865 (Washington, 1913), 8.

41. *Progressive Farmer and Southern Farm Gazette,* Vol. 28 (June 28, 1913), 731; *ibid.,* Vol. 28 (September 20, 1913), 991.

42. *Mississippi Educational Advance,* Vol. 1 (October, 1911), 23; *Mississippi Agricultural Student,* Vol. 1 (June 1, 1913), 6.

43. Annual Report, Farmers' Institutes and College Extension, 1912–1913, May 15, 1913, President's Correspondence.

44. A. A. McAlphin to Cobb, January 9, 1911, President's Correspondence.

45. *College Reflector,* Vol. 25 (April, 1912), 393; Conference for Education in the South, *Proceedings,* 1913 (Washington, n.d.), 293; *ibid.,* 1914, p. 367; G. R. Hightower to Cobb, February 19, 1913; Cobb to Hightower, March 17, 1914, President's Correspondence.

46. *College Reflector,* Vol. 28 (January 16, 1914); Cobb, "Boys' Corn Clubs," 145–47; Mississippi Teachers' Association, *Proceedings,* 1912 (Gulfport, n.d.).

47. United States Department of Agriculture, *Report On Agricultural Experiment Stations and Cooperative Agricultural Extension Work in the United States,* 1915 (Washington, 1916), II, 31. For slightly different figures, see *Progressive Farmer,* Vol. 34 (March 15, 1919), 37.

48. Population figures taken from U. S. *Thirteenth Census: Population,* I, 192–93.

49. Biennial Report of the Department of Farmers' Institutes and Extension, June 1, 1913, President's Correspondence.

50. General Education Board, *General Education Board,* 53; Cobb, "Boys' Corn Clubs," 146–47.

51. *Progressive Farmer and Southern Farm Gazette,* Vol. 28 (March 8, 1913), 29.

52. Mississippi Agricultural and Mechanical College, *Catalogue,* 1913–1914, pp. 33–35, 177.

53. Annual Report of the Department of Farmers' Institutes and Extension, April 29, 1914; *Mississippi Agricultural Student,* Vol. 1 (September 1, 1913), 6; Cobb, "Boys' Corn Clubs," 146.

54. *College Reflector,* Vol. 28 (January 16, 1914).

55. Cobb, "Boys' Corn Clubs," 146–47.

56. Bradford Knapp to B. T. Galloway, January 24, 1912, Bureau of Plant Industry Records; Cobb to Hardy, July 10, 1911, President's Correspondence; Mississippi, *Laws,* 1914, p. 94. By 1914 the General Education Board was no longer making a financial contribution to boys' club work in Mississippi. See "Rockefeller Foundation" U. S. Senate *Document* 538, 63rd Cong., 2nd Sess. (1914), 9–10.

# CHAPTER IV

# Boys' Clubs:
# The Years of Expansion,
## 1914-1919

BY the spring of 1914, corn clubs had proven their worth in Mississippi and indeed throughout the South. From its origins in Holmes County, the movement had spread eastward to Maryland and westward to Texas. Enrollment had increased from 10,543 in ten states in 1909 to 91,196 in thirteen states only four years later.[1] * But more important than any statistical measure of growth were the accomplishments of the movement. The clubs had proven that, given proper guidance and encouragement, farm boys could successfully apply the principles of agricultural science and that adult farmers could learn from the examples of their sons. The implications for the future were immeasurable, especially since the movement had the potential for almost unlimited expansion. To achieve that potential there was need for greater financial support and better organization. The historic Smith-Lever Act satisfied these needs and ushered in a new stage in the development of boys' club work.

The Smith-Lever Act led to the establishment of a new administration system for extension work in the United States Department of Agriculture. It was assigned to the newly established States Relations Service, headed by Alfred C. True, long-time head of the Office of Experiment Stations. Because of the difference in the origins of extension work in the South and in the rest of the country, two subordinate divisions were created in the States Relations Service. The Office of Extension Work South replaced the old Farmers' Cooperative Demonstration Work, while the Office of Extension Work North and West assumed the extension role of the Office of Farm Management, the agency that under the leadership of Wil-

* Notes appear at end of each chapter.

liam J. Spillman had taken the lead in establishing the county agent system in those states free from the boll weevil. Under the new arrangement, Bradford Knapp, who had directed Farmers' Cooperative Demonstration Work since 1911, became the first head of the Office of Extension Work South and "O. B." Martin, as he was affectionately known by extension workers, continued his duties with southern youth.

The Smith-Lever Act also brought together in a more formal way the federal and state agencies engaged in agricultural extension. The first step was the submission to the states of a general memorandum of understanding providing for the administration of a comprehensive cooperative extension program by the United States Department of Agriculture and by extension departments existing at, or to be established at, each of the land-grant colleges. After the various states had given their assent to this proposition, individual memorandums of agreement modeled after those negotiated four or five years earlier for corn club work were signed by the presidents of the colleges and by the Secretary of Agriculture. Among other things, they provided for the joint appointment in each state of a director of extension who would represent both agencies and who would be responsible for all extension work in that state.[2]

In Mississippi, as elsewhere, implementation of the Smith-Lever Act required action by state authorities and produced alterations in the structure of the existing organization of extension work. The governor gave his assent to the act on May 27, 1914; at the same time, he designated Mississippi Agricultural and Mechanical College the beneficiary. Legislative approval came almost two years later, April 3, 1916. The memorandum of understanding was signed by representatives of the Department of Agriculture and the college on June 28, 1915. That agreement combined under one head the extension activities previously managed by the state with those programs previously conducted wholly or in part by the Department of Agriculture, including Farmers' Cooperative Demonstration Work, boys' club work, and girls' tomato clubs, the latter headed by Susie V. Powell. Effective July 1, 1915, Edward R. Lloyd became director of cooperative agricultural extension in Mississippi.

The assistant director was Robert S. Wilson, formerly state agent in charge of Farmers' Cooperative Demonstration Work. Headquarters were at Jackson until January 1, 1916, when all personnel were transferred to the college campus.[3]

Under the new arrangement, funds for extension work and the size of the extension staff increased rapidly. Expenditures from all sources rose as follows:[4]

| | |
|---|---|
| 1914–1915 | $ 93,792 |
| 1915–1916 | 139,556 |
| 1916–1917 | 166,535 |
| 1917–1918 | 343,391 |
| 1918–1919 | 417,555 |
| 1919–1920 | 408,235 |

The size of the extension staff stationed at the college expanded in a comparable fashion. In May, 1914, the Department of Farmers' Institutes and Extension at Mississippi Agricultural and Mechanical College had only five men on its regular staff. Their efforts were supplemented from time to time by other faculty members who devoted a portion of their time to the extension program.[5] Under the new organization established in 1915, many of these men became subject matter specialists and new personnel were added. In fact, Mississippi used its first Smith-Lever funds to employ two staff members for work in home economics. Other additions followed, and by 1919–1920 the extension staff numbered approximately seventy-five, not including men and women agents assigned to counties.[6]

The delay in negotiating the memorandum of understanding between the college and the Department of Agriculture led to a temporary shift of Cobb's office from the agricultural college campus. Farmers' Cooperative Demonstration Work in Mississippi had been directed from Jackson prior to the enactment of the Smith-Lever Act. After that measure became law, authorities in Washington wanted to coordinate more closely all federally aided extension work in the state, so Cobb found himself in Jackson until January 1, 1916, when all extension officials were moved to Starkville.

During the period of change and under the new organization, Cobb's responsibilities remained much as they were before the enactment of the Smith-Lever Act, but his title was changed to assistant state agent in charge of boys' clubs. Later, in 1918, Edward R. Lloyd resigned as director of extension to take a position in private industry. Robert S. Wilson succeeded him, and Cobb became assistant director of extension, although his primary duties and interest remained with the boys' clubs.[7]

As for extension work as a whole the enactment of the Smith-Lever Act increased sharply the funds with which Cobb had to work and allowed him to expand the club force. The following figures are not totally consistent, but they are illustrative.[8]

Expenditures from All Sources, Club Work in Mississippi

| 1914–1915 | $ 5,274 |
|-----------|---------|
| 1915–1916 | 6,469 |
| 1916–1917 | 11,245 |
| 1917–1918 | 12,579 |
| 1918–1919 | 18,627 |
| 1919–1920 | 20,747 |

Manpower jumped in a comparable fashion. Since the inception of corn club work under the direction of Seaman A. Knapp, Peter P. Garner and Cobb had functioned alone, but in 1919 the club staff numbered eight.[9]

The first addition was Paul H. Sanders, who went to work July 1, 1914, as assistant state club agent in charge of pig clubs. A graduate of Mississippi Agricultural and Mechanical College with the class of 1914, Sanders had worked for Cobb as a student aide and had impressed Cobb with his ambition, ability, and energy. Sanders continued as pig club agent until July, 1917, when Cobb gave him the task of editing the *Mississippi Club Boy*, a monthly paper launched by Cobb as a vehicle for reaching the club members more effectively. Sanders resigned September 1, 1919, to become associate editor of the *Southern Ruralist*, a farm paper published in Atlanta.

Sanders' replacement as manager of pig club work was Peter E.

Sallis, Mississippi, pig club members and their animals, 1915.

Spinks, who joined Cobb's staff July 16, 1917. A native of Kemper County where he grew up on a farm, Spinks graduated from Mississippi Agricultural and Mechanical College in 1912. After a year of teaching at Lamar County Agricultural High School, he served as county agent in Winston and Tunica counties before returning to the campus. Given the title of state livestock club agent, he directed all club work involving farm animals.[10]

Before Spinks assumed direction of livestock club work, two men had participated in the formation and management of baby beef clubs. First was Frank W. Farley, who came to Mississippi in July, 1915, as an agent of the United States Bureau of Animal Industry. When he resigned, his successor was H. M. Parker, who served only a few months before his responsibilities were assigned to Spinks.[11]

After January 10, 1917, club work in field crops was directed by Julian E. Sides. Born at Lyon in Coahoma County, Sides obtained practical experience in farming after his father's death when Sides was only fourteen. In 1905 he attended a farmers' institute held by staff members of Mississippi Agricultural and Mechanical College. Convinced that the institution had something to offer farmers, Sides enrolled in 1906 and graduated four years later. After teaching in Texas, he was named county agent in Pearl River County in 1916, a position he held until he joined Cobb's staff. Late in 1919 he edited the *Mississippi Club Boy*.[12]

The availability of special funds, provided under wartime measures for the stimulation of food production, allowed Cobb to appoint district agents. The principal duty of each agent was to assist the county agents in their club work. But the district agents were also specifically charged with the task of launching the boys' community clubs and other new activities. I. B. Kerlin, the first of these agents, went to work in north Mississippi July 1, 1917. He was joined in September, 1919, by C. L. McNeil, who was to devote special attention to the arranging of county club schools in that area of the state. The first district agent in south Mississippi was Hugh L. Hopper, who took his post September 1, 1917. He resigned in 1918 and was succeeded by P. H. Easom and, effective July 1, 1919, by Fred J. Hurst, previously county agent in Pike County.[13]

Two men handled Negro club work, one of them having been employed before the enactment of the Smith-Lever Act. The first step came in September, 1913, when Major M. Hubert, who had studied at Morehouse College and Hampton Institute and who had more recently been employed by the Piney Woods School in south Mississippi, was employed as a county agent for Negro farmers in Jefferson Davis County. Five years later on July 1, 1918, C. J. Wilkes was named Negro boys' club agent for the entire state.[14]

In many ways, the enactment of the Smith-Lever Act and the better support that it provided produced no sharp break with previous procedures in club work. Purposes, according to Bradford Knapp, remained as they were earlier. In Mississippi, Cobb continued to stress also the broader significance of the program, including the virtues of hard work and dedication to the task at hand, the need for farm boys to obtain a suitable education, and the wisdom of staying on the farm. "Money doesn't make the man any more," Cobb wrote in 1915. "It is what you know and can do that counts. . . . You may be ever so poor, but this does not mean . . . that the door to hope is closed to you. If you have grit, if you have the will to do right . . . your happiest dreams can come true." [15]

Later, club leaders in Mississippi pointed out that success "is due to untiring work, brains, and good business management, the knowledge of which is derived from a close study of that business." Since farming was a business, Cobb urged his boys to stay in club work, go on to the agricultural college, and make something of themselves. For those who would follow that path, opportunities as great or greater than the cities offered might be found on the farm.[16]

Corn growing was still the major concern of Mississippi's youth club leaders. Cobb continued to stress the necessity of seed selection and of planting that variety suited to a given area. He also emphasized, as he had from the outset, the relationship between his corn clubs and the increasing production of corn in the state. Pointing to the fact that output increased 109 percent between 1909 and 1917 and that the quality of the crop had improved almost as much as quantity, Cobb reiterated his belief that Mississippi would break the hold that cotton had held so long on its economy and become a major corn-growing and exporting state.[17]

While the operation of the corn clubs remained much as they had developed before 1914, in numerous ways work was improved. For example, the Boys' Corn Club Congress, which had been held in late summer on the college campus in conjunction with the annual farmers' institute round-up, became in effect a true short course for farm boys. In 1914 the session was held August 31–September 4. In attendance were county prize winners. They were housed free of charge in the college dormitory and were required to pay only their rail fare. The program was highlighted by a lecture by Perry G. Holden, an extension pioneer then in the employ of the International Harvester Company. Demonstrations and contests also exposed the boys to new ideas. But since Cobb believed that "every farmer boy . . . should have a vacation," athletic events and other recreational activities were worked into the busy schedule. Each boy received a diploma as evidence of his having attended the course.[18]

In a like fashion, the corn exhibits at the Mississippi State Fair, a major feature of the program since the early days, continued to be the culmination of a year's work, but they became larger and the show took on some new features. By 1917 the prize list amounted to $2,500. Some five hundred boys exhibited corn there, and Tait Butler, an editor of the *Progressive Farmer*, claimed that he could not "remember having seen a larger exhibit of corn at any other show in the South. . . ." [19] The next year Cobb added a club boys' camp to the fair's attractions. A large tent housed two prize winners from each county. Cobb informed the boys that the camp provided a "means by which you may obtain the greatest possible benefit from your visit, at the least cost of money, and with the least worry and physical exertion. It is free to you." A similar camp was held at the 1919 fair, but the boys that year were provided better quarters in a building on the grounds. The rent was donated by a Grenada banker. By that year, the prize list exceeded $3,000. [20]

Continued, too, was the offer by the state fair management of an automobile and other prizes to those county superintendents who were outstanding in promoting club work. Despite the gradual shift of responsibility for club activity from school personnel to the county agents, the award was made as late as 1919. [21]

The raising of funds for awards continued to take up much of Cobb's time. Bankers were still a major source of aid. Probably most outstanding in this regard was J. T. Thomas of Grenada. In 1919 his bank alone offered eleven prizes to club boys from that area. [22] Other businessmen were almost as generous, even if their award programs were less comprehensive. In 1916, for example, the De Laval Separator Company offered a one hundred-dollar scholarship at Mississippi Agricultural and Mechanical College. The president of a private college in Meridian gave a fifty-dollar scholarship at his institution. In 1918 a book publisher offered a library valued at a hundred dollars to the community club that made the best record. One of the outstanding if unusual prizes was an eight-wheel log wagon, awarded by the James and Graham Wagon Company of Memphis to the first winner in the five-acre contest conducted by the Mississippi Corn Improvement Association. In other instances, businessmen provided not only prizes but aid of more general use to the program. For instance, J. T. Thomas gave a one-ton truck, equipped with a moving picture projector, generator, and screen. Not only Cobb but other extension personnel as well found these useful tools in presenting their messages to audiences. [23]

The gradual withdrawal of country school teachers from club work was one of the more significant alterations in procedures that came after 1914. Many teachers had performed yeoman service for years, but all too often some lost interest or were disinclined to give the work the time it required. Moreover, the school term did not fit perfectly the needs of club work, and the customary brief tenures in the profession further reduced the effectiveness of teachers. Accordingly, there developed a tendency to make club work a part of the duties of the county agents. In 1916 the agent in Covington County reported that he devoted most of his time to boys' and girls' clubs. A year later, the agent in Harrison County claimed that adult farmers were so deeply in a "rut" that it was impossible to work with them, so he spent his time with the boys who were much more responsive. By the early 1920s, it was estimated that across the South the county men were devoting about one third of their time to youth programs.[24]

Another significant innovation was the launching of club work with Negro boys. Under Cobb's leadership, in fact, that work began even before the Smith-Lever Act. Major M. Hubert had been employed as a county agent in 1913, but in addition to his work with adult farmers he organized the first clubs among Negro boys.[25] The increase in membership, however, was not great until the later years of the decade. In 1915 Cobb reported only 145 black participants in the state; the figure for 1916 was 458. But in 1919 Cobb counted 4,977 members, of whom 2,779 were growing corn. The others were producing Irish and sweet potatoes, pigs, and other farm crops. These groups were known as Farm Makers' Clubs to distinguish them from those for white boys.[26]

Cobb reported little difference in the performance of Negro and white club members. In 1916 white boys produced an average of forty-three bushels of corn per acre with an average net profit of $20.03 per acre. Figures for the Negroes were thirty-five and $24.12. In Negro club work, the support of preachers was much more important than was true with white boys, and it was always more difficult to raise money for use as premiums in the Negro program.[27]

In some parts of the state, white boys still displayed a distressing reluctance to take up club work. That tendency was especially noticeable in the Mississippi Delta and other areas where the plantation system was most firmly established. Writing from Tunica County in 1916, County Agent Peter E. Spinks reported that, since the farm labor there was performed by Negroes, white boys were not raised to work and to know how to perform farm tasks. Under those conditions, he found it "impossible to take a boy thusly reared and interest him in the production of an acre of corn." [28]

The best indication that the club movement was approaching maturity after 1914 was the expansion of the work to include programs with field crops other than corn and with different types of livestock. Of the new areas of work, because they pointed toward the diversification so badly needed in Mississippi, pig and baby beef clubs were most important.

In contrast to the view expressed by some writers,[29] pig clubs originated in Mississippi. It was apparently Hugh Critz, superintendent of Starkville schools, who must be given credit for the idea. Late in 1909, he suggested to W. H. Miller, superintendent of schools in Oktibbeha County, that the latter organize such a club among interested pupils. Miller took the suggestion and worked out the details. As plans developed, any pupil enrolled in the county schools was eligible to participate. The contest consisted of feeding a purebred pig born between October 1, 1909, and April 1, 1910, in such a manner as to produce the maximum average gain per day. Prizes ranging downward from twenty-five dollars were offered to the four top contenders and were to be awarded at a show held in the fall in conjunction with the county fair. Miller provided contestants with feeding instructions and other advice during the spring and summer of 1910. When the results were in, it was found that the winner of the first prize was a little girl whose eight-and-a-half-month-old Poland-China weighed 328 pounds.[30]

The Oktibbeha experiment soon had its imitators. In fact, pioneer pig clubs in Louisiana were a direct result of the Mississippi club. In the summer of 1910, Ira W. Carpenter, director of the Calhoun, Louisiana, Agricultural School, visited Oktibbeha County, learned of Miller's club, and in October, 1910, launched in Ouachita Parish a similar project with twenty-one members. When that club received considerable publicity, a second club in Louisiana was organized in Caddo Parish by E. W. Jones, superintendent of schools there.[31]

Despite the pioneer character of the early pig club work in Mississippi, little more was done until 1914. There was a contest in Oktibbeha County in 1911, much like the one a year earlier, but later the project died.[32] Elsewhere in the South, however, the work went forward. As early as June, 1911, Texas claimed forty-one clubs with 1,250 members. In 1912 the United States Bureau of Animal Industry began to participate in pig club projects, usually in conjunction with the agricultural colleges, and by the end of 1913 it was playing a role in Alabama, Louisiana, and Georgia.[33]

Cobb took the first step in making similar arrangements in Mississippi. Late in 1913 he began discussions with the Bureau of Animal Industry that culminated with the appointment of a pig club agent in the state, effective July 1, 1914. The memorandum of understanding between the bureau and the Mississippi college stated that the objects of the work were "to stimulate an interest in swine production and teach . . . improved methods of raising . . . hogs, to instruct the boys in the growing of forage crops . . . and the marketing of various crops by means of swine, to increase the number of hogs raised on the farm and show . . . the best methods of preparing and home-curing meats, and to instill in the boys . . . a love of animals, which will result in their taking more interest in farm life." [34]

The mode of operation, according to the memorandum, was similar to that being used in the corn clubs. An agent appointed by the bureau and the college first contacted county agents and superintendents of schools who arranged with teachers to enlist participants. When the agent in charge received lists of prospective members, he provided them with forms for formal enrollment and for record keeping. In addition, he helped members to obtain pigs and by means of bulletins and personal correspondence he instructed boys and girls in proper care and feeding methods. Exhibits of the hogs raised would be held in each county, and if possible county winners would show their stock at the state fair. The agent was to be responsible for raising funds for premiums to be awarded at those exhibits. Expenses of the programs were to be shared by the bureau and the college. The bureau agreed to pay the agent's salary and to provide stationery and other materials for the conduct of the work. The college would provide his traveling expenses, office space, stenographic assistance, and the aid of its extension staff.

For the position of special agent, Cobb nominated and higher authorities approved Paul H. Sanders. In time, Sanders became Cobb's closest co-worker, managing the pig club programs until July 14, 1917, when he was assigned other duties.[35]

Under these arrangements, systematic pig club work began in Mississippi in 1915. That year the program counted as members 1,607 boys, ten to eighteen years of age. Enrollment rose steadily to 10,559 in 1918. With the end of World War I came a sharp decline in participation, largely because of poor financial conditions which depressed prices for purebred hogs and made it difficult for club members to obtain adequate financing.[36]

To build up the enrollment Sanders spent considerable time traveling about the state, talking with superintendents, teachers, parents, and prospective members. In 1916 he spent two months on a tour throughout Mississippi. Encouraged with the response he found, Sanders concluded that Mississippi was rapidly becoming a pork-producing state. Cobb, too, actively promoted the work, organizing a club in Winston County himself. A major problem was financing. Unlike the corn clubs which required little or no investment by members, participation in the pig clubs meant that members had to raise the price of a purebred pig. Businessmen agreed to help solve that problem. In December, 1915, the Jackson Board of Trade, for example, offered to loan 150 members the necessary funds, terms being twelve months at 6 percent. These loans were available to those boys who were recommended by some reputable person, whose parents agreed to waive all rights to the stock involved, and who indicated their willingness to raise their animals in accordance with instructions provided by Cobb's office. Elsewhere, bankers and other businessmen adopted this plan, so that in 1916 almost eleven thousand dollars was made available to boys in need; the next year the figure was over thirty thousand.[37]

Cobb was soon able to point to significant results. He was especially enthusiastic concerning the impact of the pig clubs on the state's agricultural economy. In 1918 Cobb reported that some 90 percent of the more than ten thousand purebred hogs being raised at that time were sows; assuming that these produced average litters, between sixty and eighty thousand quality pigs would be scattered throughout the state. Speculative though those figures may have been Cobb was able to quote concrete facts to justify his enthusiasm. By 1918, according to the county agent in Pontotoc County, fully a third of the farmers there had purebred hogs on their places. Between 1914 and 1917, the number of hogs shipped from Mississippi to the East St. Louis, Illinois, market increased from 7,242 to 88,730 and many of them topped the market, evidence of progress in which pig clubs no doubt played some role. Moreover, the first cooperative marketing of hogs in Mississippi, from Yazoo City, stemmed from pig club work.[38]

Probably more heartwarming to Cobb and his co-workers were accounts of accomplishments of individual members. Included was that of a girl from Pontotoc County, a young lady of commendable "pluck" and drive, who reportedly sold three hundred dollars worth of hogs, besides producing some pork for the family table. With her earnings and a scholarship that her energy won for her, she was able to enroll in one of the better secondary schools in the state.[39] A Yazoo County youth reported that he earned his year's college expenses from his pig club work. More typical, perhaps, was the account of a Covington County boy. With fifteen dollars borrowed from a local bank, he purchased a Duroc-Jersey pig that in time produced a litter of six. When the litter was sold and feed costs deducted, the young businessman found that he had a net profit of forty-seven dollars.[40]

Baby beef clubs in Mississippi also originated under Cobb's leadership. The first step came in October, 1914, in Covington County where Bura Hilbun, a superintendent of schools, organized a club with about one hundred members. Pupils aged eight to eighteen were eligible to enroll; their calves had to be at least four months old. Members exhibited their animals at a show held in Collins in March. The calves, which included purebreds, mixed breeds, and scrubs, were judged there, and cash prizes offered by local businessmen were awarded to the winners. The stock was then auctioned off, bringing an average of $27.80.[41]

When the work in Covington County attracted attention, agricultural leaders in the state began to consider the feasibility of launching a statewide program. The leader was Frank W. Farley, who had been sent to Mississippi by the Bureau of Animal Industry to promote the raising of better cattle in tick-free areas. He suggested to Cobb that a state baby beef club conducted at the county level through county agents would aid his work. Cobb seized the idea, and the work began systematically in 1915.[42]

The first year baby beef club members were found in eight counties. In all, 162 boys and girls enrolled and 125 submitted reports of their work, but of that group, 113 were from Covington County. Despite that unpromising distribution, the first state baby beef show was held in Jackson in October.[43]

The next year Cobb and his co-workers made plans for a sharp expansion of the work. As an added incentive, the Illinois Central Railroad offered to give five purebred beef calves as prizes in each participating county along its lines. According to details worked out for the club, any boy or girl between the ages of ten and eighteen was entitled to active membership. There were to be organizations on the local, county, and state levels. Each county club was required to hold an annual or semi-annual show. Purebred calves winning prizes at the county level would be entered in the state contest. To be considered in any of the contests, calves had to be over six months and under twelve months of age. The feeding period was 120 days preceding the county fair. Boys and girls who entered the contest were required to have their calves weighed, to maintain accurate records, and to submit monthly reports. At the shows, calves were judged on the basis of individuality, rate of gain, cost of production, and written histories of their progress.[44]

When the final reports for 1916 were in, Cobb announced that the club had a total enrollment of 617 scattered through fourteen counties. Some 330 members fulfilled all requirements and 55 exhibited their calves at a show at the state fair where they were judged by Professor H. W. Mumford of the University of Illinois. Meanwhile, the Illinois Central Railroad found that nine counties along its lines met its requirements, so the carrier's officials distributed forty-five purebred bull calves as prizes. Other businessmen also played a role in the work; bankers loaned over six thousand dollars to members to allow them to purchase the stock they entered in the contest.[45]

Still, baby beef clubs failed by a wide margin to gain the popularity of the pig clubs, and membership fell off during the later years of the decade. In the summer of 1917, Cobb reported a total enrollment of 262; a year later he counted only 274, and almost 50 percent of that membership was found in three counties—Wayne, Pontotoc, and Lee.[46] In 1919 there were 379 boys and girls enrolled but only a few reported, and there were no baby beef reports in 1920. The initial cost of the calf, combined with longer time span needed to produce a return on the investment, were factors that restricted the spread of the work. Finally, the onset of the postwar recession depressed beef prices to such a degree that both the boys and the bankers were hesitant to undertake the financing necessary for the operation of the program. Nevertheless, Mississippi extension personnel hoped to reestablish the work when economic conditions improved.[47]

Despite the interruption in the work after the war, the launching of a baby beef program in Mississippi could only have had a catalytic effect on livestock production in the state. It also stimulated the holding of junior livestock judging contests. The first of these was staged in Jackson in the fall of 1916. Teams from nine agricultural high schools competed for a trophy offered by the sheriff of Hinds County. The affair attracted considerable attention, and Frank W. Farley, who in conjunction with Cobb promoted it, proposed that a nationwide junior judging contest become a feature of the International Live Stock Show, a suggestion that in time was accepted by officials of that exhibition.[48]

In addition to clubs for youthful producers of pigs and baby beef, Cobb took the first steps in establishing club programs with other types of livestock and with additional field crops. A lamb club was begun in 1917 and enjoyed some success in Yazoo County. But in 1919 there were only thirty-five boys enrolled with some seven hundred lambs. No final reports were filed with Cobb that year because of the resignation of the county agent who had pushed the work.[49] Plans for a dairy club program were worked out in 1919, but they were not implemented until the next year, after Cobb had left Mississippi.[50]

Meanwhile, the club program was extended to include field crops other than corn. Wheat clubs, a product of World War I, were begun to aid in the expansion of that important crop in the state. By 1919 peanut and sweet potato clubs were under way, especially in the southern counties. None of these innovations achieved great significance that year; in fact, total enrollment was less than one hundred, but even that number represented a step toward the future.[51]

While Cobb and his subordinates were extending club work to include livestock and a variety of new field crops, they were also developing new ways to improve the general quality of club work. These new approaches included the organization of community agricultural clubs, the holding of club schools, and the institution of an annual junior short course in farm mechanics. Among Cobb's other innovations were the first attempt to find a place for club boys in the International Live Stock Show and the launching of a periodical expressly for the benefit of Mississippi club boys.

The organization of boys' community agricultural clubs during World War I was hailed as the one innovation that "did more than any other" to improve the work with rural youth. Aided by special federal funds appropriated for the stimulating of food production, Cobb appointed two district agents in 1917 and directed them to undertake the establishment of community clubs among boys enrolled in the various programs. As early as January, 1918, some 150 clubs had been formed and by the end of 1919 some 760 of them were in existence.[52]

According to the plans formulated in Cobb's office, community clubs could be organized with as few as five members. They had the usual elected officers and met in regular monthly sessions. Programs were outlined by Cobb's staff. The clubs served several purposes. They brought the boys together periodically and helped to develop a constructive community spirit and to break down the isolation that was so much a part of rural life. They also helped to stimulate and retain interest in the different projects among the boys, permitted group study of common problems, and brought out leadership qualities. Assuming that boys should mix work with play, the clubs also arranged picnics and athletic contests among members. Finally, by bringing the boys of a neighborhood together, the clubs provided county agents and members of Cobb's staff another medium for reaching the youth of the state.[53]

"Next to the Boys' Community Agricultural Clubs, perhaps the greatest means of promoting all phases of club work was the Club Schools," wrote a Mississippi extension official in 1919. The first two of these schools were held in Pearl River and Harrison counties in 1916; there were seventeen in 1917; and in 1918 thirty-five of them attracted a total attendance of 1,062. Essentially, the schools were short courses for club boys. Usually three-day affairs, they were held at the county level at the agricultural high school or at a centrally located public high school in those counties where no agricultural institution existed. Expenses of attending were nominal. If held at an agricultural high school, the boys were allowed to use the dormitory free of charge. In other cases, townspeople were induced to provide sleeping space. Expenses for food rarely exceeded two dollars per day.[54]

In the operation of the schools, principals and agriculturalists of the agricultural high schools generally assumed primary roles. The county agent, however, usually participated, and in most cases one member of Cobb's staff was present. The instruction took the form of classroom work in the forenoon, but after dinner teachers took the boys into the fields for demonstrations in the handling of farm crops, terracing, seed selection, identification and harvesting of legumes, innoculation of hogs, vaccination of cattle, and other aspects of modern agriculture. Recreational activities broke the routine of instruction. Evenings were taken up by lectures or by some kind of entertainment. Not only were the boys who participated in the schools enthusiastic about them, but the adults also displayed a healthy interest. According to a writer from Chickasaw County, where a school was held in the early summer of 1918, "The community of Buena Vista seemed to think mighty well of the idea of a . . . community club meet, and the citizens of the village quickly made up $75.00 to furnish a barbecue on the last day." [55]

In 1919 Cobb added a final innovation for the training of farm boys. In June he announced that during the summer there would be held on the campus of Mississippi Agricultural and Mechanical College, under the supervision of the Department of Agricultural Engineering, a course in junior farm mechanics. Any regular member of the boys' clubs in the state was eligible to attend, and Cobb asked that every county be represented. While attending the ten-day affair, the boys would be housed in the college dormitory and would eat in the mess hall. Each boy was required to pay only a six-dollar fee to cover the cost of board. The "official uniform" was blue overalls and caps, the latter available on campus for twenty-five cents. To advertise the event, the college issued a booklet discussing the institution, outlining the instruction to be offered, and inviting boys to attend. In it Cobb wrote, "You have dreamed of a day when you could have the joy of taking a real vacation. We are offering that and at the same time an opportunity to learn the things about machin-

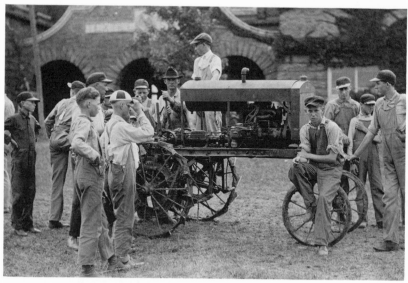

Students studying a tractor at the Junior Short Course in Farm Mechanics at Mississippi Agricultural and Mechanical College, 1919.

ery that you have always wanted to know. This course in Junior Farm Mechanics has been very carefully planned for club boys and it is my pleasure to extend to you a most cordial invitation to come." [56]

Cobb anticipated that 200 boys would attend; when the school opened August 18, a total of 568 boys were on hand. Participants constituted a cross-section of Mississippi's youth. Included in the group were the "son of one of the leading bankers of the state and the son of a 'one-gallus farmer.' " The course was "the first of its nature ever attempted," according to the United States Department of Agriculture. The instruction offered fell into three categories— farm implements, farm power, and farm practices. No lectures were given, but under the guidance of instructors the boys were able to study a diversity of machines, gasoline engines, and tractors, and to learn how to construct fences, lace belts, and perform other farm tasks of a like nature. According to a report from one of the boys, the most important thing he learned was how to time the valves and magneto of a gasoline engine; another participant went home so enthusiastic that he was able to induce his father to purchase a Fordson tractor. By any measure, the pioneer effort was a resounding success, and extension personnel resolved to offer a similar course the following year. [57]

One purpose of the short course for boys was to interest them in Mississippi Agricultural and Mechanical College with the hope that they would enroll there. The relationship between extension work and attendance at the land-grant colleges had been important to extension workers from the outset, and Cobb's interest was no exception. Accordingly, in 1917 he began a systematic program of bringing delegations of club boys from the different counties to the campus, showing them the school and its experimental plots, barns, and animals. Usually, county agents accompanied the groups and helped to entertain them while they were on campus. [58]

Early in 1918 Cobb announced preliminary plans for what would later become one of his major contributions to club work, not only in Mississippi but nationally. It was the sending of state club winners to visit the International Live Stock Show in Chicago, an idea that in time would grow into the National 4-H Club Congress held annually in conjunction with that premier livestock exposition. The

Delegation of Mississippi club boys and their leaders enroute to International Live Stock Show in Chicago, 1919. Cobb's assistants, Julian E. Sides and Peter E. Spinks, are in the third row, second and third from the left, respectively.

project originated in conversations that Cobb had with other state leaders at their annual planning sessions in Washington. From Cobb's point of view, the offering of such trips would serve at least two purposes. It would be a tremendous incentive to the boys to do better work and in the long run, by exposing Mississippi boys to the best of American livestock, it would contribute toward agricultural diversification in the state. Among his contemporaries, John Swaim, club leader in Oklahoma, was most enthusiastic, and the two resolved to take the first step in 1918.

As plans matured in Mississippi, twelve boys were to be sent to Chicago. They included eight pig and corn club winners chosen from the congressional districts, three finalists in different contests from the Grenada area, and one boy from the state at large who had made the best combined corn and pig club record. Expenses were to be met by bankers in Grenada, Biloxi, and elsewhere and by contributions from other businessmen, including the well-known firm of Clay, Robinson and Company of National Stock Yards, Illinois. The trip to Chicago would be made via the Illinois Central's crack train, the Panama Limited.[59]

By March Cobb had decided to add another individual to the party. He would be the winner in the five-acre contest conducted by the Mississippi Corn Improvement Association. According to the rules of that organization, any white farmer in the state was eligible to compete in the contest.[60]

When the time came for departure to Chicago, only nine of the planned twelve boys made the trip, because of illness and the cancellation of the statewide contest usually held at the state fair. The remainder, however, gathered at Jackson, at the agricultural college, and other points where they were met by Spinks, Cobb, and other club personnel who gave them final instructions before sending them on their way. J. E. Sides of Cobb's staff accompanied the boys, each of whom carried with him a cornstalk as a symbol of club work and of his state. Enroute to Chicago, the Mississippi farm boys were favorably impressed by the flat corn lands and huge red barns of rural Illinois. In the city they were housed in a YMCA hotel.[61]

During their stay in Chicago, the boys mixed business with pleasure. They attended the International Live Stock Show purely as visitors since they had not been officially welcomed by the exhibition's management. In fact, Cobb and John Swaim had been rebuffed by Iowa's Charles F. Curtiss and other officials when the southerners suggested that their boys might participate in various events connected with the show. Nevertheless, the boys were able to view the livestock and some of the programs that were a part of the affair. Officials of Wilson and Company, meat packers of Chicago, showed the boys through their plant and served a dinner for them that proved to be the first of a continuing annual event. Later the boys toured the city, visited the Chicago Zoo, Lincoln Park, the lakefront, and were guided through Marshall Field's emporium.

The experience was educational, both for the boys and for those who came into contact with them. The Mississippians saw much that was new to them, and they returned with a greater appreciation for the club work that had made their trip possible. Similarly, northerners who met the boys learned something of Mississippi and its people, and a few of them began to lay plans for a more formal participation by club boys from throughout the nation in future Internationals.[62]

In Mississippi Cobb and his co-workers almost immediately began to lay plans for a trip to Chicago in 1919. Businessmen in the state were especially enthusiastic. An official of the Tupelo Fertilizer Company wrote that his firm was happy to donate the approximately one hundred dollars needed to send one boy to Chicago in order to encourage "the corn club boys to do their best work in 1919." A Jackson banker noted that "Mississippi will never amount to anything as long as we confine ourselves to one crop; and we find it in the history of all countries that they prosper if the agricultural interest is diversified. . . . I think every boy in Mississippi should be encouraged . . . and we are glad to aid in this effort." [63]

In the end, fourteen Mississippi youths attended the 1919 International, including one boy only eleven years of age. They were chosen in roughly the same manner as in 1918. Joining them was the county agent whose pig club boys had made the best record at the Mississippi State Fair.[64] In Chicago the boys again met no formal reception by the management of the International but they found themselves in company with boys from several other states. Guy L. Noble, an official of Armour and Company, had induced that firm to grant five thousand dollars for approximately forty all-expense paid trips for boys from its procurement area. Four boys appeared from Arkansas. In all some 150 boys attended. Again they were treated to a tour of the city, and Noble was able to obtain one-time passes to the International for each of the boys. Later, when the National 4-H Club Congress would be firmly established, its officials would label the 1919 gathering as the first annual tour of club boys, a designation that unfortunately overlooks the presence in Chicago in 1918 of that year's tiny group of boys.[65]

In August, 1917, began the publication of the *Mississippi Club Boy*, a four-page monthly issued by Cobb's office. For years Cobb had used a multigraph machine to produce the circular letters so important in the work, but he was convinced that a periodical would be more useful in maintaining contact with members, county agents, and others. Such a magazine, Cobb thought, would fit into "boy psychology." Recalling his own emotions as a farm boy, he believed that receiving a paper would help meet the ordinary boy's "desire for recognition" and "feeling of importance." Finally, since Cobb expected to print reports of donations by bankers and other businessmen, he recognized that the magazine might well play an important promotional role.[66]

Paul H. Sanders of Cobb's staff was assigned to edit the *Club Boy*. Under his direction, according to Cobb, the magazine was "a boy's paper, published by the club workers of Mississippi, for the advancement of the farmer boys of our state." Most articles in the paper were prepared by the men involved in club work and by other extension specialists who wrote items pertaining to their areas of special competence. From these pieces, the boys learned how to prepare proper rations for beef calves, build a hog house, and manage a hundred other tasks connected with the farm. The *Club Boy* was sent free of charge to all club members. It also went to those persons who supported club work, including businessmen, school personnel, and farm paper editors. Cobb also had every reason to believe that it was read by parents, thereby contributing to general enlightenment of the countryside. In short, the *Club Boy* was the "connecting link between the boy and the various organizations and persons which are so deeply interested in him." [67]

Reportedly, the *Club Boy* served its purpose well, attracting attention throughout the United States and in Canada as well. Writing in 1920, after Cobb had left Mississippi, H. E. Savely, one of the pioneers in southern extension work, said that the paper "stands out throughout the United States as a magazine unique of its kind. In my mind it is the best . . . that I have seen. I hope that the Mississippi Extension Division will keep it . . . and that it will continue to serve the club boys of the State just as it is serving them today." [68]

Unfortunately, the *Mississippi Club Boy* was not to survive. In August, 1921, it was merged with the *Mississippi Demonstrator*, a periodical that sought to perform essentially the same function for the entire extension service. That magazine expired in July, 1924, because of a shortage of funds. [69]

At times Cobb found himself engaged in work only indirectly related to the boys' clubs. In 1916, for example, he served with others from the extension force in a better-farming campaign conducted in north Mississippi under the auspices of the Farm Development Bureau of Memphis. The same year he spoke before the Mississippi Bankers' Association, urging them to take a still greater role in agricultural improvement. Cobb also participated in farmers' institutes, although they were destined to disappear from the state soon. [70] In 1919 Cobb found himself in a meeting with railway development agents of the Gulf and Ship Island and the Illinois Central railroads where the subject of discussion was methods by which livestock production might be further increased in the state. He also continued his work with the Mississippi Corn Improvement Association and was in charge of the group's five-acre contest for men which had been launched by college personnel and the association in an effort to break the complete dominance of cotton in the Mississippi Delta. Club work faced serious handicaps in that area, so Cobb and his associates inaugurated the five-acre contest as a means of showing Delta planters that they could at least produce feed for their work stock. [71]

Among the external forces affecting boys' clubs was World War I. The coming of that struggle placed new tasks upon the boys' clubs and contributed to rapid expansion of membership. When the United States entered the war, the nation was in something of a food crisis. Wheat production in 1916 was down sharply from the year previous; potato output was off a half. The Food Production Act of 1917 recognized the role that the extension program might play in meeting the nation's food needs, so under that measure and others emergency funds were channeled into extension work. The largest portion of these funds went for enlarging the force of county agents, but some money was available for youth work.[72]

In Mississippi emergency funds were available from July, 1917, to June, 1919, and amounted to $145,000 in the last fiscal year. With a share of these funds, Cobb enlarged his staff by the addition of two district agents; more important were the renewed efforts of the club staff to increase the membership, improve still further the quality of the work, and institute new programs to meet wartime needs. In 1918 officials in Washington established a goal of 20,000 members in Mississippi; by July Cobb was able to count over 23,000 members, an increase of more than 100 percent over 1917.[73] Wheat clubs were the major new product of the war period, but since increased pork production was also essential pig clubs received added attention. Cobb's office also cooperated with the Boys' Working Reserve, a nationwide program to mobilize youth to forward the war effort.[74] When the war ended, Cobb praised his members for having done "so much to produce an ample supply of food and feed while the soldier boys were over there fighting." They had done, he said, "just what we expected of them." [75]

That statement might well have summarized Cobb's estimate of his long experience with his boys. Through club work they had not only showed clearly the way to increased output of corn in Mississippi but they had also contributed in a major way to the expansion of pork production and to diversification in the state. Other accomplishments were perhaps even more important. Club work had made leaders out of many country boys. As Cobb surveyed the results of the program in 1918, he found that one former club boy was an army captain in France, another was executive officer aboard a naval vessel, three were county agents, and another served in Cobb's office, and a large number, including at least one Negro, were already successful farmers. The impact of the clubs on formal agricultural education was unmistakable A majority of the boys enrolled in the state's agricultural high schools were club members. Professor J. C. Robert, dean of Mississippi's College of

Agriculture, claimed that former club members stood out clearly in his classes. In those communities where club work existed, Cobb found a new spirit of cooperation, not only among the boys but also among their elders, and the old rural isolation, once so much a part of farm life, was less in evidence.[76]

Statistics showed clearly the growth of the club movement since 1914 and suggested that the program in Mississippi, despite the state's unique problems, compared well with clubs across the South. Total membership in Mississippi rose from 3,140 in 1914 to 23,275 in 1918 and then fell off to 17,356 the next year. The contraction resulted from a reduction in funds for the support of the work following the termination of the wartime emergency and the collapse in prices for farm commodities, especially for pork and beef, that came in 1919. Corn growing retained its premier place among club activities, but the pig clubs had 4,226 members in the peak year of 1918. The following table provides a picture of the expansion of the clubs after the Smith-Lever Act and under Cobb's stewardship and compares the progress in Mississippi with that of the South as a whole: [77]

| Year | Total Membership, Mississippi | Total Membership, South | Corn Clubs, Mississippi | Pig Clubs, Mississippi | Corn Yield, Mississippi | Corn Yield, South |
|---|---|---|---|---|---|---|
| 1914 | 3,140 | 110,000 | 3,140 | ........ | ....... | ....... |
| 1915 | 5,996 | 62,922 | 4,082 | 1,607 | 49.8 | 51.4 |
| 1916 | 8,317 | 75,605 | 4,220 | 3,022 | 42.5 | 44.4 |
| 1917 | 11,099 | 115,746 | 5,012 | 4,227 | NA | 48.0 |
| 1918 | 23,275 | 407,540 | 5,072 | 4,226 | 52.3 | 42.8 |
| 1919 | 17,356 | 168,738 | 5,837 | 2,644 | 51.5 | 48.0 |

While such statistics indicate the growth of boys' clubs, the deeper significance of the work and the lessons it taught farm boys were best described in their own accounts. Typical of many was that of Roy Ashley, a fifteen-year-old boy from Mize. After spending 1910 in the corn club, he re-entered the program in the fall of 1913. He began by plowing his land to a depth of thirteen inches. A winter crop of rye and oats provided feed for the boy's calf and two pigs. In the spring, he plowed the plot and enriched the soil by adding manure, an oak leaf compost, and commercial fertilizer.

Planting his crop on May 1, the boy cultivated it every week until early in July when it was "laid by." A final application of commercial fertilizer was made at that time. In October, when the crop was harvested, Ashley found that he had produced 106 bushels per acre, while the average in the community was only 15. Moreover, the young man was a businessman; he graded his corn and sold it for seed, receiving a total of $161.50, "plus the nubbins." He intended to invest his earnings in a purebred Hereford bull. In quiet confidence, the boy wrote, "I can beat Papa making corn." [78] There he had summarized very well a primary goal of club work.

## NOTES TO CHAPTER IV

1. United States Department of Agriculture, *Report of Agricultural Experiment Stations and Cooperative Agricultural Extension Work in the United States,* 1915, P. II, p. 31.

2. William A. Lloyd, "County Agricultural Agent Work under the Smith-Lever Act, 1914 to 1924," United States Department of Agriculture, *Miscellaneous Circular* 59 (Washington, 1925), 7; Reck, *4–H Story*, 125.

3. United States Department of Agriculture, *Report on Agricultural Experiment Stations and Cooperative Agricultural Extension Work in the United States,* 1915, P. II, p. 23; Mississippi, *Laws*, 1916, pp. 184–85; E. R. Lloyd, Annual Report of the Cooperative Extension Work, May 10, 1916, Mississippi Extension Service Records; *Progressive Farmer*, Vol. 30 (August 7, 1915), 19.

4. United States Department of Agriculture, *Report on Agricultural Experiment Stations and Cooperative Agricultural Extension Work in the United States,* 1915, P. II, p. 345; *ibid.,* 1916, P. II, p. 391; *ibid*; 1917, P. II, p. 399; United States Department of Agriculture, *Cooperative Extension Work in Agriculture and Home Economics*, 1918, p. 151; *ibid.,* 1919, p. 54, *ibid.,* 1920, p. 44.

5. President's Report, Mississippi Agricultural and Mechanical College, May 19, 1914, President's Correspondence.

6. President's Report, Mississippi Agricultural and Mechanical College, July 8, 1915, President's Correspondence; Mississippi Agricultural and Mechanical College, *Catalogue*, 1919–1920, pp. 12–16.

7. *Mississippi Club Boy*, Vol. 2 (February, 1919), 2; undated memo on administration, Mississippi Extension Service Records; *College Reflector*, Vol. 29 (December 11, 1915).

8. United States Department of Agriculture, *Report on Agricultural Experiment Stations and Cooperative Agricultural Extension Work in the United States,* 1915, P. II, p. 345; *ibid.,* 1916, P. II, p. 391; *ibid.,* 1917, P. II, p. 399; United States Department of Agriculture, *Cooperative Extension Work in Agriculture and Home Economics*, 1918, p. 151, *ibid.,* 1919, p. 54; *ibid.,* 1920, p. 44.

9. Mississippi Agricultural and Mechanical College, *Catalogue*, 1918–1919, p. 12.

10. Names of Men Who Have Served as Members of the State Club Staff, Mississippi Extension Service Records; *Mississippi Club Boy*, Vol. 3 (October, 1919), 2; List of Student Employees, May, 1913; C. A. Cobb to G. R. Hightower, September 19, 1914, President's Correspondence.

11. Names of Men Who Have Served as Members of the State Club Staff; F. W. Farley to C. J. Goodell, February 15, 1913, Mississippi Extension Service Records.
12. *Mississippi Club Boy*, Vol. 3 (September, 1919), 2; Extension Workers in the Service prior to and including 1914, Mississippi Extension Service Records.
13. Mississippi Extension Work in Agriculture and Home Economics, *Annual Report*, 1918 (n.p., n.d.), 51; Names of Men Who Have Served as Members of the State Club Staff; C. J. Goodell, Items of Extension History, with penciled notes, Mississippi Extension Service Records; *Mississippi Club Boy*, Vol. 3 (September, 1919), 2.
14. Mississippi Extension Work Among Negroes, undated memo; C. A. Cobb to James E. Tanner, October 21, 1940; G. C. Cypress to C. J. Goodell, Mississippi Extension Service Records.
15. *Progressive Farmer*, Vol. 31 (January 8, 1916), 18; *The Bulletin*, Vol. 10 (October, 1915), 3.
16. *Mississippi Club Boy*, Vol. 1 (May, 1918), 2.
17. J. E. Tanner to C. J. Goodell, March 17, 1939, enclosing Cobb memo, Mississippi Extension Service Records; *Progressive Farmer*, Vol. 30 (March 27, 1915), 308; Memphis *Commercial Appeal*, September 5, 1916, clipping in Cobb Papers.
18. *Mississippi Boys' Corn Club Congress* (n.p., n.d.); *Progressive Farmer*, Vol. 29 (August 29, 1914), 906.
19. *Mississippi Club Boy*, Vol. 1 (December, 1917), 1–2.
20. *Ibid.*, Vol. 1 (June, 1918), 4; *Progressive Farmer*, Vol. 34 (May 24, 1919), 46; *ibid.*, Vol. 34 (October 4, 1919), 35, 46.
21. *Progressive Farmer*, Vol. 31 (August 8, 1916), 18; *ibid.*, Vol. 34 (October 18, 1919), 28.
22. *Mississippi Club Boy*, Vol. 3 (October, 1919), 3; *Southern Ruralist*, Vol. 26 (December 15, 1919), 778.
23. *Progressive Farmer*, Vol. 31 (July 1, 1916), 18; Mississippi Extension Service, Press Release, April 9, 1916, President's Correspondence; C. A. Cobb to R. V. Scott, October 11, 1968, April 22, 1971, Cobb Papers.
24. Evans, "Recollections of Extension History," 16; William B. Mercier, "Status and Results of Extension Work in the Southern States, 1903–1921," United States Department of Agriculture, *Department Circular* 248 (Washington, 1922), 10; Mississippi State University, Extension Service, Annual Narrative and Statistical Reports, Covington County, 1916, Harrison County, 1917.
25. Mississippi Extension Work Among Negroes, undated memo; C. A. Cobb to James E. Tanner, October 21, 1940; G. C. Cypress to C. J. Goodell, January 23, 1940, Mississippi Extension Service Records. For a general discussion of work with Negroes, see O. B. Martin, "A Decade of Negro Extension Work, 1914–1924," United States Department of Agriculture, *Miscellaneous Circular* 72 (Washington, 1926).
26. Mississippi Agricultural and Mechanical College, *Biennial Report*, 1915–1917, pp. 200–201; Mississippi Extension Work in Agriculture and Home Economics, *Annual Report*, 1919, pp. 34–35.
27. Mississippi Agricultural and Mechanical College, *Biennial Report*, 1915–1917, p. 201; Mississippi Extension Work in Agriculture and Home Economics, *Annual Report*, 1919, pp. 29, 35; Cobb interviews; Cobb to I. W. Hill, March 11, 1919, Cobb Papers.
28. Mississippi State University, Extension Service, Annual Narrative and Statistical Reports, Tunica County, 1916.
29. Frederick W. Williamson, *Origin and Growth of Agricultural Extension in Louisiana, 1860–1948* (Baton Rouge, 1951); United States Department of Agricul-

ture, *Yearbook*, 1915 (Washington, 1916), 173; *The Outlook*, Vol. 111 (October 13, 1915), 347.

30. Hugh Critz to W. R. Perkins, May 17, 1938, Mississippi Extension Service Records; *Progressive Farmer and Southern Farm Gazette*, Vol. 15 (September 3, 1910), 616; *ibid.*, Vol. 16 (May 6, 1911), 14.

31. Ira W. Carpenter to C. J. Goodell, August 23, 1939, Mississippi Extension Service Records; *Progressive Farmer and Southern Farm Gazette*, Vol. 16 (June 17, 1911), 24–25; United States Department of Agriculture, *Yearbook*, 1915, p. 173.

32. Undated memo, Tanner Papers; Hugh Critz to W. R. Perkins, May 17, 1938, Mississippi Extension Service Records.

33. United States Department of Agriculture, *Yearbook*, 1915, p. 173; *Progressive Farmer and Southern Farm Gazette*, Vol. 16 (June 17, 1911), 565; *Wallaces' Farmer*, Vol. 38 (November 28, 1913), 1624.

34. W. F. Ward to G. R. Hightower, June 16, 1914, enclosing memo, President's Correspondence.

35. List of Student Employees, May, 1913; C. A. Cobb to G. R. Hightower, September 19, 1914, President's Correspondence; C. J. Goodell, Items of Extension History, with penciled notes, Mississippi Extension Service Records; Mississippi Extension Work in Agriculture and Home Economics, *Annual Report*, 1918, p. 50.

36. *First Annual Livestock Show, November 24–25, 1922* (Agricultural and Mechanical College, n.d.), 30.

37. Mississippi Extension Department, Press Release, March 10, June 3, 1916, Mississippi Extension Service Boards; *Progressive Farmer*, Vol. 30 (December 18, 1915), 17; *Mississippi Club Boy*, Vol. 1 (December, 1917), 1–2; Report of Lafayette County Agent, May 6, 1918, Mississippi State University, Extension Service, Annual Narrative and Statistical Reports; C. A. Cobb, "Boys' Clubs—What They Can and Do Accomplish," Agricultural Extension Committee of the National Implement and Vehicle Association, *Agricultural Extension* (Chicago, 1916), 74–77.

38. J. E. Tanner to C. J. Goodell, March 17, 1939, enclosing Cobb memo; Report of County Agent, Pontotoc County, 1918, Mississippi State University, Extension Service, Annual Narrative and Statistical Reports; Cobb to I. W. Hill, March 11, 1919, Cobb Papers.

39. Report of County Agent, Pontotoc County, 1918, Mississippi State University, Extension Service, Annual Narrative and Statistical Reports.

40. *Progressive Farmer*, Vol. 31 (June 3, 1916), 21; *ibid.*, Vol. 31 (December 16, 1916), 19.

41. *Progressive Farmer*, Vol. 30 (April 24, 1915), 16; Bura Hilbun to C. A. Cobb, July 24, 1916, Tanner Papers.

42. F. W. Farley to C. J. Goodell, February 15, 1939, Mississippi Extension Service Records; U. G. Houck, *The Bureau of Animal Industry of the United States Department of Agriculture* (Washington, 1924), 248.

43. Undated memo; Summary of Baby Beef Club Work for 1915, Mississippi Extension Service Records.

44. Mississippi Extension Department, Press Release, April 7, 1916, President's Correspondence; *Progressive Farmer*, Vol. 31 (December 2, 1916), 17.

45. *Ibid.*, F. W. Farley to C. J. Goodell, February 15, 1939; Results of Baby Beef Club Work in Mississippi, Year ending November 1, 1916, Mississippi Extension Service Records.

46. Mississippi Agricultural and Mechanical College, *Biennial Report*, 1915–1917, p. 201; *Mississippi Club Boy*, Vol. 2 (July, 1918), 1.

47. Mississippi Agricultural and Mechanical College, *Biennial Report*, 1919–1921, p. 41; *First Annual Livestock Show, November 24–25, 1922*, p. 31.

48. Frank W. Farley, telegram, n.d., Tanner Papers; *Hinds County Gazette*, April 10, 1942.

49. *Progressive Farmer*, Vol. 34 (March 15, 1919), 37; Mississippi Extension Work in Agriculture and Home Economics, *Annual Report*, 1919, pp. 30–31; Cobb to I. W. Hill, March 11, 1919, Cobb Papers.

50. *Mississippi Club Boy*, Vol. 3 (January, 1920), 1, 4.

51. *Progressive Farmer*, Vol. 34 (March 15, 1919), 37; Mississippi Extension Work in Agriculture and Home Economics, *Annual Report*, 1919, pp. 29–30; Cobb to I. W. Hill, March 11, 1919, Cobb Papers.

52. Mississippi Extension Work in Agriculture and Home Economics, *Annual Report*, 1916, p. 51; *ibid.*, 1918, p. 31; *Mississippi Club Boy*, Vol. 1 (January, 1918), 2.

53. *Ibid.*, Vol. 1 (June, 1918), 4; Mississippi Extension Work in Agriculture and Home Economics, *Annual Report*, 1919, p. 31; J. E. Tanner to C. J. Goodell, March 17, 1939, enclosing Cobb memo, Mississippi Extension Service Records; Cobb to I. W. Hill, March 11, 1919, Cobb Papers.

54. *Progressive Farmer*, Vol. 34 (March 15, 1919), 37; *Mississippi Club Boy*, Vol. 1 (August, 1917), 1; Mississippi Extension Work in Agriculture and Home Economics, *Annual Report*, 1919, pp. 31–32. One of the pioneer schools is described in Mississippi State University, Extension Service, Annual Narrative and Statistical Reports, Harrison County, 1916.

55. *Mississippi Club Boy*, Vol. 1 (June, 1918), 1, 4.

56. *Progressive Farmer*, Vol. 24 (June 7, 1919), 41; *ibid.*, Vol. 24 (July 19, 1919), 29; C. A. Cobb to W. H. Smith, July 7, 1919, President's Correspondence; "A Vacation Course in Junior Farm Mechanics," Mississippi Agricultural Extension Department, *Extension Circular* 24 (Agricultural College, 1919).

57. *Ibid.*; *Mississippi Club Boy*, Vol. 3 (August, 1919)', 1, 2; *Progressive Farmer*, Vol. 24 (October 4, 1919), 34, 46; Undated memo, Howard Quattlebaum to I. B. Kerlin, August 12, 1920, Tanner Papers; *Southern Ruralist*, Vol. 26 (September 15, 1919), 444.

58. *Mississippi Club Boy*, Vol. 1 (September, 1917), 1; *ibid.*, Vol. 2 (August, 1918), 1.

59. Cobb interviews; *Mississippi Club Boy*, Vol. 1 (January, 1918), 1; *ibid.*, Vol. 1 (February, 1918), 1; *ibid.*, Vol. 1 (March, 1918), 2; *ibid.*, Vol. 2 (October, 1918), 2; C. A. Cobb to J. E. Tanner, July 18, 1939, Mississippi Extension Service Records.

60. *Mississippi Club Boy*, Vol. 1 (March, 1918), 1.

61. *Ibid.*, Vol. 2 (December, 1918), 1, 3.

62. *Ibid.*, Vol. 2 (December, 1918), 1, 3; *ibid.*, Vol. 2 (January, 1919), 1, 4; *ibid.*, Vol. 2 (April, 1919), 3; Clyde H. Duncan, *Straight Furrows: A Story of 4–H Club Work* (Albuquerque, 1954), 104; *Amory Advertiser*, July 20, 1967, p. 11.

63. *Mississippi Club Boy*, Vol. 2 (February, 1919), 2; *ibid.*, Vol. 2 (June, 1919), 1.

64. *Ibid.*, Vol. 2 (February, 1919), 2; *ibid.*, Vol. 2 (June, 1919), 1; *Progressive Farmer*, Vol. 34 (October 18, 1919), 28; Mississippi State University, Extension Service, Annual Narrative and Statistical Reports, Jones County, 1919.

65. *Mississippi Club Boy*, Vol. 3 (January, 1920), 1; Duncan, *Straight Furrows*, 104–105; Reck, *4–H Story*, 173–74, 186.

66. C. A. Cobb to R. V. Scott, February 19, 1968; Cobb to I. W. Hill, March 11, 1919, Cobb Papers.

67. *Mississippi Club Boy*, Vol. 1 (August, 1917), 2; *Progressive Farmer*, Vol. 24 (March 15, 1919), 37.

68. Mississippi State University, Annual Narrative and Statistical Reports, Report of the Director, Year ending June 30, 1918; H. E. Savely to J. E. Tanner, October 5, 1920, Mississippi Extension Service Records.

69. Extension Editors, Publicity and Publications, undated memo, Mississippi Extension Service Records.

70. *College Reflector*, Vol. 30 (December 27, 1916); Mississippi Extension Service, Press Release, June 2, 4, 1916, President's Correspondence.

71. *College Reflector*, Vol. 32 (February 9, 1919); *Mississippi Club Boy*, Vol. 2 (August, 1918), 3.

72. Reck, *4-H Story*, 147. See also O. H. Benson and Gertrude L. Warren, "Organization and Results of Boys' and Girls' Club Work, 1918," United States Department of Agriculture, *Circular* 66 (Washington, 1920), 5, 6.

73. *Mississippi Club Boy*, Vol. 2 (July, 1918), 1; *Progressive Farmer*, Vol. 34 (March 15, 1919), 37.

74. *Mississippi Club Boy*, Vol. 2 (October, 1918), 2; *ibid.*, Vol. 2 (November, 1919), 3; *Progressive Farmer*, Vol. 34 (March 15, 1919), 37.

75. *Mississippi Club Boy*, Vol. 2 (January, 1919), 1.

76. J. E. Tanner to C. J. Goodell, March 17, 1939, enclosing Cobb memo, Mississippi Extension Service Records.

77. Figures for the South taken or calculated from United States Department of Agriculture, *Annual Report*, 1914 (Washington, 1914), 120; *ibid.*, 1915, p. 42; *ibid.*, 1916, p. 316; *ibid.*, 1917, p. 342; *ibid.*, 1918, p. 356; *ibid.*, 1919, pp. 374–75; *ibid.*, 1920, p. 427. For Mississippi, see Mississippi Agricultural and Mechanical College, *Biennial Report*, 1915–1917, pp. 200–201; *ibid.*, 1919–1921, p. 42; Mississippi Extension Work in Agriculture and Home Economics, *Annual Report*, 1918, pp. 49–51; *ibid.*, 1919, pp. 29–31; *Progressive Farmer*, Vol. 34 (March 15, 1919), 37. For a survey of the growth of club work during these years, see George E. Farrell, "Boys' and Girls' 4-H Club Work under the Smith-Lever Act, 1914–1924," United States Department of Agriculture, *Miscellaneous Circular* 85 (Washington, 1926).

78. C. A. Cobb to County Demonstration Agents, March 15, 1915, enclosing letter from Roy Ashley, Tanner Papers.

# CHAPTER V

# A Farm Paper in Prosperity Decade: Managerial Policy, 1919–1930

CULLY A. COBB'S career in formal agricultural extension work came to an abrupt end late in 1919. Offered the position of editor-in-chief of the *Southern Ruralist*, a farm paper published in Atlanta, Cobb tendered his resignation, effective November 15, and made ready to leave the state that he had served since 1908.

His decision to leave Mississippi was a difficult one. His work in the club program had been satisfying to himself, his superiors, and the people of the state. "The club movement as it exists to-day . . . is a monument to his efficiency," wrote one observer in 1919. In February, 1919, he had been promoted to assistant director of the Mississippi Agricultural Extension Service and, given Cobb's age and record of accomplishment, there is little question that in time he would have earned the top position. Indeed, one of Cobb's associates at Mississippi Agricultural and Mechanical College believed that Cobb's popularity in the state was such that there was not "an office within the gift of the people of the commonwealth that he could not have had for the mere asking." [1] *

But Cobb had no desire for a political career. In deciding to go to Atlanta, he was motivated by a number of factors. Included, quite obviously, was the matter of salary. Cobb never believed in "economic peonage." As assistant director of agricultural extension in Mississippi, he was receiving $3,250; the *Southern Ruralist* offered him $7,200. Moreover, his less than competitive salary in Mississippi was indicative of a major problem facing the extension service as a whole in the years immediately following World War I. During that struggle, emergency funds had been made available by the

* Notes appear at end of each chapter.

federal government which contributed substantially to the enlargement of extension programs. The evaporation of those funds that
came with peace forced a general belt tightening and a curtailment
of activities. In Mississippi, the extension budget fell from $305,000
in 1918–1919 to $238,000 in 1919–1920. Under such conditions, an
energetic and ambitious man understandably might seek greater
opportunities elsewhere.[2]

But perhaps most important in Cobb's decision was his concept
of duty and service. Throughout his career, Cobb believed that
men have a deep responsibility to use their talents and abilities in
such a way as to perform their most useful service to society. Cobb
was trained in agriculture, and he was convinced that in that area
lay his duty and his opportunity for service. In his work in the club
program, Cobb believed that he had met his responsibilities, but in
farm journalism he saw an even greater opportunity for service.
With that idea in mind, Cobb moved his family to Atlanta and took
up his new tasks on December 1, 1919.[3]

By joining the staff of the *Southern Ruralist*, Cobb became a part
of one of the oldest and most important forces for rural improvement. Farm journalism began in something like recognizable form
in 1819 when John S. Skinner launched the *American Farmer*.
During the next half century, papers appeared throughout the
settled areas of the country, with the largest numbers being found
in New England, the Atlantic Coast states, and the eastern Middle
West. Included among these early magazines were the *Union Agriculturist and Western Prairie Farmer*, a paper that 130 years later
continued to serve rural residents of Illinois and adjacent states, and
such southern periodicals as the *American Cotton Planter* and the
*Southern Cultivator*.

Between the Civil War and World War I, farm journalism went
through a tremendous expansion in both number of papers and
circulation. According to one student, approximately 3,600 farm
periodicals began publication between 1810 and 1910, the great
majority appearing after Appomattox. Most were short-lived, many
of them publishing no more than a handful of issues before suc-
cumbing. In 1913 an estimate put the total then in existence at 450,
and that figure included those highly specialized magazines which

aimed at small and select audiences. Early circulation figures were highly unreliable, but later and better statistics show a dramatic surge in the late nineteenth and early twentieth centuries. In 1881 total circulation was placed at 548,000, but the figure had jumped to 4,309,000 by 1900 and to 10,420,000 a decade later. Thereafter, the growth was gradual and reasonably steady. Standing at 14,-514,000 in 1920, circulation was 19,905,000 in 1930. By the second decade of the twentieth century, 66 percent of all farmers read farm papers, according to a survey conducted by the United States Department of Agriculture, and 44 percent subscribed to two or more.

Both circulation and impact of farm papers were less in the southern states than in the country as a whole. Circulation in the South seems to have lagged from the outset, partly because of the peculiar problems of the region. At a time when 66 percent of all farmers subscribed to at least one paper, only 45 percent of southern farmers did so. At the same time, the Department of Agriculture reported that 40 percent of the nation's farmers considered the farm press as the educational agency most useful in their operations, but in the South 67 percent expressed the belief that experience was the only effective teacher for the man on the farm.[4]

Still, farm journalism was a force of some significance in the South and the industry there shared in the general boom that came after 1880. By 1900 there were at least fifty-two farm papers published in the lower South. That number remained relatively constant during the next thirty years. A total of fifty-nine was reported in 1930. Within the region, Georgia and Kentucky were the states best supplied, each having from eight to twelve papers at different times during that span of years. South Carolina and Mississippi had the fewest farm journals, the numbers ranging from none to five.[5]

Among the fifty or so papers in the lower South, there were five that could be labeled outstanding regional publications. The group included the *Progressive Farmer* (Raleigh), *Southern Agriculturist* (Nashville), *Southern Planter* (Richmond), *Southern Cultivator* (Atlanta), and *Southern Ruralist* (Atlanta). Each had a significant circulation, each lived for at least a quarter of a century after 1900, and each offered readers a balanced diet of information pertaining to farming and rural life. In terms of circulation, *Southern Ruralist* was in 1920 the most important, having a circulation of 267,000. *Progressive Farmer* followed with 187,000, *Southern Agriculturist* had 160,000, and *Southern Planter* and *Southern Cultivator* trailed behind with 70,000 and 45,000 respectively.[6]

Among these five papers were some of the oldest and best-known farm periodicals in the United States. In fact, the *Southern Cultivator* claimed to be the oldest periodical of its type in the South, having been established in Augusta, Georgia, in 1843. In 1916 it was a semi-monthly, with a subscription rate of one dollar a year. From 1904 to 1928 its editor was George F. Hunnicutt; W. M. Goodman joined him the next year. The *Southern Planter* dated from 1867, although its owners sought to push its origins back into the antebellum period. Similar in size and frequency of issue to the *Southern Cultivator*, the *Planter* charged its subscribers fifty cents a year. Its first editor in the twentieth century was J. F. Jackson. He was followed by Meade Ferguson and T. K. Wolfe. *Southern Agriculturist* was founded in Louisville, Kentucky, in 1870. Later it was moved to Nashville. In 1911 L. R. Neal was named editor, and in the 1920s E. E. Miller and Gustavus W. Myers aided him. Like its competitors, the *Agriculturist* was a semi-monthly, but for the fifty cent subscription rate its readers received a paper of larger page size.[7]

The *Progressive Farmer* was in part a product of the farmers' alliance movement of the 1880s. Its founder was Leonidas L. Polk, perhaps the greatest of the southern alliance leaders; and after the paper was established at Raleigh, North Carolina, in 1886 it served as the voice of the agrarian crusade in that state and in adjacent areas. Polk died in 1892,[8] and in 1903 his heirs sold the paper for $6,200 to the Agricultural Publishing Company (later the Progressive Farmer Company), a firm organized by Clarence Poe, the editor from 1899. Three smaller stockholders sold their interests in 1908 to John S. Pearson and Tait Butler. These men, along with Poe, very largely controlled the paper during the next quarter of a century.[9]

Poe's paper had a circulation of only 10,000 in 1900, but it shared in the boom that came in farm journalism after the turn of the century. In 1904 the *Progressive Farmer* absorbed *The Cotton Plant* of Greenville, South Carolina, and five years later it merged with the *Southern Farm Gazette* of Starkville, Mississippi. These and other acquisitions helped to push circulation to 44,000 in 1910 and to 187,000 a decade later. The *Progressive Farmer* pioneered in publishing separate editions for different geographical areas. The merger with the *Southern Farm Gazette* encouraged Poe to establish a western edition in 1910, and by 1916 the paper had editions dated at Raleigh, Birmingham, Memphis, and Dallas. All editions carried some major features, but separate editions made it possible for the paper to meet more nearly the special needs of its readers. In contrast to its competitors, the *Progressive Farmer* was a weekly, its page size was larger, and subscriptions were $1.00 a year.[10]

The *Southern Ruralist* was established by George W. Hastings at Interlachen, Florida, in 1893 as the *Florida Ruralist*. Three years later its owners changed the name to *Southern Ruralist* and in 1900 they moved the paper to Atlanta. In 1920 the paper was published by the Southern Ruralist Company, Frank J. Merriam, president. Other stockholders included H. G. Hastings, H. W. Brown, L. D. Hicks, and C. R. Cunningham, all of Atlanta, and W. J. Mills, College Park, Georgia. In the twentieth century, at least, the paper seems to have been blessed with good management; it grew in frequency of issue, size, and circulation. Launched as a monthly, it was changed to semi-monthly in 1906. By 1919, when the subscription rate was fifty cents, readers received issues that contained from twenty-four to sixty-four pages, up sharply from the eight-page issues of 1900. Meanwhile, circulation had soared to 107,000 in 1910 and to 267,000 in 1920. Not only was the *Southern Ruralist* the largest regional paper in the South, it was bigger by a considerable margin than some of the best-known farm periodicals in the North. For example, *Prairie Farmer*, the bible of Illinois farmers, had a circulation of only 112,000 in 1920, and *Wallaces' Farmer* could claim only 65,000 subscribers.[11]

Some of the success of the *Southern Ruralist* prior to 1920 could be attributed to its editor, Horace E. Stockbridge. Born in Massachusetts in 1857, Stockbridge earned a Ph.D. degree in agricultural chemistry at Göttingen, Germany, in 1884. Returning to the United

Editorial staff of the *Southern Ruralist*, March, 1920. Front row, left to right, Paul H. Sanders, W. L. Glessner, Frank J. Merrian, A. B. McKay, Jesse H. Reed. Second row, left to right, Mary E. Creswell, Dan T. Gray, C. A. Cobb, Clark Taylor, T. H. McHatton.

States, he served one year at the Massachusetts Agricultural College before going to Japan to teach at the Imperial College of Agriculture and Engineering. In 1889 he was director of the Indiana experiment station and the next year he became president of North Dakota Agricultural College. Leaving that post, he was appointed professor of agriculture and state director of farmers' institutes in Florida in 1897, a position that he held until 1906 when he became editor of the *Southern Ruralist*.[12] During the thirteen years that he held that position, Stockbridge wrote the material appearing on the editorial page and he reportedly introduced a number of innovations in the paper which contributed significantly to its growing strength. However, "slight differences . . . concerning the editorial policy" arose between Stockbridge and the stockholders that left him with "no alternative but to withdraw." His letter of resignation was dated September 16, 1919.[13]

When Cobb went to Atlanta to take the post vacated by Stockbridge, he had no way of knowing that he was embarking upon a new career at the same time that agriculture as a whole was entering a period of depression and hardship. In fact, the decade of the 1920s and the first years of the 1930s would prove to be the most difficult for farmers since the late nineteenth century; it would also be a period of widespread agrarian discontent and ferment as farmers and their leaders reacted to adverse economic conditions and sought new answers to the old but difficult problems facing them.

The prosperity that farmers enjoyed during World War I came to an abrupt end in 1920–1921. Wheat, for example, fell from $2.16 a bushel in 1919 to $1.03 in 1921 and to $.93 in 1923. Corn collapsed from $1.52 in 1918 to $.52 only two years later. Cotton suffered an equally dramatic decline—from $.35 a pound in 1919 to $.16 in 1920—but for a variety of reasons prices of that staple rebounded in a more pleasing fashion than did wheat or corn. Among other commodities, tobacco underwent a depression in prices; the figures for 1919 and 1921 were $.31 and $.17 respectively.[14]

Prices of nonagricultural commodities also declined in 1920–1921, but they did not fall as far or as fast as did farm prices. Moreover, they tended to recover as the decade progressed, while prices farmers received lagged badly. In 1917 and 1918 the parity ratio was 118, but by 1921 it had fallen to 75. During the remainder of the decade it never exceeded 90, and following the crash of 1929 it collapsed to 64 in 1931 and to 55 in 1932. Averages for different years beginning with 1910 were as follows: [15]

| Years | Parity Ratio Averages |
|---|---|
| 1910–1914 | 99.6 |
| 1915–1919 | 106.4 |
| 1920–1924 | 86.2 |
| 1925–1929 | 88.8 |
| 1930–1932 | 66.3 |

Such figures indicate clearly that conditions in agriculture improved somewhat after 1921. It is equally obvious that farmers failed by a wide margin to share equitably in the prosperity of the Roaring Twenties and that the Great Depression of 1929 had particularly adverse effects upon them.

In this environment of inequitable prices and general hardship, farmers turned to organization with an enthusiasm that they had not shown since the agrarian crusade of thirty years earlier. Southerners tended to resist the movement toward general farm organizations, placing their faith instead in commodity cooperatives; but the Grange gained new power in the Northeast, the Farmers' Union became the spokesman for wheat farmers of the plains states, and in Minnesota and the Dakotas the Nonpartisan League moved to direct political action, laying the foundations of the Farmer-Labor Party. In the lower Middle West and in scattered areas elsewhere, the Farm Bureau flourished, a national federation of state groups having been established in 1919. That organization and others soon opened offices in Washington in order that they might push more effectively for governmental solutions for what was coming to be known as the farm problem.

Nor were politicians and others wholly deaf to the cries of outrage arising from the farm. Reacting to grassroots pressures, a number of senators and representatives from rural states organized the Farm Bloc in 1921. Earlier that year Congress created a Joint Commission of Agricultural Inquiry to study rural problems. The next year Secretary of Agriculture Henry C. Wallace called a National Agricultural Conference where some four hundred spokesmen for farmers appeared to express their views. The Northwest Agricultural Conference met in Washington in 1924 to consider means by which farmers on the northern plains might be induced to diversify their operations. Still another national conference met that year. Even businessmen began to conclude that there was something wrong on the farm. The National Industrial Conference Board published the results of an investigation in 1926. The next year that agency and the United States Chamber of Commerce sponsored a Business Men's Commission on Agriculture. The Association of Land-Grant Colleges and Universities, somewhat belatedly recognizing that there was a farm problem, released in November, 1927, a report that critics said was "strong on analysis and weak on remedy."

Such activities contributed to the enactment during the decade of a variety of measures calculated to ease rural problems. The Emergency Tariff of 1921 and the Fordney-McCumber Tariff of 1922 contained provisions supposedly favorable to agriculture; the Futures Trading Act of 1921 sought to relieve farmers' worries concerning the proceedings at grain exchanges; and in 1922 and 1924 Congress passed legislation that encouraged the formation of farm cooperatives by excluding them from prosecution under the antitrust laws. The Intermediate Credit Act established a system of credit banks that offered six-month to three-year loans to farmers at reasonable rates; it proved to be a measure especially beneficial to cattle raisers. Earlier, the War Finance Corporation had been revived and its powers broadened to allow it to aid in the export of agricultural commodities and under certain circumstances to make loans for rural rehabilitation. Finally, the Hoover administration sought to meet its campaign promises by the enactment of the Agricultural Marketing Act of 1929. That measure created the Federal Farm Board, appropriated $500 million for its operations, and directed the new agency to help farmers by encouraging the formation of cooperatives and by facilitating orderly marketing of commodities through them.

All of these pieces of legislation promised to meet some current need in agriculture and all of them reflected the prevailing philosophy of the Republican administrations in the 1920s. Warren G. Harding stated that philosophy very well in 1922. Speaking to the National Agricultural Conference, he said that it "cannot be too strongly urged that the farmer must be ready to help himself. This conference would do the most lasting good if it would find ways to impress the great mass of farmers to avail themselves of the best methods. By this I mean that, in the last analysis, legislation can do little more than give the farmer the chance to organize and help himself." The encouragement of cooperatives, the providing of better credit facilities, and the elimination of such long-standing grievances as those existing in the grain trade enabled the farmer to "help himself." Unfortunately for the farmer, and in 1932 for the Republican party, such measures and the philosophy upon which they rested failed by a wide margin to solve the most pressing problem of the times.

That problem centered on the existence of surpluses of agricultural commodities. American farmers were producing more wheat, cotton, and other staples than the market could take at prices that gave the grower a fair return or even a living income. Causes of this condition were complex; farmers and their spokesmen were more interested in solving the problem than in analyzing it. It was George N. Peek and Hugh S. Johnson, farm implement executives from Moline, Illinois, who first formulated a plan for the disposal of the surplus. "Equality for Agriculture" was their objective, and their plan for achieving it reached Congress in January, 1924, in the form of the McNary-Haugen bill. In the course of time, the bill went through a number of modifications, but the basic idea of the proposal was to segregate that portion of an agricultural staple that was sold in the domestic market from the part that went into foreign trade. The former would be sold in the United States at a fixed price—interpreted by some as the world price plus protective tariff duties. A governmental agency would buy the surplus at the domestic price and sell it in world markets for whatever it would bring. Producers of the commodity would then compensate the government for its loss through a special tax or equalization fee. Not only would the scheme presumably result in higher average prices for farm commodities, but proponents believed that it would help to control production since a larger surplus would lead to a heavier equalization fee and a resultant lower return to the producer.

Rural sentiment concerning the "Equality for Agriculture" idea was by no means uniformly favorable. Attitudes depended upon a variety of factors, including the extent to which a given commodity sold in foreign trade and the degree of agricultural distress. It was the spring wheat belt that suffered most in the early 1920s, and it was there that demands for a far-reaching program were first heard. But in 1923 hog prices collapsed in the Middle West, foreclosures increased in number, and farmers in the rich prairie states of Illinois and Iowa discovered that their difficulties were little different from those of the wheat producers. In fact, the Farm Bureau, the voice of organized farmers in the Middle West, became the primary supporter of the McNary-Haugen bill, while farther east the Grange favored its own version of the surplus disposal scheme, known as the export debenture plan. The South, on the other hand, tended to be less enthusiastic and even indifferent, at least until later in the decade. Reasonably satisfactory prices for cotton in three of the years between 1919 and 1926, the region's faith in commodity cooperatives, and its traditional hostility to the principle of a protective tariff and to any increase in federal power played roles in southern attitudes. But in March, 1926, farm leaders from the South and the Middle West met in Memphis to consider mutual problems. Thereafter, general solidarity prevailed on the proposition that farmers had to have governmental help in handling the mountainous surpluses.

If farmers were rather generally of the opinion by the later years of the 1920s that they needed the McNary-Haugen bill or some comparable measure, the nation's political leaders failed to share their convictions. The McNary-Haugen bill finally emerged from Congress in 1927, only to be vetoed by President Coolidge. A modified version got the same treatment in 1928. The president claimed that the bills as passed by Congress would create a burdensome bureaucracy, encourage speculation, favor some farm crops over others, and lead to resentment in and retaliation by those nations in which the surplus commodities were dumped. Further, Coolidge was convinced that the government could not become involved in the business of price fixing; to do so, he thought, would be to strike at the heart of free enterprise. Thus rebuffed, some farm leaders embraced Herbert Hoover's Agricultural Marketing Act as the best program they were likely to get; others began to consider seriously the domestic allotment plan that would in time become a central feature of Franklin D. Roosevelt's New Deal for agriculture.[16]

Within the framework of farm problems, proposed solutions, and political rejection of rural hopes, Cobb managed the *Southern Ruralist*. As editor-in-chief he wrote the periodical's editorials and was a major force in shaping both internal and external policies.[17] The *Southern Ruralist* was obviously a successful and flourishing enterprise in November, 1919; Cobb's task was to do everything possible to insure the continuation of that condition and, if possible, to improve upon it.

When Cobb joined the staff of the *Southern Ruralist*, he had no doubts concerning the value of the farm press, and quite understandably his faith in the industry grew during the 1920s. His experiences with the *Mississippi Club Boy* had demonstrated the useful role that a well-produced paper might play in agricultural improvement; he also recognized and appreciated the aid that farm papers had given him in the management of the boys' clubs in Mississippi. In 1928, after almost a decade with the *Southern Ruralist*, he hailed agricultural journalism as "one of the greatest educational institutions" and one that had done much for the advancement of farming and for the development of "clearer and more courageous thinking" by farmers. "Unless the agricultural public reads, studies, and keeps abreast with developments," he wrote, "the agricultural public is going to lag behind and agricultural progress will continue to drag." Moreover, farm journalism was particularly well equipped to provide rural readers with the knowledge they needed to meet the challenges of farm life. "The reputable agricultural paper," he contended, "is faithfully endeavoring to provide its readers with the latest practical and authentic information," and the agricultural editors constituted "the world's largest group of non-political and non-sectarian writers."[18]

In making up the issues of the *Southern Ruralist*, Cobb had the aid of a battery of writers who prepared regular columns on their

Plant of the Southern Ruralist Company, constructed in 1926 in Atlanta, Georgia, of Stone Mountain granite.

specialities. These writers generally were given the title of associate editor and each was paid a regular salary. Most of them were connected with agricultural colleges in the Southeast, but some worked fulltime for the *Southern Ruralist*. During Cobb's administration of the *Southern Ruralist*, there was substantial stability in this group of writers. Several of them served the paper during the entire time that Cobb was connected with it. The dairy and livestock column, for example, was written by Dan T. Gray. In 1919 he was head of the animal industry division in the North Carolina agricultural experiment station and later he served as dean of the colleges of agriculture in Alabama and Arkansas. The veterinary department was the responsibility of Charles A. Cary, professor of veterinary science at the Alabama agricultural college. The dean of southern veterinarians, Cary had served as president of the American Veterinary Medical Association, and he possessed a well-earned reputation as a farmers' institute lecturer. Frank J. Merriam, the president and principal stockholder of the Southern Ruralist Company, regularly prepared the gardening department. A native of

New Hampshire, Merriam lacked academic training in his specialty but he had years of practical experience, having been a successful truck farmer near Atlanta prior to his acquisition of the *Southern Ruralist*. In fact, according to Cobb, Merriam continued "to live out of his garden, as he is advising his readers to do." For a time, Professor A. B. McKay, Cobb's old mentor at Mississippi Agricultural and Mechanical College, wrote a column on "Gardening and Other Things." Finally, Professor Thomas H. McHatton, a faculty member at Georgia's agricultural college, was the regular writer of a horticultural column; and Frank J. Marshall, who was reported to have judged more poultry shows than any man in the South, prepared a column on his specialty.[19]

But Cobb was willing to replace his writers with stronger personnel and to add new departments when such changes seemed wise. In 1919 the farm mechanics column was written by Professor L. C. Hart of the University of Georgia, but in 1920 he was replaced by Dan Scoates. The new editor had been an associate of Cobb at Mississippi Agricultural and Mechanical College before he moved to Texas where he had a long and distinguished career at that state's agricultural college. Among other honors, Scoates served a term as president of the Society of American Agricultural Engineers. Paul H. Sanders, Cobb's subordinate in club work in Mississippi who preceded Cobb to Atlanta, was responsible for a newly established boys' and girls' club department until his resignation in 1922. His replacement was Miss Alma Simpson. In 1923 the *Southern Ruralist* pioneered in the South by establishing a department of markets. Cobb employed M. C. Gay, formerly with the United States Department of Agriculture, to conduct that column. On the other hand, "Notes Afield," a column written by W. L. Glesser, disappeared from the *Southern Ruralist* in the 1920s.[20]

Since Cobb was determined to make the *Southern Ruralist* a paper for the farm woman as well as for the farmer, he sought continually to improve the magazine's home department. Mary E. Creswell of the Georgia College of Agriculture assumed direction of that department in January, 1920, but by 1922 her duties at Athens had become too heavy for her to continue on the *Southern*

Lois P. Dowdle (later Mrs. C. A. Cobb) as editor of the Home Department of the *Southern Ruralist*, c. 1926.

*Ruralist* staff. Her successor was Lulu M. Cassidy, a graduate of the North Carolina College for Women and a former home demonstration agent. She devoted full time to the *Ruralist*, editing for a time the boys' and girls' club department as well. But when Miss Cassidy resigned in 1925, her replacement was a young lady who in the future would play a very large role in Cobb's life. Miss Lois P. Dowdle, an extension worker in Georgia and head of girls' club work in that state, had written for the *Southern Ruralist* as early as 1921. Four years later she became editor of the paper's home department.[21]

Miss Dowdle soon proved to be one of the more important members of the staff. According to Frank J. Merriam, when Miss Dowdle "sets her head to anything she is hard to turn." In any event, she was fully convinced that the "home is the most important part of the farm." By 1929 she had earned the title of editor, the home department had been moved to a more central location in the paper, indicating the increased importance placed upon her work, and she had induced Merriam and Cobb to employ three contributing editors to strengthen her department. Miss Martha J. McAlpine, a native of North Carolina who was educated at Winthrop College, contributed articles on child care, and Miss Bess Hodges, an extension specialist in Arkansas, specialized in textiles and clothing. The final addition was Dr. Marvin F. Haygood, city health officer in Knoxville, who wrote on a variety of matters pertaining to good health on the farm.[22]

Two other writers appeared regularly in the columns of the *Southern Ruralist*. Reverend W. H. Faust presented a religious piece each month, and in the mid-1920s the *Southern Ruralist* introduced its "One Gallus Department for Men," by Bill Rumpus, pseudonym for H. W. Brown. Using rural philosophy and wit and writing in an exaggerated version of the dialect supposedly common among small and backwoods farmers of the South, Rumpus commented shrewdly on a variety of topics and poked fun at himself, his associates, and life in general.[23]

Each associate or contributing editor was left free to express his own ideas, supplemented by the latest research findings of the United States Department of Agriculture and the agricultural experiment stations across the South. The *Southern Ruralist* was in many ways a typical "how-to-do-it" paper, although Cobb, through energetic leadership and careful supervision, strived always to raise it above the average category. Generally, his writers used their columns to provide farmers with information concerning newer or better methods, point out mistakes commonly made on the farm, and answer questions raised by readers. Dan T. Gray, for instance, gave farmers hints on shipping hogs by railroad car, instructed them in the proper methods for raising lambs, and pointed out that spring oats provided excellent grazing for live stock.[24] Charles A. Cary produced numerous articles of a similar nature, but he was more inclined to fill his column with answers to specific questions sent to him. Farmers wanted to know how to treat scours, hog cholera, and various kinds of worms. Cary's answers were short and to the point; he prescribed treatment, suggested that the farmer take the animal in question to the nearest veterinarian, or in some cases indicated that science had not yet found the answer.[25]

The other regular writers followed fairly closely the patterns set by Gray and Cary. In one issue, for example, Thomas H. McHatton discussed modern orchard machinery, the use and preservation of water in the orchard, and the growing of raspberries and blueberries, while Frank J. Merriam had an article on the use of tractors in gardens, followed by a series of answers to questions sent him.[26] Dan Scoates wrote on such matters as the causes of concrete failure, the installation of home water systems, and methods of controlling rats and other farm pests, as well as on the whole field of farm machinery. M. C. Gay and Frank J. Marshall generally contributed three or four articles for their columns in each issue.[27]

The boys' and girls' club department was one of Cobb's favorites. Not only did it deal with the work to which Cobb had given nine years of his life, but at the outset the department was under the editorship of Paul H. Sanders, Cobb's closest associate during his last years in Mississippi. In Sanders' first article, in fact, he discussed the short course in junior farm mechanics that Cobb had arranged. Subsequently, Sanders filled his column with stories and pictures of club work across the South, often including letters and crop histories written by club members.[28] Alma Simpson, Sanders' successor on the *Southern Ruralist* staff, generally followed the patterns that he had established.

The purpose of the home department, according to Lulu M. Cassidy, its first full time editor, was to "cull the best practical ideas and suggestions of the economic, social, and educational leaders the country over, and to present them in terse, concrete form." Besides the more mundane aspects of homemaking, she wanted to give "women, particularly young women and girls . . . a more intimate knowledge of the rapidly increasing possibilities and opportunities for womanhood."[29]

Under Miss Dowdle's editorship, the home department followed that injunction and in time it became, in terms of space, the most extensive single department in the *Southern Ruralist*. Few topics directly or indirectly related to the farm home escaped Miss Dowdle's attention and comment. In one issue, she gave mothers hints on the identification and treatment of poison-oak and urged women to set the colors in cottons before washing them; in another, she discussed the financing arrangements open to farmers who wanted to build new homes and presented a thoughtful essay on the meaning of Christmas.[30]

Bill Rumpus' "One Gallus Department" sought to introduce an element of humor into the *Southern Ruralist*, much as John Turnipseed did in the *Prairie Farmer*, but with the wit and rural philosophy Rumpus mixed shrewd comment on human nature and issues then in the news. For instance, he was moved to explain to farmers that, if they would buy "ottermobiles" and teach their wives to drive the machines, they would have a great deal of peace on their farms while the women were in town. Blackberry wine, he contended, was a certain cure for various types of the "mis'ry." Rumpus also had an explanation for the coolness of President Coolidge to such farm programs as that embodied in the McNary-Haugen bill, despite the fact that the President "was raised on a farm, an' he ought t'be part farmer himself." Rumpus wrote, "The way I figger it, when he first got to Washin'ton he was part farmer an' part politician; but since them days the farmer has died." [31]

In addition to these regular writers, the *Southern Ruralist* served as a forum for a variety of other authors to present their ideas to the paper's readers. Agricultural college personnel, officials of agricultural credit systems, and authorities from the United States Department of Agriculture prepared articles from time to time.

Cobb also opened the columns of the *Southern Ruralist* to ordinary farmers. In fact, such writers were considered of primary importance since Cobb, like C. V. Gregory of the *Prairie Farmer*, saw the farm press as a medium through which real farmers could discuss their problems and successes, exchange views, and learn from each other.[32] Nor did Cobb simply wait for farmers to write to the *Southern Ruralist*; instead, he encouraged them to do so by making a standing offer of two dollars for any letter that was published in the paper. In addition, to generate longer pieces by farmers on particular aspects of agriculture, the *Southern Ruralist* ran monthly contests in which it offered prizes of twenty-five, fifteen, and ten dollars for the best articles submitted.[33]

From time to time, the *Southern Ruralist* ran special contests among its readers. Purposes were at least twofold: to encourage farmers and their wives to undertake improvements in given areas, and to inspire others to do the same by giving them an opportunity to read of the accomplishments of the prize winners. In 1920 the *Southern Ruralist* had a "Better Kitchen" contest. Contestants were farm families who had improved their kitchens and who submitted to the *Southern Ruralist* pictures, floor plans, and other data showing arrangements before and after the alterations and who wrote articles describing them. Prizes ranged downward from forty dollars.[34]

Other contests came later. In 1925 and 1926, for example, the magazine conducted a garden contest to stimulate the growing of more and better gardens in the South. A total of one thousand dollars divided among eighteen prizes was offered to farmers in each of those years, and in 1926 the management enlarged the program by sponsoring a parallel contest for city and suburban dwellers. Contestants received entry forms from the *Southern Ruralist* office or from agricultural extension personnel in fifteen states. The magazine furnished each participant with record and report blanks. Final reports had to be attested by local school, extension, or public officials. Prizes were awarded on the basis of 75 percent for the growth and consumption of vegetables adequate to provide a well balanced diet for the greatest number of days and 25 percent for the best written report by a contestant.[35]

Miss Dowdle played a major role in a number of contests dealing with the farm home that were staged in the late 1920s. In 1926 there was a home improvement and beautification contest with fifty dollars in prizes. When it stimulated a great deal of interest, the *Southern Ruralist* enlarged the program. In 1927 and 1928 there were better-homes contests with fifteen hundred dollars given in prizes each year. These contests involved the rearrangement or improvement of homes for sanitation, convenience, and beauty, as well as landscaping and arrangement of other farm buildings around the home. In 1929 the contest dealt with bathrooms and running water; prizes amounted to one thousand dollars. Such contests reflected very well the view of Cobb and Miss Dowdle that there was a "need for having the development of the farm home keep pace with that of the farm itself if we are to have a prosperous, contented farm population." [36]

The arrangement of the *Southern Ruralist* followed an established pattern. Each first-of-the-month issue was called a "Special Number" and emphasized a particular topic. In 1925, for example, these topics were:

| | |
|---|---|
| January | Farm Crops and Fertilizers |
| February | Gardening |
| March | Farm Tools, Machinery, and Tillage |
| April | Automobiles, Trucks, and Good Roads |
| May | Forage and Ensilage |
| June | Dairying and Live Stock |
| July | Marketing and Farm Finance |
| August | Better Home Equipment and Furnishings |
| September | Small Grain and Winter Legumes |
| October | Building and Fencing |
| November | Fruit and Spraying |
| December | Poultry |

From time to time Cobb changed these monthly topics, but issues were always discussed in season and an effort was made in the course of a year to deal with the entire span of subjects interesting to farmers. The regular writers directed their columns toward the particular topic of each "Special Issue," a year's program for each writer having been carefully blocked out at a regular annual meeting called for that purpose. Mid-month issues of the *Southern Ruralist* were known as "What Farmers are Doing" issues. They em-

Emblem of the Southern Ruralist Company.

phasized the activities of farmers and carried the articles by them
which contests had generated. The subjects discussed in these issues
were also keyed to the seasonal work of the paper's readers.

In the course of the 1920s, Cobb made a number of alterations
and innovations in the *Southern Ruralist* to increase its appeal and
usefulness to readers. By the end of the decade, in terms of format,
quality of paper and printing, and new features, the *Southern Ruralist* was in reality a modern farm paper in every sense of the word.
The addition of the department of marketing reflected Cobb's view
that "successful marketing is half the problem of modern farming—
perhaps more than half." [37] Similarly, the sharp increase in the size
and importance of the home department demonstrated the effort of

Cobb and his co-workers to produce a paper that would more nearly meet the needs of all members of the farm family. That objective was also apparent in the decision in 1922 to offer to readers good literature in the form of continued stories. The first novel to be presented in the *Southern Ruralist* was Mary Roberts Rinehart's *The Circular Staircase*. It ran in serial form for twenty issues. Others followed, and in 1925 subscribers might read *The Barbarian* by Wadsworth Camp.[38]

The same desire to improve the cultural life of farmers and to enhance the attractiveness of the paper, combined with technical advances in the printing of the magazine, produced a number of other noteworthy innovations. In 1927 Cobb began putting a rotogravure cover on the paper. Pictures that appeared on these covers were selected with care, the objective being not only to attract the eye but also to convey a message. Along with the utilization of better stock, the technical improvement that made rotogravure covers possible also allowed Cobb to introduce color into the *Southern Ruralist*. Throughout Cobb's editorship, he insisted upon the use of numerous illustrations and drawings to dramatize points made in the text; color could hardly fail to increase the desired effect. Cartoons made their appearance in the *Southern Ruralist* in 1928. After their introduction, Cobb used them regularly on the editorial page, usually to emphasize a point in farm policy upon which he had commented recently.[39]

The technological improvements that made possible the rotogravure covers also permitted Cobb to present to his readers reproductions of famous paintings. The purpose, of course, was to enrich the life of the farmer by awakening in him an appreciation for art. In the fall of 1928, the *Southern Ruralist* offered its first two reproductions, Jean Francois Millet's "The Gleaners" and Agnew Reid's "The Coming of the White Man." Reproductions that appeared later included Raphael's "Madonna of the Chair" and Leonardo da Vinci's famous "Mona Lisa." Reportedly, some of these reproductions, carefully clipped from the *Southern Ruralist* and framed, could be found hanging on parlor walls throughout the South.[40]

Some of the technical improvements in the *Southern Ruralist* were the result of better quarters being obtained for the printing plant. In 1926, after many years of renting, the Southern Ruralist Company moved to a modern, larger building on Glenn Street in Atlanta, one designed and built to meet its special needs. The new granite structure not only housed the printing equipment but also provided more desirable offices for the staff.[41]

Subscribers, of course, were the lifeblood of the *Southern Ruralist*, as they are of any popular publication. The extent of the circulation determined the influence of the paper; moreover, it determined the attractiveness of the magazine as an advertising medium and largely influenced advertising rates. Accordingly, success in farm journalism depended upon the ability of management to keep subscription rates low, build up circulation, and convince advertisers that through the pages of the paper they could reach the widest possible market for their products.[42]

In developing circulation, southern farm papers proceeded upon a number of premises. Presumably, low income families were less likely to be subscribers than were those with higher incomes; fewer tenants than owners took farm papers, and relatively few Negroes were subscribers. In the main, therefore, farm periodicals in the South aimed at white, land-owning, middle-class farmers, with somewhat less attention being devoted to other groups.[43]

The management of the *Southern Ruralist* was fully aware of these general ideas and conducted its circulation campaigns in light of them. In a general way, the paper's territory was the entire Southeast, northward to Virginia and Kentucky and westward to Missouri and Texas. It had but a small following in Oklahoma. Throughout the decade, it had subscription agents roaming the territory, but men were stationed permanently in those areas, such as North Alabama, where there were concentrations of industrious, intelligent, and reasonably prosperous white farmers who owned and operated their properties and who presumably possessed sufficient buying power to make them attractive to advertisers. On the other hand, the *Southern Ruralist* did not ignore the planter groups, and it made a major effort to blanket the Mississippi Valley and Delta from the Ohio River to the Gulf of Mexico.

Like other farm magazines of the time, the *Southern Ruralist* offered premiums of various types in its efforts to attract new readers and retain old ones. At times the company offered pieces of Rogers silverware,[44] wall maps of the Southeast, rose bushes, fruit trees and other nursery stock, and club arrangements with other magazines. In 1922, for example, *Southern Ruralist* subscribers could also obtain the *Weekly Alabama Times*, *Today's Housewife*, weekly *Commercial Appeal*, and other papers.[45] Finally, the *Southern Ruralist* expanded its circulation by absorbing in 1929 *Modern Farming*, a semi-monthly published in New Orleans that claimed 63,000 subscribers.[46]

Throughout the decade, Cobb held subscription rates to fifty cents a year, a figure that paid no more than the cost of circulation. Profits in the enterprise came primarily from the sale of advertising. Sales of space were handled by an advertising manager through advertising agencies located in New York, Chicago, and other cities. Circulation claims of the paper were verified by the Audit Bureau of Circulations (ABC), an agency established for that purpose in 1914. ABC reports did more than merely count subscribers, however; they also indicated how circulation was obtained and provided data concerning the quality of circulation. The *Southern Ruralist* maintained a small classified advertising section, but it was essentially a "swap-sheet" and did little to generate earnings for the firm.[47]

In company with many farm papers of the period, the *Southern Ruralist* provided its readers with a guarantee against fraudulent advertising. The magazine pledged to "make good any loss sustained by our readers" as a result of "actual fraud." The *Southern Ruralist*'s guarantee appeared to be somewhat less binding than that of the *Prairie Farmer*, for example; and some advertisements, such as those of land companies, were not covered. In general, Cobb believed and assumed that major advertisers were reliable, and if they were not they could be hauled into court for using the mails to defraud. Occasionally, Cobb refused to take advertising because he questioned the reliability of the firm offering it. This policy reportedly cost the *Southern Ruralist* fifty thousand dollars in 1920 alone.[48]

Some types of advertising were rejected out of hand, while in a few instances Cobb offered reduced rates. In only one political contest—that of 1928—did the *Southern Ruralist* carry campaign advertising, and in that instance Cobb felt it necessary to point out to his readers that the Smith Independent Agricultural Leagues paid for the advertisement at the regular commercial rates, that the *Southern Ruralist* was nonpartisan, and that he hoped that "our readers will vote their convictions." [49] On the other hand, for years the *Southern Ruralist* carried at half rates advertisements of pure-bred livestock breeders on the grounds that such a policy contributed to the general improvement of southern agriculture. [50]

Among the advertisers in the *Southern Ruralist*, automobile makers and their suppliers, farm machinery and home equipment manufacturers, and fertilizer and seed concerns were the most important. Dodge Brothers was a steady customer, and in 1928 Chevrolet used the pages of the *Southern Ruralist* to call the attention of prospective buyers to the "thrilling performance" of its current models. Roadsters and touring cars were offered at $495. The Nash automobile was also shown extensively in the *Southern Ruralist*. Among farm machinery manufacturers, International Harvester was probably the leader, pushing its standard tread 10–20 and 15–30 tractors and then shifting emphasis to its row crop Farmalls. Fertilizer companies often used full-page advertisements in promoting the sale of their wares. Montgomery Ward, R. J. Reynolds and Company, the Louisville and Nashville Railroad, H. G. Hastings, "The South's Seedsman," Purina Mills, and a multitude of less well-known firms could be found in a typical issue of the paper. Advertising of household appliances increased sharply during the later years of the decade, reflecting the rising influence of Miss Dowdle in the paper.

Under Cobb's management, the all important circulation of the *Southern Ruralist* seemed to grow steadily. Standing at 300,000 in 1918, it fell off slightly in 1919 and declined to 267,000 in 1920, reflecting the postwar break in farm prices. But a new high of 304,000 was reached in 1921, and the increase continued until 1924 when circulation was 431,000. There was a decline during the next couple of years, but in 1927 the total was 434,000, and thereafter it climbed to 513,000 in 1930.

Other figures, however, were less favorable. In 1920 the *Southern Ruralist* was the most widely read of the five regional farm papers

C. A. Cobb as editor of the *Southern Ruralist*, c. 1928.

in the Southeast, but in 1921 it lost that position to the *Southern Agriculturist*. The *Southern Ruralist* regained its premier place in 1923 and 1924, but the *Southern Agriculturist* led during the remainder of the decade, except in 1926 when the *Progressive Farmer* forged ahead. Between 1920 and 1930, circulation of the *Southern Ruralist* increased 92 percent, while the *Southern Agriculturist* and the *Progressive Farmer* gained 293 and 191 percent respectively, though from a lower base. During those same years, the *Southern Planter* showed a 187 percent jump in circulation; the *Southern Cultivator* only 4 percent. Those papers, however, were relatively weak; so the contest in the Southeast was between the *Southern Ruralist*, *Southern Agriculturist*, and *Progressive Farmer*. That struggle was a vigorous one, and the margin between the three magazines was at times paper thin, but beginning in 1925 the *Southern Ruralist* was in third place. The table shows the course of the circulation struggle during the decade.[51]

| Year | Southern Ruralist | Southern Agriculturist | Progressive Farmer | Southern Planter | Southern Cultivator |
|------|-------------------|------------------------|--------------------|------------------|---------------------|
| 1919 | 297,000 | 144,000 | 182,000 | 90,000 | 45,000 |
| 1920 | 267,000 | 160,000 | 187,000 | 70,000 | 45,000 |
| 1921 | 304,000 | 330,000 | 191,000 | 82,000 | 45,000 |
| 1922 | 353,000 | 374,000 | 215,000 | 112,000 | 40,000 |
| 1923 | 382,000 | 374,000 | 293,000 | 119,000 | NA |
| 1924 | 431,000 | 393,000 | 361,000 | 135,000 | NA |
| 1925 | 339,000 | 398,000 | 397,000 | 159,000 | 42,000 |
| 1926 | 383,000 | 438,000 | 452,000 | 171,000 | 42,000 |
| 1927 | 434,000 | 501,000 | 472,000 | 176,000 | 58,000 |
| 1928 | 432,000 | 505,000 | 475,000 | 199,000 | 58,000 |
| 1929 | 461,000 | 530,000 | 491,000 | 202,000 | 53,000 |
| 1930 | 513,000 | 629,000 | 555,000 | 201,000 | 47,000 |

Moreover, during the 1920s the size of the issues of the *Southern Ruralist* and the percentage of total space sold for advertising declined. In 1919 issues varied in size from twenty-four to sixty-four pages, and they averaged forty-four. Figures for selected later years were:

| Year | Issue Size, Range | Issue Size, Average |
|------|-------------------|---------------------|
| 1922 | 20–36 | 27 |
| 1926 | 20–44 | 28 |
| 1930 | 20–34 | 25 |

Percentages of total space devoted to advertising, using the April 1 issues, were as follows: [52]

| Year | Space, Percent |
|------|----------------|
| 1919 | 57 |
| 1920 | 65 |
| 1921 | 67 |
| 1922 | 59 |
| 1923 | 56 |
| 1924 | 49 |
| 1925 | 49 |
| 1926 | 46 |
| 1927 | 52 |
| 1928 | 54 |
| 1929 | 38 |
| 1930 | 48 |

As the Great Depression settled over the South, with its disastrous effects upon southern farmers, the management of the *Southern Ruralist* studied the results of the past decade's operations and thought of the future. It was apparent that the rise of the great national farm magazines, including the *Country Gentleman, Country Home* (formerly *Farm and Fireside*), and *Farm Journal*, hurt such regional papers as the *Southern Ruralist*. Farmers were becoming more sophisticated in their tastes, and the glazed or coated stock, four-color covers, and smart fiction that appeared in the national periodicals appealed to them.[53] Still, Cobb and his colleagues in the competing papers in the Southeast believed that there was a place for such papers as they produced; the trouble was that the South could not support as many as existed. The states served by the *Southern Ruralist* ranked low among the forty-eight states and the District of Columbia in farm magazines circulation per thousand of farm population. In fact, Louisiana, Mississippi, South Carolina, Alabama, Georgia, and Kentucky were at the bottom of the scale; and Tennessee, Arkansas, North Carolina, Virginia, Florida, and Texas did not rank much higher.[54]

These facts seemed to call for some sort of a change in the competitive situation among southeastern farm papers. Presumably, not all of them could survive in the long run; moreover, a stronger periodical might well be able to provide better service to its readers. The management of the *Southern Ruralist* concluded that a merger was in order. When a favorable offer came from Clarence Poe's *Progressive Farmer*, arrangements were worked out and the deal consummated, effective September 1, 1930. The *Southern Ruralist* became the Atlanta edition of the *Progressive Farmer*, although for a number of years the new paper carried the titles of both of the old ones. Because of his recognized ability and because he had acquired substantial interests in the *Southern Ruralist*, Cobb became vice-president and managing editor of the Progressive Farmer-Southern Ruralist Company and editor of its Atlanta edition. Miss Dowdle also moved to the new firm to serve as the editor of its home department. L. D. Hicks, formerly general manager of the old Southern Ruralist Company, was made production manager of the firm. The merger, which was hailed by observers as the largest "ever consummated in the Southern States in point of circulation and one of the largest yet made in America," produced a new giant in farm journalism, with a total circulation of more than one million.[55]

The *Southern Ruralist* was by no means the only farm paper to disappear from the South during the 1920s and the era of the Great Depression. One student has calculated that the total number declined by more than 50 percent between 1920 and 1932. Even the *Southern Agriculturist*, the largest of the five regional papers in the Southeast in 1930, ceased publication in time. Quite obviously, the decision that Cobb and his colleagues reached in the late spring of 1930 was the correct one.[56]

Writing in the first issue of the combined paper, Cobb assured his readers that "nothing has been left undone to conserve, combine, and continue the full strength of both old papers in this, the new one. . . . With the combined editorial strength of the two and the consequent abler and better balanced editorial staff, the new publication has an unequaled ability to develop and carry out an editorial policy and program of outstanding practical value." At the same time, Cobb recognized that in a very real sense his opportunity for service had increased, and he pledged to "meet this new responsibility as intelligently, as frankly, and as courageously as we know how." [57] On the basis of his earlier career, there was little doubt that Cobb would honor that pledge.

## NOTES TO CHAPTER V

1. *Mississippi Club Boy*, Vol. 2 (February, 1919), 2; Extension Workers in the Service Prior to and Including 1919, Mississippi Extension Service Records; A. W. Garner to F. J. Merriam, n.d., A. W. Garner Papers (Mississippi State University Library).

2. R. S. Wilson, Biennial Report of Extension Work in Agriculture and Home Economics, June 8, 1921, Mississippi Extension Service Records.

3. Cobb interviews.

4. Much of the foregoing comes from Scott, *Agricultural Extension*, 18–20. For statistics and percentages, see Allen D. Wilson, "Agricultural Periodicals in the United States" (M.A. thesis, University of Illinois, 1930), Table I; C. Beaman Smith and H. K. Atwood, "The Relation of Agricultural Extension Agencies to Farm Practices," United States Bureau of Plant Industry, *Circular* 117 (Washington, 1913), 18–19, 22. According to a report by the National Fertilizer Association, the percentage of farmers who read farm papers had increased to 80 by 1929. See E. S. Bayard. "The Farm Paper—A Vital Educational Force," *American Fertilizer*, Vol. 71 (July 6, 1929), 48.

5. Wilson, "Agricultural Periodicals in the United States," Table II. States included in this group were Alabama, Arkansas, Florida, Georgia, Kentucky, Louisiana, Mississippi, the Carolinas, and Tennessee.

6. Oscar A. Beck, Jr., "The Agricultural Press and Southern Rural Development, 1900–1940" (Ph.D. dissertation, George Peabody College, 1952), 7; Wilson; "Agricultural Periodicals in the United States," Table I.

7. Beck, "Agricultural Press and Southern Rural Development," 52–58, 63–65; *N. W. Ayer and Son's American Newspaper Annual and Directory*, 1916 (Philadelphia, 1916), 147, 919, 994; *ibid.*, 1929, pp. 194, 1110.

8. Stuart Noblin, *Leonidas LaFayette Polk; Agrarian Crusader* (Chapel Hill, 1949), 152, 291.

9. Beck, "Agricultural Press and Southern Rural Development," 44–47; Clarence Poe, *My First 80 Years* (Chapel Hill, 1963), 90.

10. Beck, "Agricultural Press and Southern Rural Development," 47; Wilson, "Agricultural Periodicals in the United States," Table I; Poe, *My First 80 Years*, 104; Eugene Butler, *Dr. Tait Butler: Veterinarian, Editor and Publisher, and Agricultural Leader*, Typed Manuscript (Mississippi State University Library), 42.

11. Beck, "Agricultural Press and Southern Rural Development," 63; *Southern Ruralist*, Vol. 26 (October 15, 1919), 542; *ibid.*, Vol. 27 (April 15, 1920), 106; Wilson, "Agricultural Periodicals in the United States," Table I; *N.W. Ayer and Son's American Newspaper Annual and Directory*, 1916, p. 147.

12. *Who's Who in America*, 1920–1921 (Chicago, 1920), 2, 719; *RUS: A Biographical Register of Rural Leadership in the United States and Canada*, 1920 (Ithaca, 1920), 433.

13. *Southern Ruralist*, Vol. 26 (October 1, 1919), 486.

14. Frederick Strauss and Louis H. Bean, "Gross Farm Income and Indicies of Farm Production and Prices in the United States, 1869–1937," United States Department of Agriculture, *Technical Bulletin* 703 (Washington, 1940), 36, 40, 65, 68–69. Since the figures given above are averages, prices actually received by farmers showed even sharper declines.

15. *Historical Statistics of the United States, 1789–1945* (Washington, 1949), Series E 104. The parity ratio is the ratio of prices received by farmers to prices paid by them, using the years 1910–1914 as the base period. Figures for Mississippi crops may be found in Thomas E. Tramel and David W. Parvin, "Prices Received and Paid by Mississippi Farmers and Index of Seasonal Variations in Farm Prices, 1910–1955," Mississippi Agricultural Experiment Station, *Bulletin* 535 (State College, 1955).

16. In the foregoing, we have relied primarily upon Chester C. Davis, "The Development of Agricultural Policy since the End of the World War," United States Department of Agriculture, *Yearbook of Agriculture*, 1940 (Washington, 1940), 298–316. See page 301 for Harding's statement. See also Theodore Saloutos, *Farmer Movements in the South, 1865–1933* (Berkeley and Los Angeles, 1960), 254–73, and Gilbert C. Fite, *George N. Peek and the Fight for Farm Parity* (Norman, 1954), Chapters 3–12.

17. For Cobb's editorial policies, see Chapter VI of the present volume.

18. C. A. Cobb, "The Contribution of the Press to Agriculture," Texas Agricultural Extension Service, *Silver Anniversary: Cooperative Demonstration Work, 1903–1928* (College Station, n.d.), 24; *Southern Ruralist*, Vol. 35 (August 1, 1928), 232.

19. These men are discussed in *Southern Ruralist*, Vol. 29 (January 15, 1923), 490; *ibid.*, Vol. 35 (February 1, 1929), 576; *Who's Who in America*, 1922–1923, p. 509; Harrison Hale, *University of Arkansas, 1871–1948* (Fayetteville, 1948), 123; *RUS*, 1930, pp. 122, 460.

20. *Southern Ruralist*, Vol. 29 (January 15, 1923), 490; *ibid.*, Vol. 35 (February 1, 1929), 576; *ibid.*, Vol. 31 (May 1, 1924), 90; Bettersworth, *People's College*, 215; *RUS*, 1930, p. 604.

21. *Southern Ruralist*, Vol. 26 (January 1, 1920), 836; *ibid.*, Vol. 29 (October 15, 1922), 345; *ibid.*, Vol. 32 (November 15, 1925), 392; *RUS*, 1930, p. 192. For a discussion of Miss Dowdle's career and her marriage to Cobb, see Chapters VII and IX.

22. *Southern Ruralist*, Vol. 35 (February 1, 1929), 576; *ibid.*, Vol. 35 (February 15, 1929), p. 611; *ibid.*, Vol. 35 (January 1, 1929), 521; *ibid.*, Vol. 36 (November 1, 1929), 18.

23. *Southern Ruralist*, Vol. 35 (February 1, 1929), 576.

24. *Southern Ruralist*, Vol. 28 (January 15, 1922), 412; *ibid.*, Vol. 32 (January 15, 1926), 496; *ibid.*, Vol. 36 (February 15, 1930), 20.

25. See, for example, *ibid.*, Vol. 28 (February 15, 1922), 474–75.

26. *Ibid.*, Vol. 28 (March 1, 1922), 512–14, 516–17.

27. *Ibid.*, Vol. 32 (May 15, 1925), 105; *ibid.*, Vol. 32 (August 1, 1925), 209; *ibid.*, Vol. 32 (September 1, 1925), 249.

28. *Ibid.*, Vol. 26 (September 15, 1919), 444.

29. *Ibid.*, Vol. 29 (October 15, 1922), 345.

30. *Ibid.*, Vol. 35 (June 1, 1928), 152; *ibid.*, Vol. 35 (December 1, 1928), 458; *ibid.*, Vol. 35 (December 15, 1928), 486.

31. *Ibid.*, Vol. 35 (July 1, 1928), 197; *ibid.*, Vol. 34 (July 1, 1927), 165; James F. Evans, PRAIRIE FARMER and WLS: *The Burridge D. Butler Years* (Urbana, 1969), p. 70.

32. Evans, PRAIRIE FARMER, 67.

33. Details may be found on the editorial page of any issue.

34. *Southern Ruralist*, Vol. 26 (February 15, 1920), 1027; *ibid.*, Vol. 27 (April 15, 1920), 108.

35. *Ibid.*, Vol. 31 (March 1, 1925), 671; *ibid.*, Vol. 32 (March 1, 1926), 627.

36. *Ibid.*, Vol. 33 (June 15, 1926), 140; *ibid.*, Vol. 34 (October 1, 1927), 286; *ibid.*, Vol. 34 (December 15, 1927), 433; Vol. 35 (October 1, 1928), 240; *ibid.*, Vol. 36 (October 1, 1929), 16.

37. Quoted in Beck, "Agricultural Press and Southern Rural Development," 128.

38. *Southern Ruralist*, Vol. 29 (October 1, 1922), 330; *ibid.*, Vol. 30 (July 15, 1923), 210; *ibid.*, Vol. 32 (October 15, 1925), 322.

39. C. A. Cobb to R. V. Scott, February 10, 1971, Cobb Papers; *Southern Ruralist*, Vol. 32 (January 1, 1926), 473–74; *ibid.*, Vol. 33 (January 1, 1927), 439; *ibid.*, Vol. 35 (January 15, 1928), 164.

40. *Southern Ruralist*, Vol. 35 (January 15, 1928), 372; *ibid.*, Vol. 35 (February 15, 1929), 636.

41. *Ibid.*, Vol. 32 (January 1, 1926), 473–74.

42. Theodore Peterson, *Magazines in the Twentieth Century* (Urbana, 1956), Chapter 4, gives insights into the economics of magazine publishing.

43. Beck, "Agricultural Press and Southern Rural Development," 8.

44. C. A. Cobb to R. V. Scott, February 10, 1971, Cobb Papers.

45. *Southern Ruralist*, Vol. 31 (August 1, 1924), 189; *ibid.*, Vol. 29 (September 15, 1922), 291.

46. Beck, "Agricultural Press and Southern Rural Development," 208; *N. W. Ayer and Son's American Newspaper Annual and Directory*, 1929, p. 431.

47. Cobb interviews; Peterson, *Magazines in the Twentieth Century*, 27; Evans, PRAIRIE FARMER, 73.

48. *Southern Ruralist*, Vol. 27 (April 1, 1920), 62; *ibid.*, Vol. 27 (February 1, 1921), 839; Cobb interviews; Evans, PRAIRIE FARMER, 75–76.

49. *Southern Ruralist*, Vol. 35 (October 15, 1928), 374; *ibid.*, Vol. 35 (November 1, 1928), 397.

50. *Ibid.*, Vol. 33 (April 1, 1926), 17.

51. Wilson, "Agricultural Periodicals in the United States," Table I.

52. Calculated from issues noted.

53. Harland Manchester, "The Farm Magazines," *Scribner's*, Vol. 104 (October, 1938), 25–26.

54. Mapheus Smith, "Circulation of Farm Magazines," *School and Society*, Vol. 46 (September 11, 1937), 351.

55. *Progressive Farmer*, Vol. 45 (May, 1930), 4; C. A. Cobb to R. V. Scott, February 10, 1971, Cobb Papers. See also the advertisement for the new paper in *Printers' Ink*, Vol. 151 (June 26, 1930), 126–27.

56. Beck, "Agricultural Press and Southern Rural Development," 63, 205–11.

57. *Progressive Farmer and Southern Ruralist* (Mississippi Valley Edition), Vol. 48 (September 1–14, 1930), 9.

# CHAPTER VI

# A Voice of Southern Agriculture: Editorial Policy, 1919–1932

AS editor-in-chief of the *Southern Ruralist*, Cobb left his imprint on every department and feature of that paper. But he exercised his greatest influence on farmers and those interested in the welfare of agriculture through his editorials. His total output was prodigious. During the ten years that Cobb was connected with the *Southern Ruralist*, he wrote practically every editorial. Each issue had an average of six, spread over two pages, so in all Cobb produced something like fifteen hundred items of editorial comment. Moreover, in the last years of the paper's existence, the first page of each issue carried an article by him. After the merger with the *Progressive Farmer*, Cobb usually prepared one editorial for each issue of the Georgia-Alabama edition, and these pieces quite often appeared in other editions of that paper as well.

Like the *Southern Ruralist* as a whole, Cobb's editorials were aimed at the small white farmer. Cobb always wrote in language that his constituency could understand, but he never underestimated the intelligence of his readers. His editorials were concise, tightly argued statements concerning the issue at hand. Wit and humor, satire, and occasional anecdotes helped to emphasize specific points.

Included among Cobb's numerous editorials were comments on almost every topic of interest to southern farmers and indeed to southerners generally. Above all, Cobb was an enthusiastic booster of his native section, and he regularly called upon his readers to have faith in the future of the region. The South, he believed, continued to suffer from the adverse effects of the Civil War and the period of adjustment and privation that followed; in fact, it had taken forty years to reach the level of well-being enjoyed in 1860.

But by the 1920s, Cobb was convinced that the South was ready to take its proper economic place in the nation. The section was evolving into a region of more balanced economy as industry came in, its long coast line promised a growing place in foreign trade, its nonagricultural resources were coming into use, and its climate was to its advantage since history proved, Cobb claimed, that the "human race thrives naturally in warmer climates." [1] *

Despite his evident interest in the industrial development of the South, Cobb was a confirmed agrarian fundamentalist; and he insisted that improvement in farming was essential if the region was to realize its full potential. Agriculture had to evolve along certain clearly defined lines. Farmers needed to adopt "business principles" and to develop a "better balanced system of farming; one that will provide a living at home for man and beast with a little to spare, and sufficient further diversification to keep up the fertility of the soil and bring the worn soils back to fertility again." [2]

Logically enough, Cobb, like his well-known contemporary, Henry A. Wallace, was a vigorous opponent of one-crop farming and a supporter of diversification. This "is no new doctrine," he admitted, "but there is always a tendency to forget and backslide, or fall from grace. Cotton farmers are about like church members after all. They are all sinners against right practice." Overemphasis on cotton or any other crop, he continually pointed out, robbed the soil of its fertility, reduced the moisture-retention properties of soils, led to overproduction, concentrated risks, and forced farmers to buy at retail prices food and other family and farm needs that they could produce themselves. [3]

The latter point was especially important. Cobb was certain that rural well-being in the South depended upon the ability of farmers to "live at home." They should concern themselves less with the production of cash crops and make every effort to grow on their own properties the food and feed consumed there. [4]

For farmers to achieve the desired diversification and this ability to "live at home," Cobb advocated livestock and poultry production. "The joyous cackle of the hen and the lowing of the family cow make a cheerful contrast to the tales of woe" from the cotton

* Notes appear at end of each chapter.

sections, he wrote in 1924.[5] Dairying should be encouraged, not only to produce the balanced agriculture that the South needed but also because no "single food has been found so valuable for children as the wholesome milk of a good cow." The South was ideally suited to the production of hogs, cattle, and sheep. "No other soils equal the soils of the South in forage producing ability; no other climate equals that of the South when it comes to producing quality or variety of forage crops; and no other section can afford better pastures; and the waters of the South are as good as can be found." Nor was it true, as northerners charged, that southern cattle tended to be diseased.

If the South were to become the livestock area that Cobb believed it should be, southern farmers would need to make certain changes in their practices. Foremost was a sharp improvement in pastures through the more extensive growing of bermuda grass, lespedeza, and a variety of clovers. Second was the increased production and use of purebred sires. It was a source of considerable concern to Cobb that as late as 1920 the South still had to import much of its better quality stock from the North.[6]

Cobb called upon southern farmers to raise poultry, not only for their own tables, but also for the market. There was money to be made in chickens, he contended, if producers obtained high quality chicks of the proper breed, provided adequate housing and yard space for them, produced home-grown feed, and marketed eggs and broilers through cooperatives. The raising of turkeys also received Cobb's approval; in fact, he would later produce some himself.[7]

Besides converting cotton land to pastures and poultry runs, Cobb believed that southern farmers could grow satisfactorily a number of other field crops. Corn, of course, was a necessity as feed for livestock, poultry, and work animals, but in addition Cobb urged farmers to grow sweet and Irish potatoes, peanuts, soybeans, cowpeas, and especially garden truck for home consumption. On the other hand, he urged his readers to resist fads and warned against the commercial production of such commodities as tomatoes and lettuce, except in those limited areas where substantial markets existed.[8]

Despite all appeals by himself and a variety of educational agen-

County agent in Harford County, Maryland, inspecting the harvesting of a hay crop. Under Cobb's leadership, the *Southern Ruralist* was an enthusiastic supporter of the agricultural extension service and its work.

cies for diversification of southern agriculture, Cobb knew full well that cotton was and would remain the major cash crop across much of the country served by the *Southern Ruralist*; for this reason Cobb devoted no little attention in his editorials to the task of improving the production of that staple. Repeatedly, Cobb urged growers to strive for higher yields and better quality through the use of high grade seed and proper fertilization, modern cultural methods, and more careful handling "from the field to the bale." [9]

By the 1920s the boll weevil had spread throughout the Cotton Belt; this pest represented the most serious challenge to growers.

The coming of the pest to an area, said Cobb, tended to produce two types of farmers. "The first is characterized by those who feel that in spite of the boll weevil they can get one more full crop; the second, by those who are certain that they have grown their last crop and are mad at cotton." He rejected both views. The problem had to be faced, but it was no cause for despair. The type of balanced agriculture for which the *Southern Ruralist* called would help growers to rely less on the endangered staple, thereby building up the fertility of cotton land and helping to reduce the inroads of the weevils. In addition, Cobb advocated heavy applications of fertilizers and the use of early-maturing varieties of cotton, thorough cultivation of the growing crop, and, for those who knew how to use it, the application of calcium arsenate. In actuality, Cobb was urging those methods that Seaman A. Knapp, the father of southern agricultural extension, had suggested as early as 1903.[10]

The almost universal need for an improvement in farm practices generally played a large part in Cobb's editorial commentary. The fact that southern yields were far below what they should have been distressed Cobb, and he placed the blame squarely upon "sorry farming." Too many farmers attempted to till excessively large acreages; the result was improperly prepared seedbeds and poor cultivation. Others failed to use the proper types or quantities of fertilizer. Another common problem was insufficient horsepower, especially among small farmers who tried to plow their ground with only one or two mules. Some new tools earned Cobb's enthusiastic approval. The section harrow, he claimed, was indispensable in the proper preparation of seedbeds; and he encouraged farmers to purchase tractors, arguing that there was no validity to the widely accepted idea that Negroes could not be trained to operate them. Cobb also discussed favorably the uses of trucks on the farm.[11]

In Cobb's hopes for the future of the South, education ranked high; in fact, it would not be far wrong to say that he saw education as the ultimate salvation of the region. Apparently all southern farm papers shared this conviction. Cobb constantly urged an upgrading in the quality of teaching, an increase in teachers' salaries, and more regular attendance by the children of the South. "When the profession of teaching is suffered to decline," he wrote, "the people decline with it." In 1926 he discovered that in Georgia fifteen thousand children between the ages of ten and eighteen could neither read nor write, a situation that appalled him. Repeatedly, he denounced the southern habit of taking children out of school to pick cotton and perform other farm tasks. "Education is the American child's inalienable right, and the education of the child is the first duty of the parent and the citizen," he proclaimed.[12] Accordingly, he favored compulsory attendance and school consolidation and, forty years before it became a reality, he called for federal aid to public schools.[13]

Education, he believed, should give the student a thorough grounding in morality. There should be a close working relationship between the school and the church. Americans should never be allowed to forget that the country owed its "progress to Christianity"; the schools should implant that idea in every citizen. Higher education also should play a significant role in character building. "A college diploma is quite incomplete if it does not bear witness to the character of the graduate," he wrote.[14]

Cobb rejected the idea that city children were more intelligent than those who came from the farm. In 1925 he reported the findings of the United States Bureau of Education showing that farm children "make better progress than other children through high school." The report, he observed, served "to blow up the much advertised idea that brillance . . . has all migrated to town, leaving the runts, ne'er do wells, and morons on the farm."[15]

Vocational education especially interested Cobb. Given his earlier career, of course, he could hardly have failed to appreciate the expansion of vocational teaching that came under the terms of the Smith-Hughes Act. Nor could he have avoided the sense of pride that he showed in 1923 when his old school at Buena Vista qualified for federal and state vocational money.[16]

Cobb's ideas on higher education were those that might be expected from one who had worked his way through a land-grant institution and who had served for several years at one of them. According to Cobb, agriculture's "greatest need from the beginning has been trained leadership. Our colleges of agriculture have given us this leadership" and these "leaders have been able to inspire their

County agent in Union County, North Carolina, instructing farm boys and their father in the growing of lespedeza. As editor of the *Southern Ruralist*, Cobb continued his interest in the training of rural youth.

followers, the farmers . . . with a new sense of pride, responsibility, and opportunity . . . that laid the foundation for . . . a turning in the tide of rural life." The fact that many agricultural college graduates did not go back to the farm bothered him as it has a multitude of land-grant college administrators before and since. But Cobb believed that the country benefited when farm boys and girls educated in agricultural colleges occupied positions of importance in other lines of activity. No doubt remembering his own experience, Cobb praised the self-help program at Mississippi Agricultural and Mechanical College, explaining that such training really educated. The tendency of politicians in some states to meddle in college administration distressed him, and he called for the establishment of independent boards of trustees.[17]

While generally praising the land-grant institutions, Cobb occasionally found grounds for complaint or made suggestions for the improvement of their programs. The *Southern Ruralist*, especially after Miss Dowdle joined the staff, was a vigorous advocate of college education for farm girls. In fact, proper training was just as important for the farm wife as it was the farmer, Miss Dowdle wrote, not only because women were moving out into the world but also because of their dominant influence in the home. Cobb believed very strongly that college education should be "practical," and he recognized the service role of the university in areas other than agriculture. An economics professor at the University of Arkansas who conducted a study of freight rates in that state earned Cobb's praise. Such material, introduced into the classroom, was of far greater value than the sterile laws of classical economics, he noted. Finally, Cobb had strong ideas as to what constituted a desirable college professor. He was opposed to "teachers who preach snobbery; who are continually seeking the spotlight; who would rather be sensational than sound; who know little and practice less of that type of citizenship that makes for sound community, state, and nation building; who fancy themselves liberal, when in fact they are just plain downright loose." [18]

Agricultural extension work, "the world's greatest schoolroom," remained a prime concern. The practical farmer, Cobb believed, was the farmer who put science to work on his property, and the extension services constituted the best means to learn the uses of science. "What is a County Agent worth?" Cobb asked in 1920. Using Pontotoc County, Mississippi, as an example, Cobb found that the agent there had saved farmers more than $34,000 in one year through cooperative marketing arrangements alone, while at the same time performing all of the other functions of a county agent. Quite obviously, it paid a county to maintain an agent, and Cobb strongly urged those counties that had not yet done so to hire an agent promptly. Home demonstration agents were equally useful, he believed. Nor was Cobb willing to ignore the Negroes' need for extension work. Throughout the decade, he called for an increase in federal and state support of extension programs. Calvin Coolidge was never one of Cobb's favorites, but the President received Cobb's praise when he signed the Capper-Ketchum Act of 1928, a measure that provided more federal funds for this purpose.[19]

Extension work with rural youth was understandably one of

Cobb's favorite subjects. "As an educational institution, 4-H Club Work stands out as one of the most practical and one of the most far-reaching in its importance yet to be devised," he wrote. The work was more than vocational in character, he believed. "Through club work may be developed that moral responsibility so desired by the minister; that mental balance so sought by the teacher; and a business ability, developed by actual contact with men and things, that can be secured through no other medium." [20]

Agricultural experiment stations, Cobb knew, were the cornerstones upon which agricultural science and better farming rested. Accordingly, he praised those institutions, and never failed to urge the enactment of such measures as the Purnell Act which provided additional funds for them. [21]

Besides advocating a more balanced agriculture, better farming practices, and improved education, Cobb spoke out vigorously on a variety of other topics of concern to farmers. Apparently, the *Southern Ruralist* was less concerned with governmental issues than was the *Progressive Farmer*, for example; and Cobb was most interested in those governmental policies that had a direct impact upon the needs of farmers. Outstanding among such matters were transportation, marketing, rural credits, and the further development of Muscle Shoals. [22]

Adequate and cheap transportation, Cobb knew, was essential to the South. In the past, the railroad rate structure had discriminated against the South, burdening the region with objectionable transportation costs and forcing goods to flow to East Coast ports. Cobb praised changes that came in the 1920s, believing that they pointed to cheaper transportation in the future and to the growth of those cities situated on the Gulf of Mexico. Still, he was skeptical of the workings of the Interstate Commerce Commission and, like many other farm editors, he firmly believed that the best answer to the South's transportation problems lay in the development of a system of inland waterways. The Mississippi River and its tributaries, Cobb wrote, could become a "great highway to the seas." The *Southern Ruralist* regularly supported bills in Congress to appropriate funds for internal improvements. Occasionally, Cobb voiced his own ideas concerning plans under consideration as, for example, when he urged that multipurpose high dams be built on the Tennessee River instead of the low structures proposed by the Corps of Engineers.[23]

Cobb recognized hard-surfaced roads as a major concern of farmers, especially as automobiles on the farm increased in numbers. More than half of the automobiles in the country in 1921 belonged to rural citizens, he pointed out, and they deserved adequate roads. Like the editor of the *Prairie Farmer*, Cobb believed that the greatest need was farm-to-market roads; and he objected to the expenditure of large sums on "transcontinental highways" until farmers were provided with roads that would allow them to travel to local marketing centers with a minimum of inconvenience. The current generation, however, should be willing to bear the cost of at least the 40 percent of total construction outlays for surfacing a roadbed, he thought, since any surface put down would have to be replaced by the next generation. Some common features of existing roads distressed Cobb. For example, he objected to the practice of running major highways through the public squares of country towns and he complained about gravel roads, with their flying rocks, and about poor engineering that resulted in roads seemingly following "calf trails" instead of the compass.[24]

If transportation was important to farmers, marketing was even more so. Like many farm journalists throughout the nation, Cobb believed the key to that issue was cooperation. As head of boys' club work in Mississippi, he had been familiar with the pioneer efforts in Yazoo County in the cooperative marketing of the animals of pig club members, and he never lost the interest aroused at that time. He supported the work of the United States Bureau of Markets, favored the expansion of farmers' mutual insurance companies, and participated in and reported favorably numerous meetings that led to the flowering of cotton cooperatives in the 1920s. Such examples as the Producers' Live Stock Association of East St. Louis, Illinois, and the Staple Cotton Cooperative Association of Greenwood, Mississippi, earned his praise. Earlier, Cobb had supported enthusiastically the Capper-Volstead Act.[25]

It was his interest in cooperative marketing that converted Cobb into an early and enthusiastic supporter of the American Farm Bureau Federation. At the outset, in fact, he saw that emerging organization as a vehicle that might more effectively unite farmers for cooperative economic activity. As the decade progressed, however, Cobb noted with approval the Farm Bureau's support of many of the issues for which the *Southern Ruralist* campaigned, such as the acceptance of Henry Ford's offer concerning Muscle Shoals, development of inland waterways, lower freight rates, development of foreign markets, and enlargement of the agricultural extension service. By the later years of the 1920s, accordingly, Cobb was convinced that the Farm Bureau could become a truly national farm organization, performing a variety of functions for farmers in all parts of the country. The greatest danger to such a development, he thought, was a lack of "common sense and unselfishness" that might cause the organization, with its greater strength in the Middle West, to ignore the needs of southern farmers.[26]

Perhaps more than most men of his time and place, Cobb was fully aware of the significance of foreign markets in the welfare of the South. Moreover, that awareness caused Cobb to interest himself in the American merchant marine. The experience of World War I, he thought, showed clearly that the United States needed a large and modern merchant fleet. As a result, Cobb objected to the disposal of wartime vessels, and he believed the government should embark upon a program to encourage more ship construction. In 1928, when President Coolidge and Secretary of the Navy Curtis C. Wilbur talked of the need for a naval building program, Cobb claimed that the country would be better served by acquiring ships for useful purposes. Cobb was also aware of the problems that American shipowners faced in competition with foreign flag vessels. He proposed that the government subsidize the American merchant fleet, and he was prepared to go to government operation if there were no other way to keep the American flag on the high seas.[27]

Agricultural credit was another major problem facing southern farmers. In that area, Cobb praised the Federal Reserve System and militantly defended it against its critics. Allowed to function to its full potential, Cobb said that the program would "free the farmers of the nation from the ubiquitous money lending systems of the past, offer them the cheapest money in history . . . and round out life in their homes." In addition, it would help to reduce tenancy, one of the prime evils in southern agriculture.[28] Cobb also approved of the commodity loan program of the War Finance Corporation, and he watched with approval the proceedings in Congress that culminated with the enactment of the Intermediate Credit Act of 1923.[29]

The question of taxation occupied a prominent place on the editorial pages of the *Southern Ruralist*. Like most of his readers, Cobb was totally convinced that taxes were too high and that the existing system placed an unfair burden on the farmers. Land taxes, he claimed repeatedly, were higher than taxes on other forms of property and permitted some kinds of wealth to escape entirely.[30] The income tax, he said, "is the fairest of all." Cobb praised Governor Henry L. Whitfield of Mississippi when he forced an income tax through the legislature, and Cobb bitterly denounced Governor Theodore G. Bilbo when he proposed to replace it with a sales levy, "the most vicious form of taxation." [31]

Prior to Cobb's assumption of the editorship of the *Southern Ruralist*, the paper had largely ignored the tariff, considering it a political question beyond the proper concern of a farm paper. But unlike some northern farm editors, Cobb understood clearly that the tariff was a burden on those farmers who produced goods for export and he stated his opposition vigorously. "The farmers to a man should fight the high tariff because in the end he has all to lose and nothing to gain," he wrote. In the Fordney-McCumber Tariff, Cobb believed "the farmer has been made the goat and the next thing in order is the repeal of the legislation. . . ." A few months later, Cobb was telling his readers that the tariff reduced the export of cotton by as much as 20 percent. The Tennessean never changed his mind on the effect of the tariff, but by the late 1920s he had become convinced that, since there was no hope of reducing significantly its level, the government should institute a program that would do for the farmer what the tariff did for business.[32]

Few topics received as much attention in the *Southern Ruralist* as did Muscle Shoals.[33] The need for and the high cost of commercial fertilizer was one of the problems of southern agriculture; Cobb was one of the more powerful voices in the South that saw in Muscle Shoals a partial answer to that historic problem.

In 1916 Congress authorized the construction of Wilson Dam and related facilities on the Tennessee River near Sheffield-Tuscumbia, Alabama, to produce nitrogen for munitions and agriculture. By the end of 1918, some $107 million had been expended,

An International Harvester Company Farmall tractor at work in growing cotton in the Mississippi Delta. While mechanical power made little imprint on southern agriculture in the 1920's, Cobb encouraged readers of the *Southern Ruralist* to trade in their mules for tractors.

Wilson Dam still was not completed, and the conclusion of World War I had eliminated the government's first concern, a source of nitrogen for military use. A question thus arose as to the future use or disposition of the facilities.

Southern agricultural leaders had a ready answer to that question; the dam and other installations should be completed and used in the production of cheap fertilizer. Cobb embraced that idea and throughout the decade he supported proposals that promised to accomplish that goal and militantly fought those individuals and groups who sought to abandon the facilities at Muscle Shoals or to convert them to other uses.

Early in 1921 Cobb was urging his readers to write their congressmen and senators, asking them to support a move to appropriate the funds needed to complete construction of Wilson Dam and other installations there. But later that year, the Tennessean gave his approval to one of the most hotly debated proposals of the decade. Henry Ford, the automobile manufacturer, offered five million dollars for the entire set of federal properties at Muscle Shoals. Although Ford was vague concerning his plans, southern farm leaders understood that, among other uses, the automobile magnate would produce fertilizers. Cobb reported that he had no particular affection for Ford, but he wrote that farmers "realize, whether anybody else does or not, that the Ford offer is the only offer yet presented to Congress that promises any relief to agriculture or any assurance to the public that this great natural resource will be developed in the interest of the people." [34]

While Cobb supported enthusiastically Henry Ford's proposition, the Tennessean was harshly critical of a number of other proposals submitted to Congress. He was especially concerned that the properties would be turned over to private power interests. The Alabama Power Company, for instance, was interested in Muscle Shoals, but Cobb maintained that to transfer the facilities to that concern would betray the farmer. Not only would he get no fertilizer, but in the hands of the power company the electricity generated at Muscle Shoals would never reach rural customers. [35]

The Ford offer died in Congress; but in 1927, after an interview with President Coolidge, Cobb was hopeful that a desirable solution was in sight. The American Cyanimid Company had made a bid for the property which included the manufacture of nitrates at far below prevailing market prices in the South, and Cobb embraced that proposal. He supported it editorially for several months, only to see it also die in Congress. Instrumental in shaping congressional views on the matter was Senator George W. Norris of Nebraska, an advocate of governmental operation and production of cheap electric power. Cobb assailed Norris and his ideas, but the Tennessean would have to wait for the creation of the Tennessee Valley Authority before the issue of Muscle Shoals was finally put to rest.[36]

A multitude of other topics directly or indirectly of interest to farmers received treatment on the editorial pages of the *Southern Ruralist*. Cobb shared the view of the National Grange that the government should spend no more money on irrigation projects in the West as long as the nation continued to be plagued by overproduction. Reforestation and other types of conservation, however, received his support, and a Louisiana law that reduced taxes on developing timber lands earned his praise. In another area of rural rehabilitation, he applauded such measures as the Wisconsin Land Mortgage Association and the California Land Settlement Act that sought to facilitate the breaking up of large land units and their settlement by small farmers. In fact, Cobb approved of any arrangement that would convert tenants into owners.[37]

The wave of bank failures that swept the wheat states and parts of the South in the 1920s attracted Cobb's attention and caused him to express the view that such disasters were mainly the results of bad economics and crooked management. Banks in North Dakota, for example, were so numerous and small that they were blown over by the first economic wind. On the other hand, Cobb could point to instances of bad management in Georgia, and he thought that a deposit guaranty law, similar to the one in Mississippi, would be desirable in every state.[38]

During the debates in Congress and the nation over immigration restriction, Cobb expressed the view that quotas for the north European countries should be increased in order to "encourage the more desirable groups to come here." Conversely, he opposed any efforts to open wide the doors to other nationalities, including Mexicans, on the grounds that an increase in agricultural laborers would simply compound the problems in the countryside.[39] Waste in government at all levels bothered him and he believed one way to economize in a state such as Georgia was to reduce the number of counties, thereby eliminating a number of petty officeholders. In 1924 he urged voters to write their representatives in support of the tax reduction policies of Secretary of the Treasury Andrew J. Mellon, and two years later he suggested that farmers support Senator Kenneth McKellar's plan to reduce postal rates. In 1920 Cobb favored the return of the nation's railroads to private management, saying that officers of privately owned carriers would do all in their power to provide good service in order to avoid nationalization.[40]

Labor-management disputes did not concern Cobb as much as they did Henry A. Wallace. The Tennessean could see no reason "why the farmer should be the partisan of either the laborer or the capitalist. Neither is entitled to special privileges," he wrote. "Fate has not decreed that any particular group ride while all the balance of us walk." [41]

Nor did the *Southern Ruralist* have much to say about the Negro. Cobb, of course, was a southerner, and he seemed to take the position that his readers knew and understood the Negro and his place in southern life and that there was no need to dwell on the subject. The so-called "Negro exodus" did, however, bring forth an occasional comment. Cobb rejected the idea that the Negro was going north in search of social equality and freedom from lynching. Instead, the "boll weevil in the southern cotton field, coupled with a shortage of labor in the industrial districts, is more responsible for the movement of our negroes toward the North." In the long run, Cobb was convinced that the exodus was certain to have a beneficial effect upon the South. Citing Georgia as a case in point, Cobb noted in 1931 that in thirty years the percentage of black population had fallen from forty-seven to thirty-seven, a development that Cobb equated with progress.[42]

Nevertheless, Cobb was prepared to give advice to those Negroes who wanted to join the exodus. In 1927, he recounted the story of a Negro family from Mississippi's Sunflower County that went to the "promised land beyond the Mason and Dixon Line." The family, said Cobb, arrived in Hammond, Indiana, only to find that "the great lords of industry who had made such sweeping plans for the transit of migrating Negroes had made no plans for their housing and care upon arriving." The family, in fact, had to set up housekeeping in a box car spotted on an unused siding. The conclusion that Cobb drew was that "the Negro is best off among those who know him and understand him." At least, Cobb thought, Negroes should study the matter carefully before they decamped for northern parts.[43]

If Cobb devoted little attention to the Negro he devoted even less to the plantation. The *Southern Ruralist* was essentially a periodical for the small white farmer of the Southeast, so Cobb did not fill his paper with accounts of showplace estates. When he did mention large landed properties, it was usually to describe good farming methods used on them or to criticize them for failure to do so. For example, Cobb reported enthusiastically the operations of the giant Delta and Pine Land Company of Scott, Mississippi, but he was critical of Thomas D. Campbell, who raised wheat and flax on 95,000 acres in northern Montana. Campbell, said Cobb, was stripping the land of its fertility by raising grain year after year, and his farming business could be more accurately described as a mining operation.[44]

From time to time Cobb felt moved to comment on a variety of public issues having little or no relationship to agriculture. The rising crime rate bothered him, not only because of the growing danger to peaceful citizens but also because of the cost to the public of imprisoning the criminals. Crime, he believed, was primarily the result of little education and no religious training.[45] Hitchhikers received rough treatment at his hands, especially after a couple murdered a Georgia school official in 1925. "Better let'm walk," he urged his readers. Drunken drivers and "speed fiends" also distressed him, and he believed that liability insurance should be compulsory. The rise of bus transportation in the decade brought forth demands that the operation of the vehicles be closely regulated by the state and that the buses not be allowed to destroy the railroads or to "hog the road."[46] Cobb enjoyed the movies, one of the crazes of the 1920s, but he objected to the type of "knockdown, drag-out and shoot-em'-up" pictures that too often were the standard fare in small town theaters. Farmers deserved the best, he thought, and they should demand to see "decent pictures."[47]

In his editorials, Cobb devoted a great deal of space to the farm

home and farm life. In fact, few topics were considered as important, especially after Miss Dowdle joined the staff of the paper.
Farmers, Cobb said, should treat their wives equitably. The women
should be partners in the farm enterprise, with control over the egg
money, for example. Nor should farm wives be denied modern
conveniences. New farm equipment was important to the farmer;
a new icebox was equally important to the wife and to the farm as
a whole. Cobb, in fact, was an enthusiastic advocate of new household appliances of all kinds. Be not the "last to lay the old aside,"
he urged his readers. The radio, he pointed out, would add much
to the enjoyment of life in the farm home, but he cautioned against
expecting too much too soon from the use of electricity, citing its
cost in the 1920s. Good health was essential to the well-being of
the farm, so Cobb encouraged farmers to install screens to control
flies and other insects, and fifty years before it became a fad, he was
aware of the problems of ecology, pointing to the relationship between disease and polluted streams.[48]

The *Southern Ruralist* was also a steady friend of the rural
church. No institution made a greater contribution to farm life,
Cobb believed, so he supported plans to strengthen religion in rural
communities, urged his readers to participate in the affairs of the
church of their choice, and chided backsliders. "If absence makes
the heart grow fonder, how some people must love the church,"
he wrote.[49]

The *Southern Ruralist* was always nonpartisan, but Cobb occasionally made known his personal opinion of prominent political
leaders of his day. Woodrow Wilson was one of his favorites, and
when that wartime president died, Cobb contended that no "man
contributed more to the promotion of agriculture or to freeing it
from the fetters that have bound it down all these years." William
Jennings Bryan, according to Cobb, was a "friend of the masses"
and a "great patriot and a great Christian." [50] Presidents Harding
and Coolidge fared less well at Cobb's hands, and the Tennessean
could work up very little enthusiasm for Herbert Hoover.[51]

Cobb also expressed plainly his opinions of secretaries of agriculture. He liked E. T. Meredith, Wilson's appointee in 1920 who
had been a farm paper publisher in Iowa. "He knows what the

farmers of this country need," Cobb wrote, "and we can feel sure that he will bring to the Nation's Cabinet the same splendid executive ability and foresight which has made *Successful Farming* a leader among agricultural periodicals." [52] Cobb also approved of Henry C. Wallace, but he was considerably less enthusiastic with the appointment of William M. Jardine. That former president of Kansas State Agricultural College, Cobb believed, knew little of the realities of agriculture and, like Henry A. Wallace, the Tennessean felt that Jardine had been appointed to serve only as a mouthpiece for Calvin Coolidge. Arthur M. Hyde, according to Cobb, was a purely political appointee, with no visible qualifications for the task at hand.[53]

Despite such comments concerning some of the nation's political leaders, Cobb kept politics as such out of his editorials. The *Southern Ruralist*, he constantly reiterated, could take no political position, and thus his editorials did not reflect his own Democratic proclivities. But as Cobb's reputation as a spokesman for southern agricultural interests grew, it was inevitable that in his activities outside of the editorial office he would be caught up in the ferment among agricultural leaders of the 1920s and that by the early years of the next decade he would be recognized as far more than merely a regional, if outstanding, farm journalist.

### NOTES TO CHAPTER VI

1. *Southern Ruralist*, Vol. 33 (April 15, 1926), 33; *Progressive Farmer and Southern Ruralist* (Carolina-Virginia ed.), Vol. 45 (October 15–31, 1930), 931; *Manufacturers Record*, Vol. 93 (March 15, 1928), 65.

2. *Southern Ruralist*, Vol. 28 (April 15, 1921), 44.

3. For one of many such editorials, see *Southern Ruralist*, Vol. 35 (March 1, 1929), 655. For Wallace's views, see Malcolm O. Sillars, "Henry A. Wallace's Editorials on Agricultural Discontent, 1921–1928," *Agricultural History*, Vol. 26 (October, 1952), 132. Few issues were more widely advocated in the 1920s than diversification. Businessmen especially embraced it, believing that it constituted the most practical answer to the agricultural problems of that decade. John P. Gleason, "The Attitude of the Business Community Toward Agriculture During the McNary-Haugen Period," *Agricultural History*, Vol. 32 (April, 1958), 132. For the efforts in that direction of one railroad, see C. Clyde Jones, "The Burlington Railroad and Agricultural Policy in the 1920's," *Agricultural History*, Vol. 31 (October, 1957), 67–74.

4. *Progressive Farmer and Southern Ruralist* (Georgia-Alabama ed.), Vol. 45 (March 1–15, 1931), 6; *Southern Ruralist*, Vol. 30 (June 1, 1923), 129.

5. *Southern Ruralist*, Vol. 31 (May 1, 1924), 86.

6. *Southern Ruralist*, Vol. 27 (April 1, 1920), 33; Vol. 29 (April 1, 1922), 14.

7. *Southern Ruralist*, Vol. 29 (January 1, 1929), 474; Vol. 30 (January 1, 1929), 541.

8. *Southern Ruralist*, Vol. 26 (February 1, 1920), 944; Vol. 26 (February 15, 1920), 1008; Vol. 33 (March 15, 1927), 607.

9. *Southern Ruralist*, Vol. 32 (March 15, 1926), 666.

10. *Southern Ruralist*, Vol. 28 (January 15, 1922), 405; Vol. 29 (May 15, 1922), 92; Vol. 29 (March 1, 1923), 632; Scott, *Agricultural Extension*, 215.

11. *Southern Ruralist*, Vol. 27 (June 1, 1924), 236–37; Vol. 27 (March 21, 1921), 951; Vol. 31 (September 1, 1924), 232–33; Vol. 31 (December 15, 1924), 456; Vol. 31 (October 15, 1924), 322; Beck, "Agricultural Press and Southern Rural Development," 91. When southern farm papers talked of fertilizers, they were referring in the main to commercial fertilizers. This is a topic that was of little concern to Cobb's contemporaries in the North, at least until well into the decade. See Evans, PRAIRIE FARMER, 103.

12. *Southern Ruralist*, Vol. 26 (February 15, 1920), 1008; Vol. 33 (November 15, 1926). 378: Beck, "Agricultural Press and Southern Rural Development," 134.

13. *Progressive Farmer and Southern Ruralist* (Carolina-Georgia ed.), Vol. 45 (December 15–31, 1930), 1070; *Southern Ruralist*, Vol. 37 (May 1, 1930), 4. It is interesting to note that the *Prairie Farmer* was a bitter opponent of school consolidation until the 1940s. See Evans, PRAIRIE FARMER, 112.

14. *Southern Ruralist*, Vol. 37 (May 1, 1930), 3; Vol. 31 (December 15, 1924), 456.

15. *Southern Ruralist*, Vol. 31 (January 15, 1925), 520.

16. *Southern Ruralist*, Vol. 29 (March 15, 1923), 692. For a fuller statement of Cobb's enthusiasm for vocational training in agriculture, see his "Where Farming is Taught in Every Public School," *Forbes*, Vol. 15 (January, 1925), 464–66.

17. *Southern Ruralist*, Vol. 30 (November 15, 1923), 429; Vol. 31, (June 15, 1924), 145; Vol. 28 (July 15, 1921), 173; Cobb, "Contribution of the Press to Agriculture," 25.

18. *Southern Ruralist*, Vol. 35 (May 25, 1928), 126; Vol. 33 (January 15, 1927), 467; Vol. 36 (September 1, 1929), 13.

19. *Southern Ruralist*, Vol. 30 (April 15, 1923), 41; Vol. 26 (February 1, 1920), 944; Vol. 27 (May 1, 1920), 144; Vol. 29 (January 15, 1923), 506; Vol. 31 (June 1, 1924), 129; Vol. 35 (August 15, 1928), 257.

20. *Southern Ruralist*, Vol. 26 (February 1, 1920), 944–45; Vol. 34 (May 1, 1927), 77.

21. *Southern Ruralist*, Vol. 30 (March 1, 1924), 716–17.

22. Beck, "Agricultural Press and Southern Rural Development," 173.

23. Cobb, "Contribution of the Press to Agriculture," 28–29; *Southern Ruralist*, Vol. 30 (February 1, 1924), 618; Vol. 31 (June 1, 1924), 128; Vol. 33 (February 15, 1927), 548; Vol. 35 (August 1, 1928), 232; Vol. 37 (May 1, 1930), 4; Sillars, "Wallace's Editorials," 135; *Manufacturers Record*, Vol. 93 (March 15, 1928), 65.

24. *Southern Ruralist*, Vol. 28 (November 1, 1921), 311; Vol. 28 (July 15, 1921), 172; Vol. 33 (April 1, 1926), 16; Vol. 34 (September 1, 1927), 240; Evans, PRAIRIE FARMER, 119.

25. Cobb, "Contribution of the Press to Agriculture," 27; *Southern Ruralist*, Vol. 27 (April 1, 1920), 2, 32; Vol. 27 (May 15, 1920), 192; Vol. 27 (February 1, 1921), 838; Vol. 28 (July 15, 1921), 172; Vol. 29 (June 15, 1922), 141; Vol. 34 (August 15, 1927), 218–19; Beck, "Agricultural Press and Southern Rural Development," 127–28; Evans, "PRAIRIE FARMER, 131–37.

26. *Southern Ruralist*, Vol. 27 (February 1, 1921), 838; Vol. 29 (February 1, 1923), 544–45; Vol. 30 (January 1, 1924), 540; Vol. 33 (January 1, 1927), 450–51.

27. *Southern Ruralist*, Vol. 34 (June 15, 1927), 138; Vol. 34 (September 1, 1927), 240; Vol. 34 (March 1, 1928), 618; Cobb, "Contribution of the Press to Agriculture,"

29; *Manufacturers Record*, Vol. 93 (March 15, 1928), 65.

28. *Southern Ruralist*, Vol. 27 (May 15, 1920), 169; Vol. 28 (December 15, 1921), 374; Beck, "Agricultural Press and Southern Rural Development," 111–12.

29. *Southern Ruralist*, Vol. 28 (August 1, 1921), 190–91; Vol. 30 (April 15, 1923), 56–57.

30. *Southern Ruralist*, Vol. 32 (June 15, 1925), 150; Vol. 35 (October 15, 1928), 367; Cobb, "Contribution of the Press to Agriculture," 28.

31. *Southern Ruralist*, Vol. 34 (August 1, 1927), 198–99; Vol. 34 (February 1, 1928), 530; Vol. 35 (June 15, 1928), 170–71.

32. *Southern Ruralist*, Vol. 28 (September 15, 1921), 246; Vol. 29 (June 1, 1922), 116; Vol. 29 (February 1, 1923), 544; Vol. 32 (August 1, 1925), 207; Sillars, "Wallace's Editorials," 134–35; Cobb, "Contribution of the Press to Agriculture," 29; *Manufacturers Record*, Vol. 93 (March 15, 1928), 65.

33. Preston J. Hubbard's *Origins of the TVA: The Muscle Shoals Controversy, 1920–1932* (Nashville, 1961), discusses this issue in full detail. See also Norman Wengert, "Antecedents of TVA: The Legislative History of Muscle Shoals," *Agricultural History*, Vol. 26 (October 1952), 141–47.

34. *Southern Ruralist*, Vol. 28 (April 1, 1921), 16–17; Vol. 28 (March 15, 1922), 552–53; Vol. 31 (May 15, 1924), 110–11.

35. *Southern Ruralist*, Vol. 32 (April 15, 1925), 52–53; Vol. 32 (August 15, 1925), 244; Vol. 33 (May 15, 1926), 92–93.

36. *Southern Ruralist*, Vol. 34 (November 15, 1927), 370–71; Vol. 34 (February 15, 1928), 577; Vol. 35 (April 15, 1928), 59; Vol. 35 (February 15, 1929), 633.

37. *Southern Ruralist*, Vol. 33 (October 1, 1926), 296; Vol. 31 (April 1, 1924), 20; Vol. 33 (September 1, 1926), 242; Vol. 30 (February 1, 1924), 618–19; Beck, "Agricultural Press and Southern Rural Development," 102.

38. *Southern Ruralist*, Vol. 30 (March 15, 1924), 737; Vol. 34 (July 1, 1927), 158; Vol. 35 (May 1, 1928), 92.

39. *Southern Ruralist*, Vol. 30 (July 15, 1923), 203; Vol. 34 (August 15, 1927), 218.

40. *Southern Ruralist*, Vol. 31 (April 1, 1924), 21; Vol. 33 (April 15, 1926), 46; Vol. 27 (June 1, 1920), 236; *Progressive Farmer and Southern Ruralist* (Carolina-Virginia ed.), Vol. 45 (October 1–14, 1930), 887; (Georgia-Alabama ed.), Vol. 46 (August 1–14, 1931), 8.

41. *Southern Ruralist*, Vol. 29 (September 15, 1922), 277; Sillars, "Wallace's Editorials," 133–34.

42. *Southern Ruralist*, Vol. 30 (July 1, 1923), 182; *Progressive Farmer and Southern Ruralist*, Vol. 46 (June 1–14, 1931), 10.

43. *Southern Ruralist*, Vol. 33 (March 15, 1927), 620–21.

44. *Southern Ruralist*, Vol. 26 (March 15, 1920), 1134; Vol. 36 (September 1, 1929), 12–13.

45. *Southern Ruralist*, Vol. 35 (May 15, 1928), 122.

46. *Southern Ruralist*, Vol. 32 (April 1, 1925), 18; Vol. 35 (April 1, 1928), 3.

47. *Southern Ruralist*, Vol. 32 (May 1, 1925), 80.

48. *Southern Ruralist*, Vol. 29 (July 1, 1922), 162; Vol. 31 (August 1, 1924), 185; Vol. 29 (April 15, 1922), 42; Vol. 33 (June 1, 1926), 114; Vol. 30 (August 1, 1923), 224.

49. *Southern Ruralist*, Vol. 28 (March 15, 1922), 539; Vol. 30 (June 15, 1923), 162–63; Vol. 30 (November 15, 1923), 446.

50. *Southern Ruralist*, Vol. 30 (March 1, 1924), 716; Vol. 32 (August 15, 1925), 224.

51. *Southern Ruralist*, Vol. 35 (July 1, 1928), 183; Vol. 31 (March 15, 1925), 692.

52. *Southern Ruralist*, Vol. 26 (February 15, 1920), 977.

53. *Southern Ruralist*, Vol. 31 (March 15, 1925), 692; Vol. 31 (November 15, 1924), 396; Vol. 36 (April 1, 1929), 16; Sillars, "Wallace's Editorials," 138.

# CHAPTER VII

# The Rise of a Southern Farm Editor to National Prominence, 1919–1933

WHEN in the fall of 1919 Cully Cobb left Mississippi to become editor-in-chief of the *Southern Ruralist*, he was little known outside of the Magnolia State except among that relatively small group of men who managed the boys' club work in the South and their immediate superiors in Washington. But Cobb's reputation grew dramatically in the 1920s. By the end of the Prosperity Decade, he was recognized as one of the most eloquent voices of southern agriculture, widely accepted as a spokesman for the rural interests of that section. In fact, his reputation would in time push him onto the national stage, and in 1933 he would take a high post in the United States Department of Agriculture.

As editor-in-chief of the *Southern Ruralist* and later as editor of the Georgia-Alabama edition of the *Progressive Farmer*, Cobb was in intimate contact with a significant block of southern farm families. During his tenure with the *Southern Ruralist*, its circulation ranged between 267,000 and 513,000. The different editions of the new paper created by the merger went to more than a million subscribers.[1] * With readers that numerous, it would have been difficult for Cobb to have avoided acquiring a considerable standing among his peers, the mass of farmers of the Southeast, and the political leaders whose ears were closely attuned to the hopes and aspirations of their rural constituents.

The merger of the *Southern Ruralist* and the *Progressive Farmer* and Cobb's position with the new paper quite obviously contributed to the growth of his reputation. Not only did it connect his name with a farm paper that was preeminent in its field, but the

* Notes appear at end of each chapter.

merger also brought Cobb into a close and friendly relationship with an outstanding group of agrarian leaders, the men who made up the *Progressive Farmer* staff.

Heading the group, of course, was Clarence Poe, president of the Progressive Farmer-Southern Ruralist Company. A leading figure in southern farming circles since 1899, Poe was widely respected as something of an elder statesman in agriculture. Politicians regularly sought his views on issues and personalities. In fact, a political career for Poe himself was for many years not beyond the realm of possibility.[2]

Perhaps even better known, at least among farm educators and scientists, was Tait Butler. A native of Canada who was educated at Ontario Veterinary College, he had served as professor of veterinary science at agricultural colleges in Mississippi, Kansas, and North Carolina and had acquired an enviable reputation as a farmers' institute lecturer in the latter state. In 1895, while teaching at Mississippi Agricultural and Mechanical College, he had launched the *Southern Farm Gazette* at Starkville. Fourteen years later he returned to that paper and was with it when it merged with the *Progressive Farmer*. The remainder of his active life was spent as an editor of its Mississippi Valley edition. During his long and distinguished career, he garnered numerous honors, including the presidencies of the American Association of Farmers' Institute Workers, the American Veterinary Association, and the American Agricultural Editors' Association.[3]

Several other members of the *Progressive Farmer* family were also well known. Eugene Butler, Tait Butler's son, had studied agriculture in the land-grant colleges of Mississippi and Iowa, and by 1930 he had edited the Texas edition for ten years. Dr. Benjamin W. Kilgore, former dean of the North Carolina College of Agriculture, and his son were associated with the Kentucky-Tennessee edition, and William C. Lassetter had been managing editor of all editions of the paper since 1920.[4]

Impressive as his journalistic reputation was, Cobb's rising stature did not rest upon that role alone. He was much in demand as a speaker, a circumstance which both stemmed from his growing reputation and contributed to it. In 1922 he spoke at Virginia Polytechnic Institute, commemorating the fiftieth anniversary of that school; but no doubt more satisfying was the invitation the next year to deliver the alumni oration before the graduating class at Mississippi Agricultural and Mechanical College. Cobb loved his alma mater and felt a warm relationship with all those connected with it. Audiences at the school responded in kind. According to reports, Cobb "has a rich store of information and a good vocabulary that enables him to express thoughts in an interesting and impressive style. He is easy on the platform, has a voice that carries well, and is an artist at the business of discerning the likes and dislikes of an audience." [5]

As late as 1932, Cobb's standing as an educator and orator, combined with the general knowledge that he was among several individuals being considered for the position of Secretary of Agriculture, led to his appearance before the annual meeting of the Louisiana Teachers' Association. His topic at that gathering in Monroe was the development of agricultural education, its accomplishments, and its promises for the future, subjects upon which he had strong convictions based on experience. Later, he spoke briefly before the agricultural and home economics sections of the convention. [6]

More common and more significant were Cobb's appearances before agricultural groups of various types. In January, 1927, for example, he was one of the several agricultural leaders from throughout the nation who spoke at the annual meeting of the Southern Cattlemen's Association. Entitling his address "Some Fundamentals of a Great Livestock Industry," Cobb spelled out his ideas concerning the production of cattle and hogs in the lower South. [7] Later the same year, he participated in the West Tennessee Farmers' Institute, a rural educational gathering that had been held annually since the late nineteenth century. Cobb was also in demand at meetings of railway development agents, those officials who were charged with the task of generating traffic for their companies. In January, 1924, Cobb spoke to the Railway Development Association of the Southeast and in December he appeared at Chicago on the program of the American Railway Development Association. [8]

In 1928 in company with a number of other pioneers in agricul-

From his vantage point atop a bale of hay, Cobb instructs participants at the International Club Camp and Judging Contest at Atlanta, Georgia, 1920.

tural extension, Cobb took part in a program at Texas Agricultural and Mechanical College commemorating the twenty-fifth anniversary of the launching of demonstration work by Seaman A. Knapp. Cobb's address was entitled "The Contribution of the Press to Agriculture," but after paying tribute to Justin S. Morrill and Knapp and mentioning briefly the educational role of the agricultural press, Cobb turned to an analysis of the ills that afflicted farming. Following the Texas conclave, Cobb participated in an international meeting of agricultural leaders at Matamores, Mexico.[9]

A year later Cobb served on a panel arranged by the American Institute of Cooperation which discussed the nature and place of cooperative papers. As long as cooperative papers served simply as links between the cooperatives publishing them and their members he saw such magazines as important allies in the struggle to improve the position of farmers. But he warned that when a cooperative paper took commercial advertising, it then became simply another farm paper and a rival of such periodicals as he edited. He did not fear such new rivals, but Cobb did think that, if cooperative papers were to compete with privately owned magazines for advertisers, they should not be subsidized by the organizations they represented. To do so, he thought, would create a situation unfair to privately owned papers.[10]

The same year that Cobb appeared before the American Institute of Cooperation he also was invited to address a session of the American Home Economics Association. Again the needs of agriculture were foremost in his mind, but given the conditions then prevailing Cobb showed remarkable optimism for the future of farming.[11] Admittedly, agriculture and the nation as a whole were in depression, but Cobb saw hope for the future. "Agricultural intelligence of the present day type is a new factor," and a "trained leadership armed with facts is the beginning of progress." Moreover, we "have reached the point in national development where organization and long-time planning in agriculture are recognized as basic necessities. . . ." Finally, Cobb was cheered by the realization among businessmen that their economic well-being depended upon a prosperous agriculture. "Thinking men in industry . . . urge now the necessity of a vigorous agricultural community as the only dependable commercial safeguard against the disasters of the recent past," he told his audience.

Throughout the 1920s Cobb was an enthusiastic participant in the annual meetings of the Association of Southern Agricultural Workers. In 1920 he addressed the group on "The Southern Tenant Problem." [12] In 1927 he served as chairman of the Association's resolutions committee. His committee and the Association as a whole asked for an increase in federal funds for agricultural extension, commended the Crop Reporting Service of the United States Department of Agriculture, proposed that the land-grant colleges and other agricultural agencies give proper attention to the formulation of adequate policies concerning land utilization, and suggested that Congress produce without delay "a permanent policy of merchant marine operation." The similarity between the resolutions adopted and the views expressed in the editorials of the *Southern Ruralist* suggest that Cobb was hardly a passive chairman.[13]

In 1932 Cobb again spoke to the Association of Southern Agricultural Workers. His topic on that occasion was the worldwide position of cotton, particularly in Russia, India, and Egypt, and its competitive impact upon the southern grower, an aspect of the farm problem that received increased attention at his hands during his last years in agricultural journalism.[14]

In 1924 Cobb was invited to Columbia, Missouri, to take part in Farmers' Week, an annual program held on the University of Missouri campus by the College of Agriculture and the State Board of Agriculture. As an innovation at that gathering, Cobb's speech was broadcast by radio out into the state. At least two thousand farmers reported hearing the talk; Cobb was surprised to find radios that numerous in rural Missouri. However, as he informed David Sarnoff of the Radio Corporation of America, the experience did not convince him that radios had yet reached a degree of perfection and standardization that would allow him to recommend them without reservation to his readers.[15]

In addition to speaking before various groups, Cobb participated in a number of programs designed to benefit rural people or to shape public policy to their advantage; and he served on various committees or organizations established to promote rural interests. An example of the former was a week long cotton program conducted throughout Georgia in February, 1925. Arranged by several agricultural agencies in the state, the program sought to carry to farmers information concerning the current situation regarding cotton. Farmers were told that there was a huge carryover of cotton from 1924 and that a large crop in 1925 would have disastrous effects on prices. Cobb and the other speakers urged growers to reduce acreage but to make every effort to increase yield in order to reduce costs. Speakers also stressed a number of other aspects of the proper handling of the crop, including cooperative marketing.[16] Meanwhile, as early as 1923 Cobb was a member of the agricultural committee of the Atlanta Chamber of Commerce and later he served as a director of the Country Life Association.[17]

During the 1920s Cobb continued his interest in boys' and girls' club work and, in fact, made some important contributions to the enrichment of the program. Cobb made sure that the *Southern Ru-*

*ralist* carried club news from across the South, for a time writing a column on that topic himself. He also watched with approval as the participation of rural youth in the International Live Stock Show grew in scope and ultimately became the National 4-H Club Congress. He was especially pleased to report that in 1920 Mississippi offered sixteen prize trips to Chicago, a number that gave the Magnolia State one of the largest delegations at the conclave and that led officials to proclaim Mississippi the leading state in the nation in club work. Two years later a total of 650 boys and girls from across the country attended the exposition.[18] As evidence of his contribution to and continued interest in the rural youth program, Cobb was appointed to the National Committee on Boys' and Girls' Club Work, a post he held as late as 1939.[19]

Cobb was instrumental in establishing a new feature of club work in 1920. Convinced that no incentive was too great if it inspired club members to do their best work and still disturbed by the hesitancy of officials at the International Live Stock Show to give a proper place in the program to club boys, Cobb resolved to stage an International Club Camp and Judging Contest in Atlanta. In conjunction with H. H. Williamson, state club leader in Texas, and officials of the United States Department of Agriculture and of the Southeastern Fair, Cobb arranged the first of what would become an annual judging contest for boys. Participants competed in state teams. First prize was a trip to Europe, financed by the management of the Southeastern Fair, and the right to take part in the Royal Live Stock Show in England, considered by many to be the "greatest live stock show in the world." [20]

When the Southeastern Fair opened, October 16, 1920, fourteen teams of three boys from as many states camped on the grounds. The judging, which took most of three days, was performed by Edward N. Wentworth of Armour and Company and Earl W. Sheets and R. A. Black of the United States Department of Agriculture.[21]

Mississippi boys participated in the contest. Authorities at Mississippi Agricultural and Mechanical College were enthusiastic and made every effort to send the most competent team to Atlanta. Twenty-eight boys selected by competitive examinations at the beginning of the annual Short Course in Junior Farm Mechanics on

Winning team from Texas at the International Club Camp and Judging Contest at Atlanta, Georgia, 1920. Left to right, Jack Turner, Alva Debnam, and Gilbert Wieting.

campus were given ten days of training. From that number a team of three boys and two alternates was finally chosen. That team was given further training by sending the boys on a tour of schools and farms in Mississippi, Tennessee, Kentucky, Illinois, and Indiana. Later, they spent three days each at the Tri-State Fair at Memphis and the Mississippi-Alabama Fair at Meridian. Funds for those excursions were donated by local businessmen.[22]

Unfortunately for the Mississippi team and no doubt counter to Cobb's hopes, these efforts produced only second place. Under the coaching of W. B. Cook, assistant boys' club agent, the Texas team placed first and won the trip to Europe. Members of the winning team were Jack Turner, a sixteen-year-old from Hillsboro, Alva Debnam of Lamesa, and Gilbert Wieting of Marlin. James D. Gillespie, a native of Coleman, was picked as an alternate. In June, 1920, the four boys, accompanied by H. H. Williamson, County Agent H. B. Ross from Falls County, and I. W. Hill of the United States Department of Agriculture, started their journey. They first visited Washington, D.C., where they were introduced to President Warren G. Harding and Secretary of Agriculture Henry C. Wallace. Then they went to New York where they took passage on the *Carmiania* to Liverpool. In England they visited farms and a variety of historic spots before participating in the Royal. Then followed a tour of agricultural areas and battlefields in France and Belgium and a return to their homes in August via Glasgow and Montreal.[23]

Judging from the comments of the young men upon their return to the United States, the contest and trip achieved the results for which Cobb and his associates had hoped. Gilbert Wieting reported the trip to be "educational to me, and I don't think you could have done any greater or more successful work for promoting Boys' Club Work." Alva Debnam wrote that "I believe that this prize trip is the greatest incentive to club boys that could be offered. . . ." Fifty years later Jack Turner doubted that any "one boy, let alone four, has ever had the big push with the lasting benefits that we four have had. . . ."[24]

The contest of 1920 proved to be only the first of a series of such events. A team from Maryland won in 1921. The Southeastern Fair in time relinquished sponsorship of the event, but the contest was continued until 1939. During that span of years boys from Illinois, Iowa, Nebraska, Oklahoma, and other states won the honor of a trip to the Royal Live Stock Show.[25]

While Cobb continued to make contributions to boys' club work, he was also a major figure in his new profession, that of agricultural journalism. In 1921 he participated in the organization of the American Agricultural Editors' Association, a trade group for rural journalists. He subsequently served as vice-president and five consecutive terms as president of the association, thereby establishing close and friendly relations with some of the men most influential in agriculture.[26]

As president, one of Cobb's major contributions was the organization of a series of educational tours for the membership. Problems in American farming, Cobb believed, were directly related to farming in other areas, and he could think of no better way for rural editors to inform themselves and their readers than by seeing agriculture in other parts of the United States and in other countries. Moreover, the Tennessean was firmly convinced that agricultural journalism had a major role to play in broadening the outlook of farmers. That process could hardly fail to be enhanced by expanding the knowledge and experience of the men and women who wrote for the nation's agricultural papers.[27]

The first of five trips arranged by Cobb took some forty members of the association to England and western Europe, following an itinerary worked out in advance by officials of the United States Departments of State and Agriculture. Departing the United States June 14, 1924, the group crossed the Atlantic on the 59,956-ton *Leviathan* and began studies in England. There they toured historic sites, such as Canterbury Cathedral and Hampton Court, and visited the British Empire Exposition at London. More important to their purposes, the group attended the Royal Live Stock Show, held that year in Leicester, and toured the world-famous agricultural experiment station at Rothamstead as well as a number of outstanding English farms, where they were especially impressed with the quality of the pastures and livestock. Everywhere leading figures in English farming and the British Ministry of Agriculture welcomed the Americans and served as guides and hosts.

Leaving England on July 7, the farm journalists went to Holland and later to Belgium, Denmark, France, Germany, and Switzerland. On the continent, members of the association visited some of the battlefields of World War I, but they spent most of their time studying cheesemaking in Switzerland, synthetic nitrogen production in Germany, cooperative marketing and agricultural credit systems in Denmark, and dairying in Holland. Again, they were guided on their tours by government officials, agricultural scientists, and leading members of breeders' and growers' associations. All who made the trip agreed that they had learned much that was useful. Upon returning to the United States Cobb spoke for the whole group when he wrote, "On account of the trip we believe we are able to see our own problems—present and future—a little bit clearer than ever before and we feel that we are better able to meet those problems, and thus better serve the interest of those who read our paper." [28]

Four trips came later. In 1925 the group toured western Canada. About eighty men and women left Chicago August 22 for Winni-

Agricultural editors and friends at the Prince of Wales Ranch near Calgary, Alberta, 1925. Left to right, T. L. Wheeler, Mrs. W. L. Carlyle, John Cunningham, C. A. Cobb, W. L. Carlyle, and A. B. Calder.

peg where they took the Canadian Pacific Railroad to the Pacific Coast. They returned via the Canadian National. The itinerary for the trip was worked out in the main by Arthur B. Calder, an official of the Canadian Pacific. Enroute they visited wheat and flax farms and cattle ranches, including the 4,000-acre property of the Prince of Wales, and studied the marketing cooperatives that flourished on the prairies of Canada.[29] There was no tour in 1926, but the next year a delegation went to Mexico. Leaving St. Louis the members traveled down the Mississippi valley to New Orleans, along the Gulf Coast to Galveston, and through Texas to Corpus Christi. In Mexico, the group saw a variety of types of farming, some of them exotic and primitive, and was royally entertained by the Mexican people and by President Plutareo Calles.[30] Other trips came in 1929 and 1930. In 1929 members of the association traveled some 12,000 miles in the American Southwest and California, and in 1930 the editors went to eastern Canada and the Maritime Provinces.[31]

Important in making the trips possible was the wholehearted cooperation that Cobb was able to gain from business interests. In no case were the members of the association required to pay for their transportation. The United States Shipping Board offered passage on the *Leviathan* for the trip to Europe in return for advertising space in those farm papers whose officials were members of the association. The railroads were equally cooperative. Railroad officials were cognizant of the lingering anti-railroad sentiment among farmers, and they were interested in programs that might help to dissipate it. Moreover, Cobb had a warm relationship with the agricultural development agents of many of the carriers; these men in turn recognized agricultural journalism as a powerful ally in their work. In the case of the Mexican trip, the Missouri Pacific railroad provided an entire "Agricultural Editors' Special" train for the use of Cobb and his fellow editors.[32]

In the decade of the 1920s Cobb, along with Dean Thomas P. Cooper of the Kentucky agricultural college and C. L. Christensen of the United States Bureau of Markets, led in a fight for the establishment of a foreign agricultural service. Cobb and his friends thought that, in order for American farmers to understand better the forces of world supply and demand that affected them, the na-

Cobb with agricultural editors and President Plutareo Calles of Mexico in Mexico City, 1927. Calles is on Cobb's left.

tion should maintain abroad a corps of competent agricultural experts who could provide a stream of accurate and current information. Such data would allow producers in this country to plan their plantings more intelligently. Bills establishing such a service were in Congress at various times during the decade but they encountered the hostility of Secretary of Commerce Herbert Hoover, who steadfastly maintained that such experts should be attached to his Department. Cobb and his allies rejected that idea, insisting instead

Agricultural Editors' Special, provided by the Missouri Pacific Lines for trip through the American Southwest, 1929.

that the program could only be administered by men in the Department of Agriculture who knew and understood farming.[33] It was a signal victory for the Tennessean when in 1930 a bill was approved creating the Foreign Agricultural Service, attaching it to the Department of Agriculture, and spelling out its duties in a manner reasonably consistent with the proposals that he had made over a period of several years.[34]

By the later part of the decade, Cobb's views on a number of other issues were becoming sufficiently well known to give him considerable stature among those men who formulated national agricultural policy. On such matters as land use, for instance, he had been speaking out for some time. For years he had emphasized that land was a valuable and basic resource that should be preserved and used properly. Erosion of all kinds should be controlled and crops should be produced on land best suited to them. Cobb also believed that the size of the farm unit should be increased; many farms represented an investment too small to support a family. In 1928 he suggested that the nation desperately needed a new approach to land use, based upon a comprehensive plan formulated by the government after a thorough examination of the land, its potential uses, and present and future needs. He objected strenuously to the existing policy "to open up vast areas of new agricultural lands and bring them into cultivation when overproduction and low prices are cutting the very heart out of the industry." Moreover, there were "many countless millions of acres of marginal land throughout the nation" that should be retired and "a vigorous and permanent program of reforestation should promptly be put into effect." [35]

In 1931 the Hoover administration reached the same conclusion. With the coming of the Great Depression and the apparent failure of the Agricultural Marketing Act, the President and his associates were ready to turn to land retirement as one approach to the problem of rural distress. As a step in that direction, the Administration and the Association of Land Grant Colleges and Universities called a national conference on land utilization in Chicago in November, 1931. When it convened, some of the leading figures in agricultural economics and agricultural planning were in attendance. Among the 350 participants were Richard T. Ely, the famous economist from Wisconsin, Lewis C. Gray of the United States Bureau of Agricultural Economics, John D. Black of Harvard University, Milburn L. Wilson of Montana State College, and Elwood Mead of the United States Bureau of Reclamation.[36] Probably "no more widely representative group ever met for the consideration of national land problems," according to Lewis C. Gray.[37]

Cobb was invited to participate in the conference and to speak to the conclave. Taking note of the effects of the depression, so evident in the streets of Chicago, Cobb claimed that the existing economic distress was due to the neglect shown agriculture during the 1920s and that a revival in farming was a prerequisite to a general recovery. To produce that agricultural revival, he believed, farmers would have to be helped through the formation of a "comprehensive national agricultural policy, conceived in the light of world conditions and based upon fundamental justice to all. . . ." Quite obviously, the development of a land utilization program would be "a first step toward bringing those adjustments in agricultural programs fundamental to agricultural progress and to national economic safety." Such a program should "preserve the fertility of the soil, aid toward adjusting production to demand, and provide for the most profitable use of marginal and idle lands." [38]

On the first day of the conference, participants appointed a resolutions committee and named Cobb chairman. Among his coworkers were high officials from the agricultural colleges in Utah, New Jersey, Kentucky, Minnesota, New York and Oregon; R. W. Reynolds, agricultural development agent of the Milwaukee railroad; Howard R. Tolley of the Giannini Foundation; Milburn L. Wilson; representatives of the Farm Bureau, Grange, and various commodity groups; and businessmen speaking for banking and insurance interests.

Cobb's committee and the Conference accepted with only minor changes a total of eighteen recommendations. In general, the group proposed a "rationalization of agricultural production and land utilization, the conservation of natural resources, and the safeguarding of the national welfare in the use of land." More specifically, the Conference called for federal administration of the public domain in order to rehabilitate public ranges and protect water sheds, the consolidation of scattered state and federal lands, and the formulation of land-use policies based upon a thorough inventory of land resources and the establishment of a land-use classification system. The Conference also suggested that the government should restrict homesteading, adjust taxes on land in light of its current uses, regulate all land-settlement enterprises, undertake no more reclamation projects, take steps to control soil erosion and depletion, and withdraw marginal land from cultivation.

Finally, the Conference recommended that the Secretary of Agriculture establish two standing committees to aid in implementing its proposals. The first, a National Land Use Planning Committee, should be made up of technical personnel from the appropriate governmental bureaus and the land-grant colleges. The second group would be known as the National Advisory and Legislative Committee on Land Use, to be comprised of representatives of the national farm organizations, the United States Chamber of Commerce, state agricultural agencies, the American Forestry Association, the farm press, the American Railway Development Association, and livestock growers' organizations.[39]

The Hoover administration gave every indication of accepting the resolutions of the Conference and early in 1932 set up the two proposed committees. Cobb served on one of the committees and helped organize the other one.[40] The approach of the 1932 political campaign blocked solid accomplishments in the form of legislation, despite Hoover's sympathy with some of the proposals offered. Nevertheless, the Republican platform that year reflected the thinking of the Conference, and to a degree the New Deal of Franklin Roosevelt built its land policies on ideas and information generated by the Conference and the committees formed later.[41]

Cobb was also an enthusiastic advocate of the agricultural outlook conferences that were launched in the last years of the Hoover administration. Throughout the 1920s he was convinced that, if farmers had accurate, up-to-date information, they could and would plan their operations more intelligently. By 1930 public authorities shared his views. Accordingly, the first Agricultural Outlook Conference was held in Atlanta, November 10–14, 1930. In attendance were two hundred representatives of the United States Department of Agriculture, the Federal Reserve Board, and the agricultural colleges from seven southern states. Logically enough, the Conference concerned itself initially with the outlook for cotton in 1931. Participants pointed out that foreign consumption of the staple was declining and that the carryover on August 1, 1930, was 1.8 million bales larger than a year earlier. Reductions in acreage were clearly in order, and farmers should shift land to other uses. Data presented and discussed at the Conference on all significant southern crops were compiled and made available in order that farmers might have them while planning their 1931 plantings. Similar conclaves were held in Atlanta in the fall of 1931 and 1932.[42]

But in final analysis, programs to provide better economic information for farmers or to produce a more rational use of the nation's land resources could not solve, at least in the short run, the problem that was most critical in the 1920s and early 1930s. Nor could better farming methods, cooperative marketing, greater expenditures for agricultural experimentation and extension, and diversification—issues emphasized in the pages of the *Southern Ruralist*—meet in an effective way the basic matter of overproduction. It was perfectly obvious to Cobb, as it was to most students of the issue, that production of farm commodities was outrunning consumption.[43] How farmers might adjust their aggregate output to square more nearly with aggregate demand was the great central question.

Cobb had no ready answer to that question. During most of the decade his statements suggested that the Tennessean thought that farmers could effectively cut production through voluntary reductions in acreage and by diversifying their operations. More efficient production and marketing procedures would allow growers to reduce costs on their remaining cotton lands and maintain or increase their gross earnings from that staple. Meanwhile, every effort should be made to expand markets, especially those abroad. Cobb urged growers to inform themselves concerning foreign tastes and needs in cotton, demanded that the nation equip itself with an adequate merchant marine, and vigorously denounced those policies, such as the tariff, that interfered with the free flow of American agricultural goods to foreign markets.[44]

Central to the farm problem in the 1920s, Cobb believed, was a basic injustice in governmental economic policies. For decades government had been a partner of business, providing what amounted to a subsidy in the form of the tariff. Labor also benefited from governmental policy, especially through immigration restrictions which could only have the effect of reducing the supply of labor and driving wages upward. Cobb concluded that farmers were the only great group in society that did not benefit in some substantial way from governmental aid. The farmer was the forgotten man, forced to take for his products what the market would offer while having to purchase his every need in markets which were to some degree protected from simple supply and demand.[45]

In some measure this injustice in governmental economic policy stemmed from the inadequate representation of agriculture in Congress. Like the Populists of thirty years earlier, Cobb complained in 1921 that the nation's legislature was dominated by lawyers and bankers. In fact, he could count only twenty farmers in the lot. Agriculture fared especially poorly in the House, wrote Cobb in 1930, pointing out that the city of New York alone had more representatives than did seven predominantly agricultural western states.[46] Cobb hailed the formation of the Farm Bloc in the early 1920s as a significant forward step in counterbalancing the poor representation of agricultural interests, and for a time he considered Senator Arthur Capper of Kansas as one of the key men in Congress who might be expected to fight for rural needs.[47]

What the farmer needed above all else, Cobb reiterated time and again, was the formation by Congress of a national program for agriculture. The farmer wanted government to do nothing that it was not doing for other groups; he only wanted Congress to treat agriculture as it treated other elements in the country.[48] As Cobb expressed the matter in 1926, "The farm must demand a national economic policy that will include agriculture along with industry, labor, and capital. . . . At present, agriculture is left to root, hog, or die, while industry is protected by a tariff wall raised to the height of complete embargo in many cases, and labor is protected with stringent immigration laws, and the return upon capital has been stabilized and made as secure as it is humanly possible to do it." [49] If government did not act, he said in 1927, American farmers would "become peasants." [50]

It was Cobb's conviction that agriculture had to have governmental aid that caused him to embrace and become a militant advocate of the McNary-Haugen bill. That measure, he wrote, would "do exactly for farm products what the tariff has done for industrial products . . . and what immigrant restriction has done for the wage earners. . . ." After all, the "farmer has as much right to enjoy an 'American standard of living' as anybody else." Like many southerners, Cobb was not certain that the bill offered the best solution to the problem, or that it would operate satisfactorily for those crops that moved heavily in the export trade. But unlike many political leaders in the South, Cobb was willing to take the McNary-Haugen bill as a first step. If nothing else, its passage would indicate that the federal government recognized its responsibility to agriculture and that it was prepared to act in a positive manner to remove the injustice that had for so long burdened farmers.[51]

Cobb endorsed the McNary-Haugen bill in 1924, supported it through its struggles in Congress, and vigorously denounced those who opposed it. In 1926, Cobb went to Washington to work for the passage of the bill. There he met Henry A. Wallace and other northern farm leaders and with them helped to unify southern and midwestern efforts in behalf of the measure. Attempts to dilute the concept of the bill, such as the Curtis-Crisp proposal of 1927, disgusted Cobb; and he turned his most biting sarcasm on those, primarily easterners and business interests, who labeled the McNary-Haugen bill as uneconomic, un-American, and radical, while they themselves benefitted from such governmental policies as the tariff. He also belabored those southern politicians who for a variety of reasons opposed the bill. In 1927, when the McNary-Haugen bill first passed Congress, Cobb was amazed that such southern senators as George and Harris of Georgia and Stephens and Harrison of Mississippi voted against the bill. No doubt those men would return to their states with plausible arguments for their positions, but Cobb noted that "the most plausible individual that we have met during our sojourn in Atlanta is now doing time in the state penitentiary." Such senators, Cobb implied, should be retired by their constituents.[52]

Despite the distressing position of many southern senators and congressmen, the McNary-Haugen bill received sizeable majorities in both houses of Congress, and Cobb expressed the hope that President Coolidge would give the measure his approval. But the president blasted the hopes of the agrarians with a stinging veto. For "its inaccuracy, for its inconsistency, for rank presumption, and for injustice, we have never seen a more amazing document," Cobb wrote in reference to the veto message. He was especially outraged by the President's opposition to the bill on the grounds that it would get the government into the business of price fixing. What, Cobb demanded to know, did Coolidge think the government was doing through the tariff, the Federal Reserve System, and the Interstate Commerce Commission?[53]

When the McNary-Haugen bill appeared in Congress the next year and, after passage a second time, received the same treatment from Coolidge, Cobb washed his hands of the Vermonter. Nor was he encouraged by the outcome of the election of 1928, but he was willing to give Herbert Hoover the benefit of the doubt and to allow him time to devise his program for agriculture. That program proved to be the Agricultural Marketing Act, enacted June 15, 1929, at a special session called for the purpose.[54]

Cobb had mixed feelings concerning the Agricultural Marketing Act. It fell short of what he believed agriculture needed. It was, he said, "nothing more than a marketing measure," supplementing the Capper-Volstead Act of 1922. "We could have had the bill . . . at any time during the past few years. And if that was all we were to have, there was no use calling the special session." But still Cobb was willing to give the new measure a chance. After all, he had been a firm advocate of cooperative marketing, and the new law promised to strengthen those programs. Nothing would be accomplished by opposing it before "Hoover has full and free opportunity to prove the wisdom of his belief . . . in the measure. . . ."[55]

Moreover, Cobb was reasonably well pleased with the membership of the Federal Farm Board, the agency established to implement the Agricultural Marketing Act. It was, he wrote, "a very able group of men." The fact that Alexander H. Legg, president of the International Harvester Company, was made chairman of the Board did not disturb Cobb as it did some rural leaders; in fact, Cobb praised the industrialist as being "eminently qualified." Nor were the other members objectionable, and Cobb was glad to see that with "a couple or so exceptions, Mr. Hoover stayed clear of political debt paying."[56]

During the first months of the Board's operations, Cobb found some grounds for hope. In promoting the merger of small cooperatives into larger ones Cobb thought the agency was on the right path; in fact, Cobb had been calling for such developments for years. He was also pleased when the Board indicated an inclination to use in its work agricultural extension personnel. These men, Cobb was convinced, knew more about the realities of agriculture than any group in the country. In December, 1929, Cobb concluded that the Board was pursuing a "sensible course" and "its loans and assistance have already been of very great value."[57]

Cobb, in fact, had sufficient faith in the ability of the Federal

Judging corn in a contest sponsored by the Agricultural Department of the Southern Railway, 1925. From the left, John R. Hutcheson, Director of the Cooperative Agricultural Extension Service, Blacksburg, Virginia; E. B. Ferris, Director of the South Mississippi Branch Experiment Station, Poplarville, Mississippi; and Cobb.

Farm Board to meet some of the problems of agriculture to serve for a time on one of its committees and to allow his name to be offered for a position on the Board. Southerners tended to believe that their section, especially the Gulf and Atlantic Coast states, was inadequately represented on the Federal Farm Board. In 1931 a group of Floridians sought to promote the candidacy of Burdette G. Lewis of Green Cove Springs, Florida,[58] and later that year J. Phil Campbell of Georgia and others organized a movement to have Cobb named to the agency. Clarence Poe of the *Progressive Farmer* worked energetically in Cobb's behalf, visiting Hoover and others in Washington in the course of his efforts. Among Cobb's supporters was Robert R. Moton, principal of Alabama's Tuskegee Institute. Cobb's appointment would be "pleasing to the Negro as well as to the entire south," Moton wrote Hoover, because the Tennessean was "a man with the highest ideals" who "has not only worked faithfully for many years to help the white farmers of the south but has been equally interested in helping the Negro farmers as well." The movement failed, according to Campbell, partly because of the accusation by some that Cobb's appointment would benefit Poe's paper.[59]

But Cobb was never under any illusions concerning the ability of the Federal Farm Board to solve the basic problem of overproduction. In fact, he foresaw correctly that the operations of the Board would actually encourage greater output unless growers used restraint in their plantings. In February, 1930, he joined with other southern farm leaders in a movement to encourage voluntary reduction in acreage, and he told his readers that producers of such great staples as cotton should organize to reduce production, since in "agriculture, as in the great cables, strength lies in combining individual strength into a mighty single unit." A few months later he reiterated his belief that "a square deal for agriculture at the hands of a government that should have no favorites . . . is the greatest need of the present moment. . . ." [60]

Cobb failed to spell out the details of a government program that would give agriculture the desired "square deal" through some form of production control. At times he indicated continued faith in McNary-Haugenism and on May 4, 1933, in a speech before the

United States Chamber of Commerce, he restated the basic positions that he had taken in the pages of the *Southern Ruralist* throughout the 1920s. Agriculture was the nation's primary industry; farming had been the "object of deliberate discrimination and continuous exploitation"; and if the farmer were ever to find a way out of his difficulties "a great deal must be done by his government . . . the government that has done most to deny him his just reward." But early in 1932, with enough cotton on hand to meet demands for almost two years, he pointed out that the "matter of supply and demand is one of the greatest importance. Cotton acreage of the South must be reduced to the minimum. . . ." [61] By that time, he was willing to accept any plan, including equalization fees, export debentures, or domestic allotments, that promised salvation. Later that year Cobb tentatively placed his support behind the domestic allotment concept of William J. Spillman and Milburn L. Wilson, provided that the plan was applied at the outset only to cotton and wheat.[62]

Logically enough, Cobb watched with great interest the political events of 1932. Equally logically, in light of his reputation throughout the South and indeed the nation, some of his friends and associates in the summer of 1932 resolved to obtain his appointment as Secretary of Agriculture in case Franklin D. Roosevelt defeated the incumbent Hoover. The effort a year earlier to win for Cobb a post on the Federal Farm Board had established important contacts and had left the framework of an organization.[63] Building on that structure Cobb's supporters launched a nationwide campaign calculated to generate sufficient interest to induce Roosevelt to name him to the position.

The field promised to be a crowded one. Early speculation named such men as Senators George W. Norris of Nebraska and Harry F. Byrd of Virginia as well as a number of less well-known members of Congress.[64] Henry L. Morgenthau, publisher of the *American Agriculturist* and a close friend and confidant of Roosevelt, apparently wanted the post for himself. Rexford G. Tugwell, a Columbia University professor, was considered to be in the running. Senator Peter Norbeck of South Dakota favored John Simpson, president of the militant Farmers' Union, while William Hirth of the Missouri Farmers' Association had his supporters. Milburn L. Wilson of Montana State College, John D. Black of Harvard, and Edward A. O'Neal of the Farm Bureau favored Iowa's Henry A. Wallace, but Wallace thought the job should go to George Peek, who had worked so energetically since the early 1920s to obtain equality for agriculture. There were still other contenders, including Tait Butler, Cobb's associate on the *Progressive Farmer*.[65]

Probably as energetic as any in working for Cobb's candidacy was Miss Lois P. Dowdle, editor of the *Progressive Farmer*'s Home Department and Cobb's journalistic colleague since the mid-1920s. A formidable individual, Miss Dowdle was herself widely known and respected. Educated at Shorter College, Cornell University, and the University of Georgia, she had been a country school teacher and agricultural extension worker in Georgia, rising to head girls' club work in that state. In 1925 she resigned to accept a fulltime position on the staff of the *Southern Ruralist*, and, like Cobb, she moved to the *Progressive Farmer* following the merger of those papers in 1930. Among numerous other distinctions, Miss Dowdle served a term as president of the Association of Southern Agricultural Workers, a rare honor for a woman and a testimonial to the esteem she enjoyed.[66]

Miss Dowdle undertook the responsibility for an extensive letter-writing campaign, asking for support for Cobb and urging her correspondents to write Franklin Roosevelt in his behalf. Farm journalists, agricultural scientists and teachers, businessmen, and politicians were contacted in large numbers. In some instances, Miss Dowdle was specific concerning the type of aid needed; in writing to Virginia P. Moore, a native Tennessean, Miss Dowdle suggested that Cordell Hull should be contacted and Cobb's Tennessee origins brought to his attention.[67] She pointed out to W. B. Cook, who at that juncture was a railroad development agent in Texas, that it might be helpful if some Texans could be located to mention Cobb to John N. Garner.[68] Miss Dowdle herself wrote Roosevelt, setting forth in considerable detail Cobb's career, his contributions to agriculture, and those facets of his character and personality that she believed would make him a great Secretary of Agriculture.[69]

Not all of Miss Dowdle's correspondents were willing to support

Cobb, but very few were openly hostile. Clifford V. Gregory, editor of the *Prairie Farmer*, wrote "that there might be some candidate from the Middle West which circumstances would make it necessary for me to support." E. K. Eastman of the *American Agriculturist* stated that he liked Cobb personally, but of course he favored Henry L. Morgenthau.[70] E. S. Bayard of the *Pennsylvania Farmer* wrote that he would be happy to see Cobb named Secretary of Agriculture, but he warned that one taking the post should be independently wealthy. According to Bayard, E. T. Meredith spent some thirty thousand dollars of his own money during his term of office.[71]

Still, there was widespread support of Cobb's candidacy. In Mississippi representatives of the agricultural extension service, state departments of education and agriculture, farm bureau, bankers' association, and cooperative marketing associations met and endorsed Cobb. The editor of the Jackson *Daily News* ran an editorial praising Cobb and calling for his selection.[72] Across the country, William A. Schoenfeld, dean of the college of agriculture in Oregon and one of Cobb's warmest friends on the Pacific Coast, wrote Roosevelt, saying that Cobb had the poise, tact, character, and knowledge of agriculture to make him a great Secretary. Farm organizations on the West Coast, Schoenfeld believed, would support Cobb.[73] H. H. Williamson, Cobb's old friend from Texas, reported that he had men "behind" Congressmen Dies, Rayburn, Sumners, Jones, and Kleberg, and Senators Sheppard and Connally and that he was in contact with Vice-President-elect Garner. T. M. Campbell, Negro extension worker in Alabama, wrote that he regarded Cobb "as the best and safest man in the South for that position." [74] From South Carolina Cobb's friends reported that Senator Smith was "hot in the collar against ex-Governors and millionaire gentlemen farmers" as Secretary of Agriculture, a sentiment that promised no harm to Cobb's cause. Senators George of Georgia and Harrison of Mississippi were reported to be friendly, and the latter indicated that he would personally call upon Roosevelt in Cobb's behalf.[75]

By the middle of November, barely two weeks after the election, the campaign was in full swing. The Southern Agricultural Outlook Conference, meeting in Atlanta, adopted resolutions supporting Cobb and dispatched a delegation to Roosevelt to press Cobb's case.[76] Strong organizations were at work in Mississippi, Louisiana, Texas, South Carolina, and Arkansas, and only slightly less vigorous efforts were under way in other southern states. Later, delegations from several of these states visited Roosevelt at Warm Springs and urged the appointment of their candidate. There was also extensive support for Cobb in the Middle West. Leading his forces there were John F. Cunningham and C. L. Christensen, deans of the colleges of agriculture in Ohio and Wisconsin, respectively. Farther west Dean William A. Schoenfeld of Oregon and R. W. Reynolds, development agent for the Milwaukee railroad, were busy. Among those individuals later to be prominent in the New Deal who were reported at times to be supporting Cobb were Milburn L. Wilson, although his loyalties were apparently divided, and Howard R. Tolley.[77]

A variety of organizations also endorsed Cobb. Included among these were the American Society of Agricultural Engineers, a group that was influenced by Dan Scoates and L. J. Fletcher of the Caterpillar Tractor Company, and the American Railway Development Association, the organization of railroad men with whom Cobb had enjoyed long and friendly relations. The Association of Southern Agricultural Workers officially supported Cobb and sent a delegation to Warm Springs. The president of the American Agricultural Editors' Association, John Case of the *Missouri Ruralist*, favored Cobb, as did Thomas L. Wheeler of the influential *Indiana Farmers' Guide*. Through its executive committee the Grange gave its blessing, and the Association of Land-Grant Colleges and Universities also favored the Tennessean.[78]

As the contest continued, promoters of the Cobb candidacy were convinced that their man had a good chance. If nothing else, justice to the South would give him the job since, according to their calculations, no southerner had ever served as Secretary of Agriculture. Admittedly, Henry L. Morgenthau had considerable support, not only in the East but elsewhere as well, but they could not believe that Roosevelt would appoint a fellow New Yorker to the post, since it appeared that James A. Farley of that state would be Postmaster General. Henry A. Wallace was recognized as a serious contender, but there was a feeling among Cobb's friends that the Iowan was not "big enough" for the job and that Roosevelt would never appoint a man of such strong Republican antecedents. Moreover, it was rumored that Wallace was an emotional man and that others found it difficult to work with him. Cobb, on the other hand, was described as an agreeable and cooperative but strong-willed individual who was neither narrow nor sectional, who knew the agricultural leaders throughout the country, and who was a thorough student of farm problems, not only in the South but nationally.[79]

The support for Cobb, his friends believed, was "about as strong as could possibly be secured by any person." A number of state legislatures adopted resolutions favoring him, a variety of businessmen gave their support, Roosevelt himself claimed Cobb as a friend, and rumors out of the President-elect's headquarters were at times very encouraging. Late in December, after a committee appointed by the Association of American Land-Grant Colleges and Universities had visited Roosevelt at Albany to urge Cobb's appointment, Dean Thomas P. Cooper of the Kentucky College of Agriculture reported that Cobb was second or at the worst third on Roosevelt's list.[80]

In the end these efforts were in vain. Two weeks before Roosevelt's inaugural, the usually well-informed *Kipinger Farm Letter* reported that Cobb was Roosevelt's choice. But apparently the President-elect had decided in December to appoint Wallace, although the Iowan did not receive the offer of the post until February 12.[81] Years later Cobb expressed the view that Roosevelt's decision was purely political,[82] and there appears to be no reason to question that opinion. Wallace had a famous name, he was a midwesterner, and his Republican antecedents, instead of being a handicap, were actually to his advantage. Clearly the Democratic Roosevelt, astute politician that he was, could do no better.

But if politics prevented Cobb from becoming Secretary of Agriculture, they did not prevent him from taking a high post in the Department of Agriculture. On May 12, 1933, during the famous Hundred Days, Congress passed the Agricultural Adjustment Act. That measure, destined to be one of the New Deal's most important, marked a significant turning point in American agricultural history; thereafter, government would assume a responsibility to maintain a reasonable level of well-being on the farm. It embodied the domestic allotment concept, and the control of cotton production would be one of the measure's major purposes.[83] A strong man, and one who knew the South and all of its problems, was needed to manage the cotton program. On May 22, 1933, influenced no doubt by Senator Ellison D. Smith and other leading southern politicians, Roosevelt named Cobb Chief, Cotton Production Section, Agricultural Adjustment Administration.[84] The Tennessee-born and Mississippi-educated farm leader was ready to undertake his most difficult and demanding task.

## NOTES TO CHAPTER VII

1. Wilson, "Agricultural Periodicals in the United States," Table I; *Printers' Ink*, Vol. 152 (September 11, 1930), 114; *Magnolia Farmer*, Vol. 5 (October, 1930), 16.

2. *Progressive Farmer* (Carolina-Virginia ed.), Vol. 45 (September 1–14, 1930), 816; J. Phil Campbell to Clarence Poe, July 23, 1932, Cobb Papers. Poe told his own story in his *My First 80 Years*.

3. *Progressive Farmer* (Carolina-Virginia ed.), Vol. 45 (September 1–14, 1930), 816–18. See Butler, Tait Butler, for a sketch of Butler's life.

4. *Progressive Farmer* (Carolina-Virginia ed.), Vol. 45 (September 1–14, 1930), 818; *Who's Who in America*, 1930–1931, pp. 1274, 1330; Poe, *My First 80 Years*, 101.

5. C. A. Cobb to D. C. Hull, May 12, 1922, Mississippi State University Alumni Association Files (Alumni Office, Mississippi State, Mississippi); *Mississippi A. and M. Alumnus*, Vol. 3 (May, 1923), 111–12; Starkville (Miss.), *News*, May 18, 1923.

6. *Louisiana Club and Extension News*, Vol. 2 (October–November, 1932), 1; C. A. Cobb to C. O. Moser, November 17, 1932; C. A. Cobb, An Educated Agricultural Public, Address before the Louisiana Teachers' Association, November 18, 1932, Cobb Papers.

7. Southern Cattlemen's Association, *Fifteenth Annual Meeting, January 10–12, 1927* (n.p., n.d.); Jackson *Daily News*, January 13, 1927, p. 13.

8. *Southern Ruralist*, Vol. 34 (August 15, 1927), 211; *Manufacturers Record*, Vol. 85 (January 17, 1924), 85; *Agricultural and Industrial Bulletin*, Vol. 6 (December, 1924), 4.

9. Cobb, "Contribution of the Press to Agriculture," 24–30; Cobb interviews. For a discussion of the launching of demonstration work in Texas, see Scott, *Agricultural Extension*, 210–12.

10. C. A. Cobb, "Relations between Farm Papers and Cooperative Papers," American Institute of Cooperation, *American Cooperation*, 1929 (Washington, 1930), 257–59.

11. C. A. Cobb, "The Future Promise of Farm Life," *Journal of Home Economics*, Vol. 24 (November, 1932), 974–75.

12. *Southern Ruralist*, Vol. 26 (February 1, 1920), 945; Vol. 28 (February 1, 1922), 438.

13. C. A. Cobb and others, "Report of the Resolutions Committee," Association of Southern Agricultural Workers, *Proceedings*, 1927 (n.p., n.d.), 12–13; *Manufacturers Record*, Vol. 91 (February 24, 1927), 120.

14. C. A. Cobb, "The World Situation with Regard to Cotton," Association of Southern Agricultural Workers, *Proceedings*, 1932 (n.p., n.d.), 6–9.

15. *Southern Ruralist*, Vol. 30 (March 1, 1924), 716; C. A. Cobb, A Friendly Message from Dixie, Address, Cobb Papers.

16. *Southern Ruralist*, Vol. 31 (March 15, 1925), 692-93.

17. *Mississippi A. and M. Alumnus*, Vol. 3 (May, 1923), 112; clipping from the New Orleans *State*, November 8, 1932, p. 2, in Cobb Papers.

18. Mississippi State University, Extension Service, Annual Narrative and Statistical Reports, January 1, 1921; *Southern Ruralist*, Vol. 27 (April 15, 1920), 105, Vol. 26 (February 1, 1920), 958; International Live Stock Exposition, *Review and Album*, 1922 (n.p., n.d.), 269.

19. G. L. Noble to J. E. Tanner, June 28, 1939, Mississippi Extension Service Records.

20. *Southern Ruralist*, Vol. 34 (May 15, 1927), 96; Vol. 27 (June 1, 1920), 217, 244; Reck, *4-H Story*, 207; C. A. Cobb to J. E. Tanner, July 18, 1939, Mississippi Extension Service Records; W. B. Cook to C. A. Cobb, October 25, 1968, Cobb Papers.

21. *Southern Ruralist*, Vol. 34 (May 15, 1927), 96; Duncan, *Straight Furrows*, 107; clipping from the *Constitution*, October 19, 1920, Cobb Papers.

22. Mississippi State University, Extension Service, Annual Narrative and Statistical Reports, January 1, 1921.

23. *Southern Ruralist*, Vol. 28 (July 1, 1921), 159; Vol. 28 (July 11, 1921), 165; Texas Agricultural Exention Service, *Four Who Won* (n.p., n.d.), 6–10.

24. *Southern Ruralist*, Vol. 28 (September 1, 1921), 231; Jack Turner to C. A. Cobb, June 6, 1970. Cobb Papers.

25. Reck, *4-H Story*, 208; *Southern Ruralist*, Vol. 28 (November 15, 1921), 335; Vol. 29 (July 15, 1922), 182.

26. Lois P. Dowdle to F. D. Roosevelt, October 29, 1932, Cobb Papers.

27. C. A. Cobb to R. V. Scott, February 10, 1971, Cobb Papers.

28. C. A. Cobb to Mrs. Mary Cobb, July 12, 1924, Cobb Papers; *Southern Ruralist*, Vol. 31 (July 1, 1924), 160; Vol. 31 (September 15, 1924), 245; Vol. 32 (August 15, 1925), 218; C. A. Cobb to Dave O. Thompson, May 28, 1956, Cobb to R. V. Scott, January 31, 1972, Charles E. Hughes to Diplomatic and Consular Officers, May 20, 1924, Cobb Papers.

29. *Southern Ruralist*, Vol. 32 (August 15, 1925), 218; Vol. 32 (October 15, 1925), 313, 334; C. A. Cobb to R. V. Scott, February 15, 1972, Cobb Papers.

30. *Southern Ruralist*, Vol. 34 (May 15, 1927), 89, 91; Vol. 34 (July 15, 1927), 172, 185; *Agricultural Development Bulletin*, Vol. 3 (April, 1927), 1, 15; *Ohio Farmer*, Vol. 159 (May 14, 1927), 636; Vol. 159 (June 4, 1927), 720; clipping from Houston *Chronicle*, March 23, 1927: C. A. Cobb to R. V. Scott, February 15, 1972, Cobb Papers.

31. *Southern Ruralist*, Vol. 36 (July 1, 1929), 8; C. A. Cobb, undated memo, Cobb Papers.

32. *Southern Ruralist*, Vol. 34 (May 15, 1927), 89, 91; *Agricultural Development Bulletin*, Vol. 3 (April, 1927), 1, 15; C. A. Cobb to R. V. Scott, February 10, 1971, February 15, 1972, Cobb Papers.

33. Lois P. Dowdle to F. D. Roosevelt, October 29, 1932, Cobb Papers; *Southern Ruralist*, Vol. 31 (March 1, 1925), 650–51; Vol. 33 (September 1, 1926), 242-43; Vol. 34 (March 15, 1928), 643.

34. United States Department of Agriculture, *Yearbook of Agriculture*, 1931, p.

45; *Louisiana Club and Extension News*, Vol. 2 (October–November, 1932), 1. For later development of this governmental office, see United States Department of Agriculture, *Yearbook of Agriculture*, 1964, pp. 392, 403, 409–11.

35. Cobb, "Contribution of the Press to Agriculture," 28; Cobb interviews.

36. Paul K. Conkin, *Tomorrow A New World: The New Deal Community Program* (Ithaca, 1959), 79.

37. Quoted in Richard S. Kirkendall, "L. C. Gray and the Supply of Agricultural Land," *Agricultural History*, Vol. 37 (October, 1963), 210.

38. C. A. Cobb, "The Coordination of State and Federal Efforts in the Development of a Land-Utilization Program," National Conference on Land Utilization, *Proceedings, November 19–21, 1931* (Washington, 1932), 103–106.

39. National Conference on Land Utilization, *Proceedings, November 19–21, 1931* (Washington, 1932), 240–49; L. C. Gray, "National Conference Recommends Program of Study and Action," United States Department of Agriculture, *Yearbook of Agriculture*, 1932, 461–62; *The Constitution*, May 23, 1933, pp. 1, 4.

40. United States Department of Agriculture, *Yearbook of Agriculture*, 1933, pp. 57–59; Lois P. Dowdle to F. D. Roosevelt, October 29, 1932, Cobb Papers.

41. Rexford G. Tugwell, "The Place of Government in a National Land Program," *Journal of Farm Economics*, Vol. 16 (January, 1934), 68; Richard S. Kirkendall, *Social Scientists and Farm Politics in the Age of Roosevelt* (Columbia, 1966), 39.

42. D. W. Watkins, "The Southern Agricultural Outlook Conference," *Journal of Farm Economics*, Vol. 13 (January, 1931), 160–62; "The Agricultural Outlook for the Southern States, 1930–1931," United States Department of Agriculture, *Miscellaneous Publication* 102 (Washington, 1930), 1; *The Constitution*, November 12, 1930, p. 5; November 14, 1930, p. 2; November 9, 1931, p. 5; November 12, 1932, p. 4; *Progressive Farmer and Southern Ruralist* (Georgia–Alabama ed.), Vol. 45 (December 15–31, 1930), 7; *Manufacturers Record*, Vol. 98 (December 11, 1930), 30.

43. Cobb, "World Situation with Regard to Cotton," 9; *Southern Ruralist*, Vol. 35 (January 1, 1929), 512.

44. Cobb, "Contribution of the Press to Agriculture," 27–29.

45. *Southern Ruralist*, Vol. 36 (July 15, 1929), 12; C. A. Cobb, A National Policy for Agriculture, Address before United States Chamber of Commerce, May 4, 1933, Cobb Papers.

46. *Southern Ruralist*, Vol. 28 (December 15, 1921), 374; Vol. 36 (March 15, 1930), 4.

47. *Southern Ruralist*, Vol. 28 (June 15, 1921), 135; Vol. 32 (April 15, 1926), 565, 600. The standard biography of the Kansas farm leader is Homer E. Socolofsky, *Arthur Capper: Publisher, Politician, and Philanthropist* (Lawrence, 1962).

48. *Southern Ruralist*, Vol. 28 (November 15, 1921), 330; Vol. 34 (April 15, 1927), 35; Vol. 36 (July 15, 1929), 12; Cobb, "Future Promise of Farm Life," 974–75.

49. *Southern Ruralist*, Vol. 33 (December 15, 1926), 417.

50. Clipping from Houston *Chronicle*, March 23, 1927, in Cobb papers.

51. *Southern Ruralist*, Vol. 33 (July 15, 1926), 174–75; Vol. 33 (December 15, 1926), 417.

52. *Southern Ruralist*, Vol. 33 (July 15, 1925), 174–75; Vol. 33 (February 1, 1927), 516; Vol. 33 (March 1, 1927), 584–85; Edward L. and Frederick H. Schapsmeier, *Henry A. Wallace of Iowa: The Agrarian Years, 1910–1940* (Ames, 1968), 102.

53. *Southern Ruralist*, Vol. 33 (March 15, 1927), 620; Murray R. Benedict, *Farm Policies of the United States, 1790–1950* (New York, 1953), 227–28.

54. *Southern Ruralist*, Vol. 35 (January 15, 1929), 546; Vol. 35 (March 15, 1929), 707. The Agricultural Marketing Act is conveniently discussed in Broadus Mitchell,

*Depression Decade: From New Era Through New Deal, 1929–1941* (New York, 1947), 69–72.

55. *Southern Ruralist*, Vol. 36 (July 1, 1929), 3. Cobb's views are quoted in *Rural America*, Vol. 7 (September, 1929), 9.

56. *Southern Ruralist*, Vol. 36 (October 15, 1929), 12–13.

57. *Southern Ruralist*, Vol. 36 (November 1, 1929), 3; Vol. 36 (November 15, 1929), 3; Vol. 36 (December 15, 1929), 12.

58. Clipping from New Orleans *State*, November 8, 1932, Cobb Papers; William L. Wilson, "Southeast Seeks Representation on Federal Farm Board," *Manufacturers Record*, Vol. 100 (July 30, 1931), 30–31.

59. Lois P. Dowdle to Walter F. George, February 12, 1933; J. Phil Campbell to Clarence Poe, July 23, 1932, Cobb Papers; Robert Moton to Herbert Hoover, January 11, 1932, Robert R. Moton Papers (Hollis Burke Frissell Library, Tuskegee Institute, Tuskegee, Alabama).

60. *Southern Ruralist*, Vol. 36 (February 1, 1930), 3; *Manufacturers Record*, Vol. 97 (February 13, 1930), 69; *Progressive Farmer and Southern Ruralist*, (Georgia–Alabama ed.), Vol. 46 (February 15–28, 1931), 6.

61. C. A. Cobb, A National Policy for Agriculture, Address before United States Chamber of Commerce, May 4, 1932, Cobb Papers; Cobb, "World Situation with Regard to Cotton," 9.

62. J. W. Bradley to William A. Schoenfeld, January 24, 1933, Cobb Papers. For a discussion of the various proposals for farm relief under consideration in 1932, see William R. Johnson, "National Farm Organizations and the Reshaping of Agricultural Policy in 1932," *Agricultural History*, Vol. 37 (January, 1963), 35–42; William D. Rowley, "M. L. Wilson: 'Believer' in the Domestic Allotment," *Agricultural History*, Vol. 43 (April, 1969), 277–87.

63. J. Phil Campbell to Clarence Poe, July 23, 1932, Cobb Papers.

64. *The Constitution*, November 10, 1932, p. 1.

65. Schapsmeier, *Wallace*, 160–61; Bernard Sternsher, *Rexford Tugwell and the New Deal* (New Brunswick, 1964), 87–88; Butler, Tait Butler, 24–25.

66. Personnel Data, Mississippi Extension Service Records; clippings from *Atlanta Journal*, February 5, 1932, Lois P. Dowdle Cobb Papers (Mississippi State University Library).

67. Lois P. Dowdle to John Thompson, John E. Pickett, George Slocum, Virginia P. Moore, H. R. Tolley, November 9, 1932; Connie J. Bonslagel to Huey P. Long, January 6, 1933, Cobb Papers.

68. Lois P. Dowdle to W. B. Cook, November 9, 1932, Cobb Papers.

69. Lois P. Dowdle to F. D. Roosevelt, October 29, 1932, Cobb Papers.

70. Clifford V. Gregory to Lois P. Dowdle, November 7, 1932; E. K. Eastman to Lois P. Dowdle, November 11, 1932, Cobb Papers.

71. E. S. Bayard to Lois P. Dowdle, November 11, 1932, Cobb Papers.

72. Fred J. Hurst to Lois P. Dowdle, n.d., Cobb Papers; Jackson *Daily News*, November 12, 1932, p. 6.

73. W. A. Schoenfeld to F. D. Roosevelt, November 9, 1932, Schoenfeld to Cobb, January 12, 1933, Cobb Papers.

74. H. H. Williamson to Cobb, November 10, 1932, T. M. Campbell to R. R. Moton, November 12, 1932, Cobb Papers.

75. H. E. Savely to Cobb, November 13, 1932, Cobb Papers.

76. Lois P. Dowdle to Jeanette Rankin, November 9, 1932, Cobb Papers.

77. Dan Scoates to Lois P. Dowdle, November 14, 1932; Cobb to C. O. Moser, November 17, 1932, John F. Cunningham to John Pickett, November 22, 1932, clipping from Jackson *Daily News*, Cobb Papers.

78. C. A. Cobb to C. O. Moser, November 17, 1932; Cobb to W. A. Schoenfeld,

December 7, 1932, F. J. Tabor to Cobb, January 18, 1933, Cobb Papers.

79. T. E. Brown to F. D. Roosevelt, January 21, 1933; Lois P. Dowdle to J. Phil Campbell, January 9, 1933; H. C. Booker to Charles Jackson, December 10, 1932, Cobb Papers; John M. Blum (ed.), *From the Morgenthau Diaries* (3 vols.; Boston, 1959–1967), I, 30–31.

80. Lois P. Dowdle to Paul W. Chapman, December 3, 1932; C. A. Cobb to C. G. Smith, December 15, 1932; Lois P. Dowdle to J. Phil Campbell, January 9, 1933, Cobb Papers.

81. Russell Lord, *The Wallaces of Iowa* (Boston, 1947), 324; Schapsmeier, *Wallace*, 161; Raymond Moley, *The First New Deal* (New York, 1966), 251–52.

82. Cobb interviews.

83. Mitchell, *Depression Decade*, 186–88.

84. New York *Times*, May 23, 1933, p. 14; *The Constitution*, May 23, 1933, pp. 1. 4; *Progressive Farmer*, Vol. 48 (July, 1933), 3.

# CHAPTER VIII

# "To Put Agriculture on a Paying Basis" The New Deal Years, 1933-1937

ARRIVING in Washington late in May, 1933, Cully A. Cobb was making his way toward Union Station's central terminal when he was recognized by a reporter assigned to catch new federal appointees as they arrived in the Capital. In a manner that Cobb would encounter many times during the next four years, the newsman greeted him with a barrage of questions. Quite possibly the interviewer doubted the ability of this Georgia farm editor to work with the men in Washington, and perhaps he wanted to provoke Cobb into a rash statement that would make attractive copy. But refusing to be rattled, Cobb ended the interview by stating flatly that his only job and his only interest was to help put American agriculture on a paying basis.[1] *

That first interview said much of Cobb and of his record with the Agricultural Adjustment Administration. His view of the farm problem was simple, clear-cut, and, unlike those of some of his new associates, completely unclouded by questions that transcended economic considerations. To Cobb the issue was obvious: American farmers were mired in the worst depression in history, and the job at hand was to reverse that situation in the shortest possible time. If there were social injustices or other problems in agriculture, they were not of immediate concern to him.

That agriculture was in desperate straits in the spring of 1933 was obvious to all. The 1920s had not been a prosperous decade for farmers; the Great Crash of 1929 had simply caused a sharp deterioration in an already bad situation. Overproduction and underconsumption of agricultural commodities were commonly cited as ma-

* Notes appear at end of each chapter.

Cobb at his desk in the Department of Agriculture, 1933.

jor causes of rural problems; but individual farmers, faced with declining prices but fixed obligations, had no recourse except to increase production and hope for the best. As a result, parity, a statistical measure which compared a farmer's buying power with that of the economy as a whole, continued to drop. By 1932 it had fallen to fifty-eight, indicating that rural dwellers had less than three-fifths of the buying power that they had enjoyed twenty years earlier.[2]

Cotton farmers and the South as a whole were in a particularly difficult position in the spring of 1933. Gross farm income from cotton and cottonseed had fallen from $1.5 billion in 1928 to $464 million in 1932, the lowest figure in thirty years. While the coming of the Great Depression had played a role, this disastrous drop was caused in large measure by a 50 percent increase in cotton acreage between 1921 and 1926 and by a decline in the late 1920s in foreign consumption of American cotton. The 1931 crop was a giant one, amounting to 17 million bales. On August 1, 1932, the carryover was 12.9 million bales, nearly a year's supply under even normal conditions. The end result was a dramatic fall in the price of cotton and a growing disparity between prices received and prices paid by cotton farmers. In June, 1932, cotton sold for 37 percent of the average price for the 1910–1914 period; and even with a relatively short crop of 13 million bales in 1932, the price in February, 1933, was only 44 percent of the prewar average.[3]

A number of factors peculiar to the Deep South complicated further the cotton situation. That area produced some 80 percent of the nation's cotton; no other large section of the country was as dependent upon a single crop. As a result, the collapse in cotton prices produced a dramatic effect upon merchants, professional people, and manufacturers of commodities sold to farm people. The matter of race was an ever-present problem, and closely intertwined with it was the tenant system, an arrangement on the land that was unknown outside the South. There was no question that with unscrupulous landlords sharecropping could be cruel and oppressive; it was equally true that in a very real sense the traditional sharecropper was not a farmer but rather a farm laborer. In any event, few southerners were in a position to grow cotton on a large scale without the tenant system. Finally, there was the traditional southern resistance to change and the section's deep suspicion of outside influence. Even in the middle of a death struggle with its economy, the South was not prepared to accept anything that resembled a social revolution, especially if change were proposed by those whose contacts with southern realities were superficial.[4]

In the course of his campaign for the presidency, Franklin D. Roosevelt made known his awareness of and concern for the problems of rural America. His election, it came to be understood, would bring changes. Roosevelt's answer to the farm problem was not spelled out, but the rural vote in November indicated that farmers had faith in the New York governor's ability and good will. Meanwhile, for a decade, such agricultural economists and farm leaders as Milburn L. Wilson, Charles J. Brand, Chester C. Davis, and George N. Peek had been studying and formulating a variety of approaches to the dilemma of farm prices. After the failure of the McNary-Haugen bills in the 1920s and after Herbert Hoover's Agricultural Marketing Act had demonstrated its ineffectiveness, the idea of governmental control of farm output gained converts among farmers, economists, and political leaders. Apparently, Roosevelt adopted the domestic allotment plan in principle on the eve of his nomination, but his position remained flexible, and it was not until March, 1933, that final outlines of the Administration plan were hammered out.[5]

The end result was the enactment on May 12, 1933, of the Agricultural Adjustment Act. To administer the new law, Roosevelt established the Agricultural Adjustment Administration (AAA) and placed it under the direct supervision of the Secretary of Agriculture. The act consisted of a conglomeration of old ideas mixed with a goodly portion of new approaches. Its basic purpose was to raise gradually the purchasing power of farmers to parity or, stated differently, to restore the buying power that farmers had enjoyed during a base period, August, 1909–July, 1914. In practice, the AAA used three general methods to reach its goal. First, producers of so-called basic commodities, including cotton, were asked to sign voluntary agreements to limit production. Cotton growers who did so were in the fall of 1933 made eligible for nonrecourse, stabilization loans from the Commodity Credit Corporation, an agency established for that purpose. Secondly, the government provided subsidy payments of different kinds to cooperating farmers, funds for the purpose being raised by a tax levied on prime processors of the given commodities. Finally, the AAA promoted the organization of those who handled farm products and exempted resulting associations from the antitrust laws in an effort to achieve more orderly marketing.[6]

The organization of the Agricultural Adjustment Administration was complex, and it underwent changes during the years that Cobb served in Washington. At the outset, immediately below the Administrator and reporting to him were six divisions: Consumers' Counsel, Information and Publicity, Production, Processing and Marketing, Finance, and General Counsel. The first division heads, and in the same order, were Frederick C. Howe, Alfred D. Stedman, Chester C. Davis, William I. Westervelt, Oscar Johnston, and Jerome N. Frank. Beneath these divisions and reporting to the head of Production and the head of Processing and Marketing were a number of subdivisions or sections responsible for specific farm commodities. The most important of these were those for corn and hogs, wheat, and cotton.[7]

The first Administrator of the AAA was George N. Peek, a seasoned veteran of the struggle for agricultural reform. Given a position of authority, however, he proved to be inflexible and soon found himself in conflict with Rexford G. Tugwell, Assistant Secretary and later Undersecretary of the Department of Agriculture. Peek resigned in December, 1933, and was succeeded by Chester C. Davis, whose experience and wide contacts with different groups in agriculture made him a logical choice for the post.[8]

The AAA proved to be a complex mechanism whose operation was complicated by constant shifting of responsibilities and personnel and by substantial usurpation of authority by officials within its structure. Because both Henry A. Wallace and Peek wanted to avoid building a new, giant bureaucracy, there was an effort to minimize the staff and to coordinate the functions of the six divisions in order that they might more effectively aid the work of the commodity divisions. Wallace also ordered that insofar as possible units of the AAA utilize the talents of existing agencies of the Department of Agriculture, such as the Bureau of Agricultural Economics, so that duplication of effort might be minimized.[9]

On paper Wallace's organizational structure had much to recommend it, providing as it did for a streamlined staff that hopefully would collectively plan and administer the overall program. But in practice the results were often less than ideal. The diffusion of authority required a close working relationship among all units of the organization. Harmony did not always prevail. Ordinary human jealousies, the understandable desire of men to protect their spheres from encroachment by others, and the development of an idealogical split within the AAA tended to make difficult the achievement of the desired coordination.

One result was that the heads of the commodity subdivisions tended to become powerful men in the AAA.[10] Given the nature of the organization and the lack of clear lines of authority, the stronger of them soon learned that they could assume almost complete responsibility for implementing the Agricultural Adjustment Act insofar as it pertained to their commodities. After all, the commodity chiefs pointed out, they were experts in their special areas and were best equipped to manage their programs. But such an attitude, given the other sources of friction within the AAA, made the agency ripe for disruptive controversies.

Cobb's appointment on May 22 as chief of the cotton subdivision was a completely understandable one. He was a southerner, a fact of life that the position demanded, and he was well known throughout the South and among a wide range of farm leaders across the nation. His contacts with the land-grant colleges and with the agricultural extension service, two groups that would play a major role in agricultural adjustment, were of long standing. Cobb was also well known among the various professional and other organizations related to the cotton industry. Perhaps even more important were the political realities. The unsuccessful effort to obtain the position of Secretary of Agriculture for Cobb had shown that the Georgia farm editor had powerful friends. Moreover, Cobb knew and was respected by many of the prominent southern senators and congressmen, including several congressional committee chairmen, without whose support very little legislation could be enacted. No doubt both Roosevelt and Wallace were fully aware of the political ramifications of the situation. Finally, Cobb had an appealing perspective; his practicality might balance the idealism of some of his associates.[11]

Although Cobb's view of his task as he arrived in Washington was clear and easily stated, his personal philosophy was more complex. Cobb later stated that he took up his duties with a deep sense of patriotism. His country was in trouble, and he hoped that his expertise might be useful in finding answers to the problems that plagued farming. His sympathy for the farmer was sincere, since he had known rural poverty himself, but unlike some of his colleagues he knew that southern agriculture did not consist simply of two groups, plantation owners and sharecroppers. His greatest concern was always for that large, if often ignored, number of small landowners who, like his father and like a majority of the subscribers to the *Southern Ruralist* a decade earlier, worked all or most of their own land. Finally, although before 1933 Cobb had reconciled himself to the need for temporary government-implemented production controls in agriculture, he was a firm exponent of the free enterprise system, believing it to be the source of America's greatest strength. His fear in 1933 was that, with the country's economy in turmoil, the nation could turn to ill-founded ideologies. Specifically, he was convinced that there was no small danger that communism could ride in on the coattails of chaos and misguided solutions.[12]

To his tasks as head of the Cotton Section Cobb brought certain characteristics and beliefs that shaped his manner of managing his office. Cobb believed he had a moral obligation to get on with the job at hand and to do so with as much efficiency and as little waste of public funds as possible. When bureaucracy interfered with what he conceived to be the efficiency of his office, he had no misgivings about going to higher authority, to powerful figures in Congress, or to the public. Ordinary operating procedures, he thought, should be expedited and useless steps, even if legally proper, should be eliminated. For example, Cobb saw no reason to submit countless minor questions to the office of the General Counsel when common sense and practicality had already dictated the decision. Further, Cobb had no faith in the ability of the bureaucracy to handle the details of every issue that might arise. Extenuating circumstances and unique local conditions always existed, he thought, and because of them matters would be best handled if local control were maximized.

When Cobb arrived in Washington to take his post, the basic outlines of the program to be undertaken had been worked out, but in hammering together the "nuts and bolts" of the first cotton program he played a not insignificant role. In addition to providing his associates with a veteran's views on the cotton situation, he took a firm and decisive stand on the issue of the field force to be used in implementing the program.[13]

An effort of the magnitude envisioned by the Agricultural Adjustment Act would obviously require a sizable number of men on the ground. When it was suggested that personnel of the agricultural extension service might be utilized for the purpose, some of Henry A. Wallace's closest advisors objected, contending that county agents and their superiors were too closely connected with the American Farm Bureau Federation and too conservative and perhaps too limited in their outlook to give the program the fresh, enthusiastic support that it needed. Rexford G. Tugwell, for example, was reported to have said that he did not have "a damned bit of confidence in any" of the state directors of the extension service;[14] presumably, his view of the ordinary county agent was on a par.

Cobb, on the other hand, vigorously defended the extension service and argued that its use in this new role was essential if the crop reduction program were to have a chance of success. Cobb's loyalty to the extension service and to the land-grant colleges with which it was associated was understandable, of course, given his long contact with them. But his reasoning on this issue went deeper than mere sentiment. Cobb knew the extension service's reputation among southern farmers, and he was convinced that, given the nature of southerners, only men of established stature in their communities working with local participation could get the necessary cooperation. Under the best of circumstances, the government's program would meet a certain amount of reluctance and suspicion, attitudes that county agents would be best able to overcome. Moreover, there was the urgent need for speed. With summer just a few days away and with cotton growing nicely, it was imperative that the program be launched immediately. Since the extension service had an organizational structure that reached into a majority of counties, it seemed ridiculous to Cobb to talk of establishing a new hierarchy. Finally, Cobb opposed the idea of a new federal force on the grounds that, as he later recalled, the entire plan espoused by Tugwell and his supporters seemed suggestive of a program for permanent government management of agriculture. In the end, Cobb was to prevail. Years later, an elder statesman in agriculture would write, "I have always felt that by his determined stand . . . Cobb did both the Colleges and the A.A.A. a very great service." [15]

Cobb's victory meant that the field work would be handled through the state extension offices located on agricultural college campuses and supervised on the local level by county agents. Frequently, these men enlisted the aid of vocational agriculture teachers from the public schools.

Keys to the success or failure of the entire program were the county and community committees. These groups, either chosen by the county agents or elected by participants in the program, evaluated their neighbor's production records and made allotment decisions. Later, they were given the additional responsibility of checking on compliance with regulations. State boards and the Washington office of the AAA were administrative centers and appeal agencies for farmers who had complaints.[16]

Cobb was an avid defender of the committee system. It squared well with his idea of local control. Furthermore, he saw the committee arrangement as a means of enlisting community leaders in the program, securing their compliance, and through them the support of their neighbors. While some critics would denounce the committees and contend that too often they represented only one stratum of the agricultural population, Cobb recalled his experiences twenty years earlier with the corn clubs in Mississippi and concluded that no program could succeed in the countryside unless it involved and was accepted by the local rural leadership. If such leaders were fair men, he reasoned, the program would be fair. If they were not, no program could function without an army of federal supervisors and enforcers.

During discussions concerning the establishment of the committees, Cobb stressed the necessity of doing as much as possible to protect the interests of small farmers and others at the lower end of the economic and social scale. Efforts should be made, he contended, to include responsible small farmers and tenants on the committees. Unfortunately, in practice results were often less than satisfactory. Factors intangible and difficult to define came to the surface, including legal considerations, the lack of organizational experience among small farmers, and perhaps most frustrating, a discouraging lack of community and cooperative spirit among poorer rural dwellers.[17]

Regardless of a real concern for middle-sized and smaller producers of cotton, Cobb and his superiors in the AAA recognized that the program of crop reduction would have no chance of success unless the great planters were induced to cooperate. Not only did they produce a considerable portion of the total output of cotton, but the involvement of large owners would inevitably increase the acceptability of the program. Accordingly, to cotton growers the AAA offered two alternatives, a cash-payment and a cash-and-option plan. Under the first plan, a farmer received a cash payment for those acres that he agreed to take out of production. If he had resources with which to speculate, a tradition in the South among men of means, a grower could take part of his benefit in cash and receive in addition an option to government surplus cotton at six cents a pound. He could later sell his option cotton at the current market price through the secretary of agriculture.[18]

After these and other plans had been worked out, the Cotton Section was ready to turn to its first task, the arranging of contracts with those farmers who agreed to cooperate. The job was complicated by the need to destroy a portion of the growing crop, a shocking proposal to many Americans. Moreover, time was of the essence. The enactment of the Agricultural Adjustment Act and the working out of details had consumed more than three months. Across the South cotton was blooming, and in southern Texas harvest was not far in the future.

The task was largely educational in nature. Farmers had to be contacted and convinced that it was to their advantage to destroy a crop in which they had already invested time and money. The first step was to arrange a series of state and regional meetings with agricultural leaders and officials of related industries to explain the program to those having substantial interests in different phases of the cotton business and to obtain their pledges of support. Simultaneously, the Cotton Section held conferences with extension service personnel to make certain that those who would do much of the field work both understood and approved of the program. Some extension people, in fact, had let it be known that they would find it difficult to reconcile destruction of crops with the work to which they had previously devoted their time.[19]

In both types of meetings, Cobb played a major role. Probably few people in the Department of Agriculture had greater rapport with such divergent groups as businessmen, leading farmers, and extension personnel; Cobb spent no little time talking with them, discussing the program, and seeking their advice while generating enthusiasm for it. As Cobb told a group of agricultural leaders attending a cotton conference in Washington in June, 1933, "You . . . have been asked to come here today and give us the benefits of such suggestions and recommendations as in your judgment will be helpful in formulating plans and policies to guide those of us in charge of cotton administration in carrying out the provisions of the Agricultural Adjustment Act." [20] Certainly in Cobb's mind his time was well spent, since the meetings afforded him excellent opportunities to establish direct contact with some of the types of leadership whose support he knew was absolutely essential.[21]

By the last week of June the field force was considered sufficiently well informed to take the message to the mass of cotton farmers. County agents and members of county committees held county and community meetings across the South, explaining the program and arguing that farmers would benefit by cooperating. According to reports, few growers expressed open hostility to the program, perhaps in part because of timidity or bewilderment; but they wanted clarification on such matters as the division of payments between interested parties, the uses to which land could be put, and the differences between the alternatives offered them.

Having worked with farmers for years, Cobb was fully aware of the problems county agents and the committeemen faced. He was also deeply appreciative of their efforts. As he later wrote to Texas extension personnel, "You have been in the front lines and continuously under fire . . . and have my admiration and sincere appreciation for the fine and efficient way you have carried on." [22]

Cobb's suggestions to those who conducted the local meetings reflected both his high hopes for the success of the program and his understanding of the nature of the ordinary southern farmer.

Having participated in a multitude of rural meetings himself, he knew the strengths and weaknesses of the typical cotton producer. He urged county agents to make every effort to develop faith among farmers that the program would succeed. Without that conviction, he felt, explanation of details would be useless. The country churches, black and white, he said, were a medium through which farmers might be reached. Vocational agriculture teachers might be able to influence fathers through their sons. Negro members of the extension service should be used, and without making a major issue of the matter Cobb pointed out that there could be no racial discrimination in the program.[23]

Thus the monumental task began. In the field, or on the "firing line" as Cobb referred to it, county agents, aided by 247 emergency agents appointed for the purpose and 20,000 local leaders, asked farmers to sign offers to plow up from 25 to 50 percent of their growing crop. Some farmers signed on the spot, but most needed time to consider the matter. Many appeared later at their county agent's offices, but others had to be visited in their homes by committee members. After offers and statements of fact were checked locally, they were forwarded to Washington.

Problems enough there were, stemming in the main from ordinary misunderstandings and the simple enormity of the task. From his Washington office, Cobb urged the field workers to push on with the task as rapidly as possible while he tried to minimize bureaucratic problems. For example, when reports from the field indicated that the sign-up was falling behind schedule because the government printing office was unable to keep up with the demand for forms, he authorized the state extension directors to make their own printing arrangements with private firms.[24]

While the work progressed in the field, Cobb was assembling a clerical staff in Washington. During the last days in June and the first week in July, some 1,400 clerks were employed and instructed in their tasks. Soon the offers from farmers began to pour in. After the offers were approved by Cobb's office, farmers were directed to proceed with the destruction of their cotton. Local committees verified the results, and Cobb's office then issued final contracts, and the disbursing office mailed out the checks to the county agents who distributed them. On July 28, at a ceremony at the White House, President Roosevelt handed the first check to William E. Morris, a tenant farmer from Nueces County, Texas. By August 1, Cobb's office, working three shifts a day, was processing over sixty thousand offers in a twenty-four hour period, but still the task was so great that mailing of checks lagged. In September farmers began to complain, claiming that the government had failed in its promise that payments would be in their hands earlier than they could have expected to harvest their cotton. It was this agitation, combined with the desire to stabilize cotton prices, that induced the administration to establish the Commodity Credit Corporation to make ten-cent-a-pound nonrecourse loans on cotton grown in 1933 to those producers who agreed to cooperate with the government's soon-to-be-announced cotton reduction program for 1934–1935.[25]

The plow-up program was a crucial first test for the concept of production control and for the AAA as a whole. The idea of deliberate destruction of food and fiber during times of privation and misery was hard for many Americans to understand and accept. In fact, there is little doubt that many ordinary farmers who cooperated completely with the government never did fully grasp the significance of their participation. As Cobb had suggested at the outset, these people simply put their faith in those local leaders who assured them that by plowing under cotton they were contributing to their future and that of the cotton industry as a whole.[26]

As AAA officials gathered data to evaluate the plow-up program, it became evident that indeed the effort had succeeded. Some 73 percent of all cotton land had been placed under contract with the government. In all, 10.5 million acres of cotton had been destroyed. Original objectives had called for almost that exact figure. Figuring an average yield of 190 pounds per acre, the destroyed acreage represented almost four million bales of cotton that did not reach an already glutted market. At least for a time, the price of cotton also suggested that the plow-up had achieved its goal. From the disastrous six cents a pound level prevailing in the spring, the price climbed to around ten cents. Although economists had hoped for a higher figure, the increase was great enough to be considered highly encouraging. Moreover, the program had pumped directly

President Franklin D. Roosevelt delivering the first check in the 1933 cotton plow-up campaign to William E. Morris, tenant farmer from Nueces County, Texas, July 26, 1933, roughly two months after the campaign was launched. Behind the President, from left to right, are Representative Marvin M. Jones of Texas, Cobb, and E. R. Eudaly, AAA Administrator for Texas.

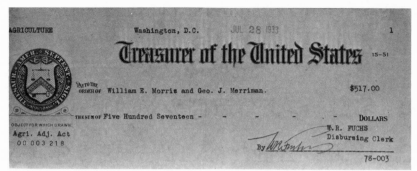

First check dispensed in the 1933 cotton plow-up campaign. It was also the first machine written check issued by the federal government.

$112 million in benefit payments into the southern economy.[27]

Other measures also showed that the plow-up had had beneficial effects. Quite obviously, aggregate farm income in the Cotton Belt went up. Throughout the South in the fall and winter of 1933–1934 business reported gains; in fact, by some indicators the southern states seemed to be doing better than much of the remainder of the country. New car registrations and sales of fertilizer and work animals showed substantial jumps. Department store sales in the Sixth Federal Reserve District were up 23 percent over the previous year and the Atlanta Federal Reserve District Bank pointed to average daily deposits that surged upward by 52 percent, while the nation as a whole had only a 34 percent gain. No one would contend, of course, that these hopeful signs could be attributed solely to the effects of the plow-up, but on the other hand few would deny that destruction of a portion of the growing crop had had a beneficial effect upon them.[28]

Perhaps even more important was the effect that the plow-up had on other areas of the New Deal's program in agriculture. Cobb's Cotton Section was the first major segment of the AAA to produce sizable benefits for farmers; the success of the plow-up could hardly have failed to encourage those who administered and participated in other programs. In fact, at a news conference, President Roosevelt remarked that the success of the plow-up guaranteed the success of the AAA program throughout the country. In addition, the cotton plow-up had an impact upon the corn and hog program. By reducing the output of cottonseed oil, the government had enlarged the market for pork fat, thereby improving the position of hog producers.[29]

Regardless of whatever success the plow-up had achieved, experts knew that the 1933 program represented no more than a first step toward a solution of cotton's problems. The achievement of parity was still far in the future, and the world supply of cotton remained oppressively large. Consequently, Cobb and his superiors resolved to implement a more comprehensive cotton control program in the 1934 and 1935 crop years. Participation in the pioneer program in 1933 had been voluntary, although admittedly pressure of one nature or the other had induced some men to cooperate who otherwise would have abstained; but AAA men believed that compulsory restrictions on output were now necessary. This decision stemmed from the realization that farmers tended to take their worst land out of production and to fertilize heavily the remainder and that, if supply and demand were to be brought into something approaching the desired balance, production of noncooperating farmers would have to be controlled. Accordingly, in April, 1934, Congress passed the Bankhead Cotton Control Act. By the terms of that measure, cotton ginned by a farmer in excess of his allotment would be taxed at the rate of 50 percent of the average market price. Administration of the new law was delegated to Cobb's office.[30]

The goal of the new program was to cut cotton acreage from the anticipated 42 million acres to 25 million acres in 1934 and to 31 million acres the next year. Experts figured that production would be slashed by 6 million bales in 1934. For land taken out of production, or "rented" to the government, farmers received two payments, a cash rental fee and a parity payment. The former was computed by multiplying the average yield in pounds per acre over the years 1928–1932 by 3½ cents, the amount not to exceed $18 an acre. This sum was payable in two installments, in the spring and fall. A parity payment of not less than 1 cent a pound would be paid in December on that cotton grown on the allotment acreage, or 40 percent of the farmer's base acreage.[31]

Cobb's Cotton Section used essentially the same procedures and machinery to implement and administer the new acreage control program as it had used during the plow-up. Additional staff was added in Washington and elsewhere to compensate for heavier work loads and new responsibilities, but the general functions of the state extension offices, county agents, and county and local committees and their relationships to the central office remained unchanged. Again Cobb insisted that great attention be devoted to an educational campaign to enlighten farmers concerning the changes in the program, and he participated actively in the effort.[32]

At year's end the results of the 1934 program were deemed reasonably satisfactory. Anticipating an unrestricted yield of 13 to 18 million bales from 42 million acres, the Cotton Section had hoped to reduce production to 9 million bales from 25 million acres. When final figures were available, even the Cotton Section was pleasantly surprised. The yield for the year was slightly over 9¼ million bales, a decrease of almost 3¼ million bales from the output of 1933 and far below the production that would have been certain in the absence of restrictive controls. Acreage had been cut from 42 million to 27 million. Benefits to cotton farmers as a whole also indicated reasonable success. By December the average price of cotton was over twelve cents a pound, up a solid two cents from 1933. In addition, farmers had received over $115 million in government payments.[33]

Regardless of such statistical measures of success, it was the 1934–1935 program that brought to a head a conflict that had existed in the Department of Agriculture from the outset. It has become customary to label the two groups as conservatives or agrarians and liberals. The former included in the main men who had served for years in the Department of Agriculture and those newcomers like Cobb who came from a farm, land-grant college, and extension service background. On the other hand, the liberals, "boys with their hair ablaze"[34] as one critic labeled them, tended to be recent arrivals in Washington and generally were products of eastern universities and of urban environments. Given that mixture, conflict was probably inevitable. To the liberals, the conservatives were rural rustics and often reactionary southerners besides; the conservatives saw many liberals as conceited easterners whose arrogance was exceeded only by their ignorance of the realities of farming. There was, of course, some truth on both sides. The agrarians were conservative, and it was certainly true that few of the liberals had much acquaintance with cranky Farmalls or the proper procedures for birthing a litter of pigs. At any rate, the conservatives decided rather early that they could learn little from men who sought to protect the rights of "macaroni growers." [35]

Bickering between the groups began almost as soon as the Roosevelt administration took office and continued with growing intensity until the issue was finally settled in 1935. Cobb's first impression of the liberals was a mixed one. He could not object to their zeal or to their conviction that the farmer was one of America's forgotten men. On the other hand, he was thoroughly convinced that, with their urban and eastern backgrounds, their knowledge of the practicalities of at least southern agriculture could only be limited. Moreover, as time passed, he became increasingly suspicious of the ideologies voiced by some of them.[36]

The leader of the Department of Agriculture liberals was Rexford G. Tugwell, a former Columbia University professor and a favorite of President and Mrs. Roosevelt and of Secretary of Agriculture Henry A. Wallace. Tugwell's appointment as Assistant Secretary of Agriculture was the first in a governmental career that spanned three decades and included service in a diversity of areas. Tugwell's interests were as varied as his service record. He was deeply interested in the process of change in a society and was equally intrigued by administrative challenges. A fascinating but brusque personality, Tugwell enjoyed toying with new ideas. Once in a position of authority in government, he tended to experiment with his theories.[37]

Given this lofty idealism, Tugwell and Secretary Wallace were intellectually congenial. At the same time, with their agrarian background and long acquaintance through agricultural journalism, Cobb and Wallace were able to maintain a satisfactory working relationship. But the vast differences in cultural and educational background of Tugwell and Cobb, coupled with Tugwell's inflexible personality, soon led to clashes and mutual dislike between the two men. Cobb fervently believed that the American system of government was the ideal one and that the economy needed only adjustment of the machinery. Tugwell, on the other hand, saw a multitude of inequities and was prepared to accept sweeping changes in order to rectify the situation. Often his solutions detoured into areas that Cobb simply could not accept. In Cobb's mind, it became increasingly clear that Tugwell, if allowed to institute his ill-founded and patently dangerous schemes, could do great harm not only to agriculture but also to the country as a whole.[38]

The General Counsel of the Agricultural Adjustment Administration was Jerome N. Frank, a brilliant legal mind who, like Tugwell, became an inspirational leader of the liberal group. Frank was recommended for the post by Harvard University's prestigious Felix Frankfurter. To aid him in his labors, Frank brought into the Department of Agriculture a group of young, alert, and vigorous lawyers, many of whom would gain national reputations later. Among the Frank recruits were Abe Fortas, Alger Hiss, Gardner Jackson, Lee Pressman, John Abt, and Margaret B. Bennett. These young attorneys, in many ways the epitome of the zeal that characterized the New Deal, went to work with great zest. As a result, the office of the General Counsel soon acquired a reputation for favoring dramatic change rather than a sober, considered approach to the problems at hand.[39]

While he usually found Tugwell to be objectionable, Cobb appreciated and admired the intellect of Jerome Frank. Frank and Cobb were never close friends, but Cobb found Frank's quick mind much more tolerable than the abrasive attitude of Tugwell. The law had always interested Cobb, and at the outset he and Frank had many friendly exchanges of opinion on the subject. As time went on, however, it became evident to Cobb that Frank was dominated by Tugwell and the working relationship between Cobb and Frank soon deteriorated to bitter feelings.[40]

The innovations of the New Deal generated a multitude of criticisms, and probably the Agricultural Adjustment Administration had more than its share. Beginning with the whole concept of government-sponsored production controls, the critics of the AAA moved on to specifics as the 1933 program got under way. According to these observers, there were numerous inequities in the arrangements, needless delays in the mailing of checks, and an assortmont of intra- and inter-agency feuds that worked hardships on various groups and generally handicapped proceedings. The AAA itself recognized that many of these criticisms were valid. After all, it was a new and complex agency, pioneering in many areas, and problems were inevitable. While pushing forward with their main tasks, men in the AAA attempted to improve operations. For example, it was the AAA and the Cotton Section that urged the Treasury to turn finally to mechanical check writing to speed payments to farmers.[41]

The most complicated issue, and one that would ultimately produce a famous confrontation between the liberals and conservatives in the Department of Agriculture, was that involving the southern tenant problem. The tenant system was a notoriously complex institution which could not be defended on social and many economic grounds. Some men in the Department of Agriculture felt very strongly that the government should now make a major effort to eliminate the whole problem. Since southerners and conservatives in the Department of Agriculture were fully aware of the place of tenancy in southern farming, most of the criticisms of the institution that were aired in Washington in the 1930s were voiced by northerners and liberals, many of whom had only recently discovered the details of its nature. As a result, the reformers quickly fell victim to southern fear and distrust of "outside" critics, and ground was prepared for conflict.

It was perhaps no exaggeration to say that Cobb was the AAA official best informed on the tenant problem. He had been a part of it, he had lived with it from childhood, and as a club leader and farm journal editor he had worked to cure its ills. Cobb also had clear and distinct views on the subject. The sharecropper system, he knew, had been an inevitable product of circumstances in the post-Civil War period; its effects upon the economic progress and development of the South had been adverse; and in the hands of unscrupulous men it could be oppressive indeed. But he also knew that not all landowners were unscrupulous, that not all tenants in the South fit the classic picture of sharecroppers, that landowners large and small faced risks unknown to typical sharecroppers, and that sharecroppers could on occasion be unscrupulous themselves.

Furthermore, Cobb was certain in his own mind that the middle of a great depression was no time to undertake a comprehensive overhaul of economic and social relationships in the South. To do so, he thought, would certainly alienate those elements and their political spokesmen whose support was absolutely necessary and thereby doom the entire program to failure. In the short run, at least, the problems of even the typical sharecropper could best be met by reviving the economy of which he was a part.[42]

The liberals had expressed dissatisfaction with aspects of the Cotton Section's work almost from the outset, but the conflict flowered over disputes concerning the 1934–1935 program. The acreage reduction contract, they claimed, failed to protect the interests of sharecroppers and gave landowners a club with which they could control and perhaps abuse their labor. The liberals pointed out that under the new program, the government signed contracts only with owners, cash tenants, and managing share tenants. Share tenants were defined as those who furnished the work stock, equipment, and labor needed to produce a crop and who managed operations on their farms. In actuality, these tenants were the southern counterparts of the northern renter and were relatively rare in the South. Both they and cash tenants shared equitably in the benefits provided by the 1934–1935 program. On the other hand, ordinary sharecroppers, who in many instances furnished only labor and had no real role in managing a property, did not sign contracts and were allocated no part of the rental payment and only a pro rata share of the parity payment. This, the liberals contended, was manifestly unfair. It meant that in many instances sharecroppers would have less total income than they would have earned had their landowner not cooperated in the acreage-reduction program. Moreover, since the croppers did not sign the contract, liberals argued that there was little reason to believe that they would receive even their proper share of the parity payment. That payment was paid to the landowner, who was then required by the contract to distribute on a pro rata basis a proper portion of it to his croppers. But that provision of the contract, liberals said, was largely unenforceable.[43]

The liberals also pointed to what they claimed were questionable provisions of Paragraph 7 of the 1934–1935 contract. According to that section, "producers" were required to make every effort "in good faith" to minimize the "labor, economic and social disturbance, and to this end, insofar as possible . . . effect the acreage reduction as nearly ratably as practicable among tenants" and to maintain the normal number of tenants on their properties. They were also directed to permit tenants to continue to occupy their homes during the life of the contract, unless they became "a nuisance or a menace," and to make available to tenants an adequate supply of firewood and, in return for labor, needed garden and pasture land for dairy cattle. These ambiguous provisions, said the liberals, were probably unenforceable and were almost open invitations to landlords to drive from the land those croppers no longer needed and those who for some reason were objectionable.[44]

As head of the Cotton Section, Cobb realized that he bore responsibility for the 1934–1935 contract, and he was not surprised when the liberals concentrated their fire on him. Nor was he surprised by the nature of their criticisms. After all, he had spent considerable time with the very issues the liberals were now discussing. There were peculiarities and inequities in southern agriculture, and the 1934–1935 contract had been drawn with them in mind. Not even Cobb would maintain that the contract was a perfect instrument, but given the realities of southern agriculture and politics he believed that it represented a reasonable compromise under which the primary task at hand, the rejuvenation of cotton farming, might be continued.[45]

The cold war between the liberals and conservatives flared into open hostilities in 1934 when it was reported that an Arkansas planter was in the process of evicting some of his tenants, presumably because they had joined the Southern Tenant Farmers' Union. Hiram Norcross, a wealthy landowner from Tyronza, had apparently been informed by his county agent that under Paragraph 7 of the cotton contract he was free to choose his labor and, as long as he maintained the normal number of tenants on the property, the AAA would not object if he replaced some with others. In any event, the alleged evictions received immediate and widespread press coverage, much of it hostile to Norcross and to the Department of Agriculture.[46] The liberals now had what they conceived to be an excellent

Cobb with ball players at the 1933 World Series, Washington Senators vs. New York Giants. Players from left to right are E. V. Chapman, C. S. Myer, and H. M. Critz, all of whom had played ball for Mississippi Agricultural and Mechanical College.

example to prove the validity of their charges against the 1934–1935 contract, Cobb's leadership of the Cotton Section, and the Department of Agriculture conservatives in general.[47]

Cobb's first reaction to the Norcross case was to attempt to ascertain the facts. Extension personnel in Arkansas, after investigation, reported that the community and county committees were satisfied that Norcross was honest and that such changes as he had made among his tenants were fully justifiable.[48] Cobb then attempted to learn something of the men who reportedly were organizing sharecroppers in eastern Arkansas and who apparently were supplying much of the ammunition for the attack on Norcross. An extension official in Tennessee notified Cobb that Dr. William R. Amberson, a professor at the University of Tennessee Medical School who had written Wallace and AAA officials concerning the Norcross situation, according to police reports, was "a full-fledged communist" and "very dangerous." From other sources and from information received earlier, Cobb concluded that the Southern Tenant Farmers' Union was an insidious socialist organization with good intentions but poor leadership and that unfortunately it had been infiltrated by a few communists. Finally, Cobb sent E. A. Miller, a Cotton Section official, to Arkansas to make a firsthand investigation. Miller's report substantiated the findings of the county agent and the local committees at Tyronza. According to Miller, there had been no wholesale evictions on the Norcross place; in fact, Norcross had increased the number of his tenants. Miller also reported that Harry L. Mitchell and Clay East of the Southern Tenant Farmers' Union had checkered reputations and that it was his impression that leading members of the community were essentially correct in their evaluation of the men and their activities.[49]

Cobb must have known that the Miller report was not totally accurate or complete. But he also knew that the situation in Arkansas was extremely complex. Outside influence had blown the episode out of all perspective, and more was involved than simple justice to Arkansas sharecroppers. Cobb hoped that the emotions generated by the Norcross affair would wear themselves out without doing irreparable harm to the whole cotton program. Certainly, he was un-

willing to endanger that effort by meeting directly the now vigorous attacks of the liberals upon him and the Cotton Section, thereby
generating still more dissension and adverse publicity. At the same
time, he hoped that the national coverage and controversy arising
from the Norcross case would induce local leadership, which he
still considered to be absolutely essential, to fulfill its responsibilities
somewhat more judiciously than apparently had been the case at
Tyronza. Insofar as the Norcross incident itself was concerned,
Cobb was determined to examine it on its merits, and if Norcross
had violated the contract he would be held accountable.[50]

If Cobb was unwilling to create a war over the Norcross affair
and over the interpretation of Paragraph 7, the liberals in the Department of Agriculture were less restrained. The office of the General Counsel became the center of an energetic attack upon the
infamous paragraph, the Cotton Section, and Cully Cobb. Gathering his young lawyers and others of like mind about him, Jerome
Frank hoped to use the Norcross case for a departmental showdown.

The final barrage between the liberals and the Cotton Section
seems to have intensified in December, 1934, and accelerated rapidly
in January, 1935. Up to this point the liberal effort seems to have
been marked by a general lack of coordination and little success.
By combining their efforts and concentrating on the Norcross case,
the liberals now committed themselves to a single and, eventually,
final test.

Because of its question of benefit payments, the Norcross case
eventually went before the Committee on Violations of Rental and
Benefit Contracts for a decision on whether to withold Norcross'
payments. That committee consisted of a single liberal and two conservatives, but Frank hoped to use the hearing as a basis of his initiative. While the issue was being debated by the committee, other
seemingly coordinated liberal efforts began to appear. Paul Appleby,
in a memorandum edited by Assistant to the Administrator William
Byrd, informed Cobb that he was adamantly opposed to the Cotton
Section's view on tenant matters and suggested in strong terms that
Cobb begin revamping the entire payment procedure.[51] Meanwhile,
Mary Conner Myers, an attorney from Frank's office, was finishing
what promised to be an expose of plantation conditions in Arkan-

sas.[52] Paul Appleby, with the endorsement of Chester Davis, asked Frank Tannenbaum of the Brookings Institute to file a report on possible solutions to the tenant problem.[53] As the final thrust, Frank set his lawyers, primarily Alger Hiss and Francis Shea, to work drafting a final opinion of the troublesome paragraph.[54]

Unfortunately for the liberals, coordination was not easily achieved, and their efforts did not all produce the desired results. Appleby's memorandum to Cobb concerning the reorganization of the payment system only served to alienate further the chief of the Cotton Section. The Myers' report, however controversial it may have been, would not be ready for several weeks and could be of no immediate use to the liberals.[55] Appleby and Frank must have been bitterly disappointed when Tannenbaum reported that the solution to the tenant problem did not lie in a restructuring of the cotton contract but in a "comprehensive land settlement program." Liberals were further hampered, although hardly surprised, by a pro-conservative decision on the Norcross case by the Committee on Violations.[56] The success of the entire liberal effort was now reduced to a single issue—the General Counsel's interpretation of Paragraph 7.

Although Hiss and Shea spent several weeks in January, 1935, writing the interpretation, the liberal view was well known within the AAA. It was also an unguarded secret that the new decision was to be announced in the immediate future.[57] This lack of security may have been a mistake on Frank's part. By adopting such an open course of action, he gave the conservatives time to think through their alternatives and perhaps to map their strategy. With their preliminary moves complete, both sides readied for the ultimate test of strength.

There has been some question concerning the exact sequence of events leading up to the famous purge.[58] According to the two top officials in the Cotton Section, it began dramatically with a telegram to the extension directors in three southern states on February 2. In a message drafted by Paul Appleby and based on the Alger Hiss-Francis Shea opinion, the liberals informed the extension people that Paragraph 7 as now interpreted would require landowners to retain not only the same number of tenants but also the same identical tenants. This new interpretation was to be submitted to the Administrator the following Monday, February 4, and they should begin to implement the new policy at that time.[59]

To the men of the Cotton Section, Appleby's telegram was objectionable on both administrative and practical grounds. Cobb was certain that if southern landowners were told that they could not choose their labor, they would surely reject the government's program and the cotton control effort would be lost. Administrative problems in enforcing such an interpretation were almost beyond comprehension. In fact, Alger Hiss himself doubted the feasibility of enforcement; he was apparently more interested in the theory of the law than its execution.[60] Finally, the new turn of events suggested that the authority of the Cotton Section was being sharply challenged and subordinated to that of the office of the General Counsel in ways that Cobb regarded as intolerable.

Chester Davis, AAA Administrator, was touring the West when the crisis began to erupt, and it was not until February 2 that he returned to Washington, thoroughly outraged with the turn of events.[61] The Cotton Section had always regarded Davis as a friend, but now the Administrator appeared to be less than resolute. Davis had served often as a peacemaker between the rival factions, and he was not eager to ignite the fireworks. Wofford B. Camp, Cobb's subordinate who was acting head of the Cotton Section in Cobb's absence, had no qualms about forcing the issue. Going to Davis' office on February 4 with complaints from extension personnel already in hand, he demanded that the liberals be fired. He got no satisfaction.

According to Camp, he had foreseen that result. Believing that he knew Cobb's views on the matter and knowing Cobb's relationship with leading southern congressmen and senators, Camp had already arranged a meeting with some of them in Cobb's office. Present were Senators Smith of South Carolina, Harrison of Mississippi, and Robinson of Arkansas, as well as Congressman Fulmer of South Carolina and others. The group proved to be a very attentive audience; and Camp, who under any circumstances was plain-spoken, presented the Cotton Section's view of the existing crisis, named those he considered responsible, and spelled out what he and Cobb believed would be the consequences if the liberals were allowed to go unchecked. Moreover, he suggested that the liberals had in mind additional changes for southern agriculture, changes which Camp labeled bizarre and even dangerous.

When the conference ended, the political leaders told Camp that they intended to take the matter directly to the President. Later they informed Camp that they had done so and that they had informed Roosevelt that no significant piece of legislation would come out of Congress until matters were resolved in the Department of Agriculture.[62]

The end result was a general house cleaning. Among those fired by Chester Davis, who was given the job by Wallace, were Jerome Frank, Lee Pressman, Frederick Howe, Gardner Jackson, and others. Some liberals, such as Victor Christgau, resigned in protest, and still others were transferred to other agencies.[63] The question of the interpretation of Paragraph 7 was settled promptly. In a telegram to the Memphis Chamber of Commerce and subsequently released to the press, Wallace stated that the troublesome clause meant that landowners were required to retain the same number of tenants, not the same tenants.[64] The Cotton Section had won its battle.

Tenant problems, of course, did not disappear with the purge of the liberals. In fact, the number of complaints and the amount of publicity about sharecroppers increased substantially. The critics of the AAA claimed that landowners, now virtually assured of freedom from prosecution, had begun a "reign of terror."[65] The conservatives within the AAA were equally sure that the sudden surge of complaints was caused by the activities of the ousted liberals and to such groups as the National Negro Congress, the Southern Conference for Human Welfare, and the Southern Tenant Farmers' Union. Regardless of the cause for the dramatic increase in complaints, Cobb was determined to make every effort to insure that all groups involved in cotton production obtained reasonable justice. With the liberals out of the way, he now felt that the time was opportune to create new machinery for handling landowner-tenant controversies.[66]

A week after the purge Cobb organized the Landlord-Tenant Relations Unit, complete with a legally constituted hearing body in Washington for receiving complaints. The predecessor agency, the Committee on Violations of Rental and Benefit Contracts, had become involved in the departmental feud and was now disbanded. The new agency was a typical Cobb creation. It was attached to the Cotton Section and was therefore subject to general supervision by the parent agency. The organization consisted of county and state units and an advisory committee in Washington composed of men able to work with "all groups." State directors of extension were thoroughly briefed on the new agency's functions and responsibilities. Among other tasks, the unit was given the chore of supervising a survey of the tenant situation to "answer the unfavorable comments that are being made." [67]

In general, Cobb thought the new Landlord-Tenant Relations Unit functioned admirably. The advisory committee in Washington removed the burden of the complaints from the Cotton Section itself and gave landlords and tenants an office to which they could appeal decisions from lower levels. Still, since an official of the Cotton Section served on the advisory committee, it tended to reflect Cobb's views. Moreover, the survey of the tenant situation conducted by the unit seemed to prove to Cobb what he thought was an accurate picture of southern farm tenancy: specifically, that tenancy produced extremely complex problems on the land but that the AAA had not worsened the overall conditions of tenants, as critics had contended.[68]

In the summer of 1935 Cobb played a major, if behind the scenes, role in arranging a farmers' march on Washington. Such an expression of rural sentiment, he thought, would be of value in demonstrating farmer support for the AAA and for the cotton program in particular; it might also help to put to rest the last vestiges of the liberal-conservative conflict. Moreover, a farmers' march made up of ordinary men from the countryside might dispel the notion that southern agriculture consisted of only two groups, unscrupulous landlords and oppressed sharecroppers.

The idea of a farmers' march originated in the spring of 1935 in conversations between Cobb and H. H. Williamson, Cobb's old friend from Texas. There were some obvious problems connected with the project, including the objections that might be raised if it

Wofford B. Camp in one of his cotton fields near Bakersfield, California. Camp, who was Cobb's chief assistant in the Cotton Section in the 1930's, is one of the largest farmers in the nation, annually producing some 9,000 bales of cotton on 3,000 acres of land. He also grows potatoes, sugar beets, and grapes, with smaller acreages in alfalfa and truck crops.

became commonly known that Department of Agriculture personnel had anything to do with sponsoring the event. But while on a
trip to Texas, Wofford B. Camp met Clifford H. Day, a diplomatic
Texan from Plainview who possessed considerable leadership ability. Day agreed to be the "front man" and to recruit farmers to
make the trip. Hopefully, a trainload could be gotten together and
transported to Washington where they would publicly endorse the
AAA's work and personally thank the President and Congress for
the interest they had shown in rural problems.

The organization of the project proceeded rapidly. The Missouri
Pacific Railroad's W. B. Cook, another of Cobb's friends from the
1920s, arranged transportation. Participants had to pay other expenses out of their own pockets, but farmers came forward in numbers that surprised even the promoters of the enterprise.[69] Meanwhile, the idea spread to other areas of the South and into the
Middle West where Wayne Darrow, a minor official in the AAA's
Division of Information, perhaps played some role.[70]

Little information concerning the march was given to the press.
Organizers of the affair feared that premature reports might dis-
credit the enterprise; moreover, they believed that a certain amount
of surprise in Washington might increase the impact of the march.
Some farmers did give interviews and a few of them demonstrated
both rural wit and an awareness of the purpose of the affair. One
Georgia farmer, asked whether the AAA had done anything for
him, stated that while he now was doing well, when "Herbert
Hoover turned me loose and Franklin Roosevelt picked me up, I was
hunting cottontail rabbits on the halves with a borrowed bitch." [71]

The bulk of the marchers arrived in Washington on May 13.
Some came by bus or in private automobiles, but the majority traveled by special trains, the Pullman cars serving as hotels while the
men were in Washington. The major scheduled event of the march
was a mass meeting in one of the halls of the city. Hopefully, such
a conclave would attract public attention and induce high officials,
perhaps even the President, to meet with the farmers. Since no other
facilities were available, the leaders obtained the Daughters of the
American Revolution Independence Hall for the gathering, two of
the participants paying the rental fee out of their own pockets.[72]

Those officials in Washington who were unaware of the nature of the march were understandably concerned. Both Wallace and Chester Davis worried about possible political repercussions, while the remnants of the old liberal element in the Department of Agriculture were partly correct when they labeled the affair an attempt to shift public attention from the tenant problem.[73] Some officials, it appeared, feared violence. Cobb watched affairs calmly, giving no indication that he was a foremost promoter of the enterprise, but he was amused to see those who had feared the farmers scurry across town to join the masses when it was evident they meant no harm.

The mass meeting in Independence Hall on the morning of May 14 proved to be a typical farmers' meeting on a grand scale. Some four thousand farmers joined in expressing their approval and general support for the program of the AAA. Among the luminaries who spoke to the gathering were South Carolina's Senator "Cotton Ed" Smith, Congressman Marvin Jones of Texas, and Secretary Wallace. But the highlight of the affair came in the afternoon, when the visiting farmers were invited to the lawn of the White House where they met President Roosevelt and heard him deliver what some called the first speech of the 1936 campaign.[74]

The months that Cobb remained in Washington after the famous purge and activities related to it were anticlimatic, although there were substantial changes within the Department of Agriculture. In February, 1935, the Agricultural Adjustment Administration was reorganized, and the title of Cobb's office was changed to the Division of Cotton. The next year in the Hoosac Mills case, the Supreme Court struck down the Agricultural Adjustment Act. Congress reacted quickly, producing in February, 1936, the Soil Conservation and Domestic Allotment Act, a measure which provided benefits for those farmers who cut acreages of soil-depleting crops, including cotton, and instituted soil-building practices. Funds for the program were appropriated directly from the federal treasury. Under the new law, Cobb's office became the Southern Division. Finally, in June, 1936, Howard R. Tolley succeeded Chester Davis as Administrator.[75]

For Cobb these changes produced few alterations in purpose or operating procedures. The basic task of restricting production to effect price remained. Cobb had a special interest in the 1936 law since its emphasis on soil conservation squared well with his continuing concern for increasing yield averages and adequate utilization of the idle acres.

Cobb felt some loss when Davis resigned; Cobb and Davis shared many of the same attitudes and convictions, but Tolley was of different mind and background. Moreover, while Tolley was considered a better administrator than Davis, he was inclined to give Cobb less autonomy in managing the cotton office.[76]

One of Cobb's later innovations in procedure dealt with the problem of compliance. The task of insuring the accuracy of farmers' statements concerning performance was always compounded by the enormity of the program, the rural environment, and by human ingenuity in concealing unreported acreages. Verification by community and county committees and the supervision of those committees by personnel of the extension service, reinforced by local pressure and later by ticket systems for marketing allotment cotton, were the basic methods for insuring compliance. Cobb was convinced that in the overwhelming majority of cases the system functioned reasonably well, and he was certainly never in favor of creating a great federal force to do the job, as some of his liberal associates had earlier proposed. Still, he was not completely satisfied and in seeking new methods for verifying compliance, he experimented with aerial photography. When studies showed the accuracy of such work, Cobb made plans to supplement existing procedures with the aerial surveys, a practice soon adopted in other programs of the AAA.[77]

Results of the programs during Cobb's last two crop years suggested that in the main the crop reduction effort was proceeding satisfactorily, although final figures for 1935 fell short of the planners' original objectives. Farmers signed some 1.3 million contracts which reduced output by an estimated 5 million bales and provided growers with benefit payments totaling $168 million. The AAA estimated that the 1935 program reduced the carryover to approximately 9 million bales, exceeding the AAA goal by more than 3 million.[78] Price of cotton fell slightly in 1935, but when benefit payments were added, growers realized about twelve cents a pound on their crops. In 1936 under the Soil Conservation and Domestic Allotment Act, farmers in the Southern Division diverted over 8.5 million acres of cotton land to soil-building uses and earned $103 million in total benefit payments.[79]

The appearance of numerous problems in 1936, however, suggested that the Soil Conservation and Domestic Allotment Act could be nothing more than a temporary expedient. In operation the measure proved to be inadequate for effectively controlling production–adverse weather conditions probably did as much to limit output in 1936–and under it compliance was especially difficult to verify. Some attempts were made in 1937 to strengthen the program carried on under the measure. Government planners emphasized the element of flexibility introduced in these modifications, particularly in the options open to producers. These changes did bring improvements in the program,[80] but even as these stopgap changes were being implemented, a more comprehensive approach was being planned. The Agricultural Adjustment Act of 1938 was on the horizon.

Cobb left the Department of Agriculture before the new law was finalized, although he took part in its planning. In the spring of 1937, he informed his superiors that he would terminate his appointment, effective September 1, 1937.[81] Cobb wanted to return to private life and to his own business. But his decision rested on other grounds as well. Cobb felt strongly that government service in a position such as he had occupied for four years should never be considered a permanent arrangement. Both the agency and the officeholder would benefit from a change. Moreover, Cobb had gone to Washington to help implement a highly experimental program in which he had great faith; that program had functioned for four years and was seemingly on the right path. Cobb believed that his task, as he had understood it when he went to Washington, was largely completed.

In leaving the Department of Agriculture, Cobb recognized that he had not achieved all of his goals, but in his own mind he believed that he had done all that he could. Certainly, he had used his expertise in cotton production as well as the influence of southern leaders in Congress, the press, and agricultural leadership in the

South to fight for the economic health of his section. To a measurable degree, he had succeeded. Agriculture was again on a paying basis.

## NOTES TO CHAPTER VIII

1. Cobb interviews.
2. Basil Rauch, *The History of the New Deal, 1933-1938* (New York, 1944), 7–8; Mitchell, *Depression Decade*, 67–69, 180–81, 226–27; Henry I. Richards, *Cotton under the Agricultural Adjustment Act: Developments up to July 1934* (Washington, 1934), 4–5.
3. History of the Division of Cotton from May 12, 1933, to January 6, 1936, MSS in Cobb Papers. Copy in U.S. Department of Agriculture Library, Washington, D.C.
4. U.S. Department of Agriculture, *Agricultural Statistics*, 1938 (Washington, 1938), 95–97; W. J. Cash, *The Mind of the South* (New York, 1941), 169–70, 405–407; William A. Percy, *Lanterns on the Levee* (New York, 1941), 275–84.
5. William E. Leuchtenburg, *Franklin D. Roosevelt and the New Deal, 1932–1940* (New York, 1963), 10–11; Arthur M. Schlesinger, Jr., *The Coming of the New Deal* (Boston, 1959), 38–39; Schapsmeier, *Wallace*, 155–56; William D. Rowley, *M. L. Wilson and the Campaign for the Domestic Allotment* (Lincoln, 1970), 165–76; Daniel R. Fusfeld, *The Economic Thought of Franklin D. Roosevelt and the Origins of the New Deal* (New York, 1956), 233n.
6. Schlesinger, *Coming of the New Deal*, 39; Edwin G. Nourse, Joseph S. Davis, and John D. Black, *Three Years of the Agricultural Adjustment Administration* (Washington, 1937), 23; Mitchell, *Depression Decade*, 192–94.
7. Nourse and others, *Three Years of the Agricultural Adjustment Administration*, 51–55; Richards, *Cotton under the Agricultural Adjustment Act*, 14–17; David E. Conrad, *The Forgotten Farmers: The Story of Sharecroppers in the New Deal* (Urbana, 1965), 37–40.
8. Fite, *Peek*, 251–54, 265–66; Sternsher, *Tugwell*, 198–202.
9. Conrad, *Forgotten Farmers*, 40; Van L. Perkins, *Crisis in Agriculture: The Agricultural Adjustment Administration and the New Deal, 1933* (Berkeley and Los Angeles, 1969), 90–97.
10. Conrad, *Forgotten Farmers*. 38, 45; Donald H. Grubbs, *Cry from the Cotton: The Southern Tenant Farmers' Union and the New Deal* (Chapel Hill, 1971), 32–33; Perkins, *Crisis in Agriculture*, 90–96.
11. Interview with Victor Christgau, August 10, 1971; H. A. Wallace to C. A. Cobb, May 19, 1933, Cobb Papers.
12. Cobb interviews.
13. Interview with Victor Christgau.
14. Evans, "Recollections of Extension History," 43; Schlesinger, *Coming of the New Deal*, 60.
15. Cobb interviews; Evans, "Recollections of Extension History," 43; "Memorandum of Understanding Between the Cotton Section AAA and the Extension Service, U. S. Department of Agriculture, Concerning the Field Work Incident to the Administration of the Cotton Act of 1934," May 31, 1934; Cully Cobb to C. C. Davis, June 26, 1933, Records of the Agricultural Stabilization and Conservation Service, Production Control Program, 1933–1940, Record Group 145 (National Archives, Washington), hereinafter cited as RG 145, PCP, NA.
16. Conrad, *Forgotten Farmers*, 42; Richards, *Cotton under the Agricultural Adjustment Act*, 18–19.

17. Cobb interviews.
18. Richards, *Cotton under the Agricultural Adjustment Act*, 7–14; Perkins, *Crisis in Agriculture*, 103–104.
19. History of the Division of Cotton, 12–14; Richards, *Cotton under the Agricultural Adjustment Act*, 21–22; Nourse and others, *Three Years of the Agricultural Adjustment Administration*, 70–74; C. C. Davis to C. A. Cobb, December 1, 1933, Records of the Agricultural Stabilization and Conservation Service, Central Correspondence Files, 1933–1947, Record Group 145 (National Archives, Washington), hereinafter cited as RG 145, CCF, NA.
20. Cotton Conference, Washington, D.C. June 3, 1933, typescript in RG 145, CCF, NA.
21. Cobb interviews.
22. C. A. Cobb to H. H. Williamson, December 11, 1934, RG 145, CCF, NA.
23. C. A. Cobb to C. C. Davis, October 31, 1933, RG 145, CCF, NA; Cobb interviews; interview with H. H. Williamson, July 17, 1971; "Agricultural Conservation—The Gospel of Economic Salvation, Address by Cully A. Cobb at Pilgrim Baptist Church, Chicago, Illinois, July 18, 1937," Cobb Papers. This speech was delivered to a Negro congregation. Cobb gave many such addresses at Negro churches. The addresses tended to concentrate on the Bible, morality, and explanations of the AAA.
24. Richards, *Cotton under the Agricultural Adjustment Act*, 23–24; interview with H. H. Williamson; Cobb to Peek, July 6, 1933, RG 145, PCP, NA; Cobb to Davis, July 26, 1933, RG 145, CCF, NA.
25. Richards, *Cotton under the Agricultural Adjustment Act*, 48–56; Conrad, *Forgotten Farmers*, 46; History of the Division of Cotton, 19; Cobb to Davis, July 26, September 9, 1933, RG 145, CCF, NA.
26. Rauch, *History of the New Deal*, 101; Perkins, *Crisis in Agriculture*, 113, 117–18.
27. Richards, *Cotton under the Agricultural Adjustment Act*, 39, 63–66; History of the Division of Cotton, 19–20; Henry I. Richards, *Cotton and the AAA* (Washington, 1936), 119.
28. Richards, *Cotton under the Agricultural Adjustment Act*, 79–82.
29. *Ibid.*, 79; Cobb interviews; Cobb to T. O. Asburg, September 27, 1933, attached to Cobb to Davis, September 27, 1933, RG 145, CCF, NA.
30. Nourse and others, *Three Years of the Agricultural Adjustment Administration*, 95–100; History of the Division of Cotton, 41, 46, 48, 50, 54.
31. History of the Division of Cotton, 46–47; Conrad, *Forgotten Farmers*, 54–55.
32. History of the Division of Cotton, 12–14, 48–50.
33. U. S. Department of Agriculture, *Agricultural Statistics*, 1938, pp. 95, 97; History of the Division of Cotton, 41–46, 52.
34. Quoted in Schlesinger, *Coming of the New Deal*, 46.
35. As quoted in Lord, *Wallaces of Iowa*, 358; Conrad, *Forgotten Farmers*, 105–14.
36. Cobb interviews.
37. Sternsher, *Tugwell*, 46–50, 91–141; Schlesinger, *Coming of the New Deal*, 5, 55, 72–74, 93, 123–24, 351, 380.
38. Cobb interviews; interview with W. B. Camp, October 22, 1971. Camp recalled later than on one occasion he saw the text of a plan which would have turned control of all American agriculture over to the Secretary of Agriculture.
39. Schlesinger, *Coming of the New Deal*, 49–51; Conrad, *Forgotten Farmers*, 38; Grubbs, *Cry from the Cotton*, 31–32.
40. Cobb interviews.

41. *Ibid.*; Conrad, *Forgotten Farmers*, 71–72; Grubbs, *Cry from the Cotton*, 19–33; H. H. Williamson to Cobb, June 27, 1933, Cobb to Davis, October 31, 1935, RG 145, CCF, NA; Cobb to Victor Christgau, September 8, 1934, Mary B. Hall to Cobb, March 22, 1934, Davis to Jerome Frank, July 27, 1933, RG 145, PCP, NA.

42. Cobb interviews; Cobb to Davis, September 28, 1933, RG 145, PCP, NA.

43. Grubbs, *Cry from the Cotton*, 17–24; Conrad, *Forgotten Farmers*, 56–63; Gladys L. Baker, " 'And to Act for the Secretary'; Paul H. Appleby and the Department of Agriculture, 1933–1940," *Agricultural History*, Vol. 45 (October, 1971), 247–48; Alger Hiss to Jerome Frank, January 26, 1935, RG 145, CCF, NA; Margret B. Bennett, Memorandum to the Secretary, January 12, 1935, Records of the Office of the Secretary of Agriculture, Case Files of the Office of the Solicitor, Record Group 16 (National Archives, Washington), hereinafter cited as RG 16, FOS, NA.

44. U.S. Department of Agriculture, Form No. Cotton 1, *Cotton Contract*, 1934–1935; Grubbs, *Cry from the Cotton*, 41–42, 45–46, 48–52; Conrad, *Forgotten Farmers*, 56–58, 145; Alger Hiss to Jerome Frank, January 26, 1935, RG 145, CCF, NA.

45. Cobb interviews; Baker, "Appleby and the Department of Agriculture," 247; Cobb to Davis, October 26, 1934, RG 145, CCF, NA; Cobb to unknown (probably Davis), November 27, 1934, RG 145, CCF, NA.

46. For a more complete treatment of the Norcross case, see Grubbs, *Cry from the Cotton*, 45–64; Conrad, *Forgotten Farmers*, 84–88, 130–45, 178–79, 188; Baker, "Appleby and the Department of Agriculture," 248–49; Norman Thomas, *The Plight of the Sharecropper* (New York, 1934), 11–12, 35–36; Memphis *Press-Scimitar*, December 21, 1934; Edward J. Meeman to H. A. Wallace, December 24, 1934, RG 145, CCF. W.A. Meeman was the editor of the Memphis *Press-Scimitar*.

47. Victor Christgau to Davis, January 14, 1935, RG 145, CCF, NA; Conrad, *Forgotten Farmers*, 103, 105–19.

48. *Ibid.*, 98–100; Cobb interviews; Cobb to D. P. Trent, May 1, 1934, RG 145, PCP, NA.

49. S. M. Landers to Cobb, n.d., RG 16, FOS, NA; E. A. Miller to Cobb, March 16, 19, 24, 26, 1934, RG 145, PCP, NA.

50. Cobb interviews; Cobb to Davis, January 5, 1935, RG 145, CCF, NA. Cobb informed Davis emphatically that the Cotton Section would not allow Norcross to carry out his threat to withhold his tenants' parity payments.

51. Paul H. Appleby to Cobb, December 27, 1934, RG 145, CCF, NA; Appleby to Cobb, December 27, 1934, attached to Appleby to Byrd, December 28, 1934, RG 145, PCP, NA. Appleby's rough draft of a memo to Cobb was sent to Byrd who added to the original letter. Cobb eventually received the Byrd-edited version.

52. Grubbs, *Cry from the Cotton*, 48–52; Mary Conner Myers to Jerome Frank, January 18, 1934, RG 16, FOS, NA; Memphis *Press-Scimitar*, February 22, 1935; Jerome Frank to Cobb, January 15, 1935, RG 145, CCF, NA.

53. Frank Tannenbaum to Appleby, December 29, 1934, RG 145, CCF, NA.

54. Alger Hiss to Jerome Frank, January 26, 1935, RG 145, CCF, NA.

55. The Myers report was not finished until after the purge of the liberals and was not released by the AAA. A search for the report by competent scholars has failed to produce the document. Grubbs, *Cry from the Cotton*, 52; Conrad, *Forgotten Farmers*, 140.

56. Grubbs, *Cry from the Cotton*, 48–52; Tannenbaum to Appleby, December 29, 1934, RG 145, CCF, NA; "Memorandum for the Secretary," January 10, 1935, RG 145, PCP, NA.

57. Frank to Christgau, January 11, 1935, Christgau to Cobb, January 14, 1935, RG 145, CCF, NA.

58. Baker, "Appleby and the Department of Agriculture," 249–51; Conrad, *For-*

*gotten Farmers*, 141–48; Grubbs, *Cry from the Cotton*, 53–58. These writers generally agree that Paragraph 7 served as the final issue between the rival factions. Their versions differ from that of Camp and Cobb primarily in the significance of Chester Davis' role.

59. Camp interview; Cobb interviews. The authors were unable to locate this telegram in the National Archives or in the files of the Extension Service of the states concerned. However, it should be noted that Camp, who was on the scene at the time, was most deliberate and precise in his recollection of events.

60. Alger Hiss to Frank, January 26, 1935, RG 145, PCP, NA; Conrad, *Forgotten Farmers*, 145.

61. Baker, "Appleby and the Department of Agriculture," 250.

62. Camp interview. The president's appointment list of February 5 indicates no meeting with southern congressional leaders. However, the nature of the topic under discussion may have necessitated no face-to-face confrontation. The Memphis *Commercial Appeal*, November 22, 1946, partially credited the purge to Senator Robinson. Wallace later recalled that there was little doubt that the southern leaders would kill the program unless the liberals were discharged. See, for example, Wallace's statement in *U.S. News and World Report*, Vol. 36 (January 8, 1954), 42.

63. Baker, "Appleby and the Department of Agriculture," 250–51; Conrad, *Forgotten Farmers*, 147–49; Grubbs, *Cry from the Cotton*, 55–56; R. G. Swing, "Purge at the AAA," *Nation*, Vol. 140 (February 20, 1935), 216; Washington *Post*, February 6, 1935; Rexford G. Tugwell Diary, February 10, 1935, Rexford G. Tugwell Papers (Franklin D. Roosevelt Library, Hyde Park, New York).

64. Henry Wallace to Memphis Chamber of Commerce, February 12, 1935, RG 16, FOS, NA.

65. Grubbs, *Cry from the Cotton*, Chap. 4; Conrad, *Forgotten Farmers*, Chap. 9.

66. Cobb interviews; Cobb to Davis, February 13, 1935, D. W. Watkins to Cobb, February 14, 1935, Cobb to Davis, February 14, 1935, RG 145, PCP, NA. In a memo to Davis on February 13, Cobb conceded that too few convictions for violation of contract had been achieved and he stressed the need to "proceed most vigorously . . . to preserve the integrity of our program."

67. Quoted in Conrad, *Forgotten Farmers*, 189–90; Cobb to Davis, February 13, 14, 1935, RG 145, PCP, NA.

68. Cobb interviews; Williamson interview; Conrad, *Forgotten Farmers*, 190–96. The findings of the survey, the W. J. Green Report, were criticized sharply for errors in technique and biased samplings and consequently were never released for publication.

69. Cobb interviews; Williamson interview.

70. [Gladys Baker], Discussion with Wayne Darrow, June 22, 1964; Wayne Darrow, Farm March–1935. Tyescripts in U.S. Department of Agriculture Library, Washington.

71. Williamson interview.

72. *Ibid.*; Darrow, Farm March–1935, p. 3.

73. Williamson interview; Christgau interview; Cobb interview; Darrow, Farm March–1935, pp. 2–3; M. S. Venkataramani, "Norman Thomas, Arkansas Share-croppers, and the Roosevelt Agricultural Policies," *Mississippi Valley Historical Review*, Vol. 47 (September, 1960), 238.

74. New York *Times*, May 14, 15, 1935; Washington *Evening Star*, May 14, 1935; Washington *Post*, May 14, 15, 1935; Williamson interview; Cobb interviews.

75. Mitchell, *Depression Decade*, 205–206; Richard S. Kirkendall, "Howard Tolley and Agricultural Planning in the 1930's," *Agricultural History*, Vol. 39 (January, 1965), 29.

76. Cobb interviews; Camp interview.

77. D. W. Myer to H. H. Williamson, May 14, 1935, RG 145, CCF, NA; Cobb to Davis, January 7, 1936, RG 145 PCP, NA.

78. History of the Division of Cotton, 64; Ward Buckles, Financial Statement, November 27, 1935, RG 145, PCP, NA.

79. U.S. Department of Agriculture, *Agricultural Statistics*, 1938, p. 95; U.S. Agricultural Adjustment Administration, *Report*, 1937–1938 (Washington, 1939), 258, 289.

80. *Ibid.*, pp. 30–32, 34.

81. Cobb to H. R. Tolley, July 31, 1937, RG 145, CCF, NA.

# CHAPTER IX

# A Farm Leader in "Retirement":
## Since 1937

WHEN Cully A. Cobb left the Agricultural Adjustment Administration, he was only fifty-three years of age, still in the prime of life. He had spent twenty-nine years in agriculture, and by any reasonable standard he was a success in his chosen field. Beginning as a poor boy from Tennessee, he had advanced from principal of an obscure agricultural high school in rural Mississippi to one of the more important and controversial offices in the United States Department of Agriculture. That career in agriculture was now at an end, but Cobb had no desire to retire, even had his personal finances permitted that luxury. Instead, he now matured plans to return to Atlanta. There he anticipated completing the rearing and educating of his two sons and devoting any spare time that might remain to church, civic, and similar activities.

The prospects of the company to which Cobb returned in September, 1937, appeared to be less than bright. The firm was the Ruralist Press, Inc., a commercial printing corporation. Its chief customer had been the *Southern Ruralist*, the farm paper for which Cobb had worked in the 1920s. The older concern had been incorporated in Georgia in 1907 with an authorized capital of $500,000. Nineteen years later the charter had been extended and the authorized capital increased to $1,000,000 in common and preferred stock. Shares had a par value of $100. When the merger of the *Southern Ruralist* and the *Progressive Farmer* was consummated in 1930, the Southern Ruralist Company ceased to exist. However, the Ruralist Press, Inc., which had been a subsidiary of the Southern Ruralist Company, continued to operate as a commercial printing firm, having its headquarters in Atlanta and using the plant that had also previously produced the *Southern Ruralist*.[1] *

The Ruralist Press could hardly have faced a more difficult situation than that which Cobb found upon his return to Atlanta. The depression affected the printing industry as it did all other lines of business, and soon the firm was struggling for its very existence. Apparently, inept leadership also handicapped the company; at least, Cobb was convinced that Frank J. Merriam, who headed the firm earlier, suffered from a serious lack of business judgment, while President H. G. Hastings had large and absorbing interests elsewhere. In any event, by 1935 the company found itself almost a year in arrears on interest due on $115,000 bonded indebtedness, in debt some $83,000 to paper manufacturers, and with other obligations which it was unable to meet. There followed in rapid succession an attempt to scale down the creditors' claims and then in March, 1936, a reorganization of the firm under the provisions of the federal bankruptcy laws.[2]

Arrangements were worked out quickly. Some creditors were issued 7 percent preferred stock. Others were at least partially satisfied and their claims cancelled with funds raised from the sale of Progressive Farmer Company stock, which made available $90,000, and with a loan obtained from the Reconstruction Finance Corporation. That 5 percent loan, dated August 12, 1936, amounted to $180,000, of which only $158,000 was drawn. It was payable at a rate of $7,500 semi-annually, beginning August 12, 1937, and if the company prospered payments on the loan were required to be equal to 50 percent of net income.[3]

Cobb watched these proceedings from afar. While on the *Progressive Farmer* staff and later in Washington, he kept himself informed as to developments, but he played only an advisory role in the management of the firm as it went through its own economic wringer. He was, after all, only a minority stockholder, having thirty-four shares of common stock out of the five hundred outstanding. These he had acquired in the 1920s; in 1927 he had valued them at $26,605.[4]

It was after the reorganization of the Ruralist Press that Cobb re-

* Notes appear at end of each chapter.

solved to return to active participation in the company and, in fact, to assume direction of it. Between November, 1936, and March, 1937, he bought 223 shares, paying from $60 to $90 a share for them. These purchases gave him a total of 257 shares, half a dozen more than were needed for control. In January, 1937, he was elected a director of the company and in August he became president, at a salary of $700 a month.[5]

The concern that Cobb now controlled and headed was relatively small and weak. Total assets as of August 31, 1937, were listed at $527,742. Current liabilities amounted to $44,319, and $120,000 of the RFC loan was still outstanding. Capital stock consisted of 842 shares of 7 percent cumulative, participating preferred stock and 500 shares of common, both having a par value of $100. During the preceding twelve months net sales had equalled $565,264, operating profit $69,218, and net income $45,633.[6]

What the firm needed, Cobb was convinced, was energetic but conservative leadership; and he set out to provide it. Within the plant, he tightened controls to achieve more efficient operation and gradually eliminated considerable waste and many superfluous workers. Purchasing was centralized to obtain better control over the cost of materials. A vigorous sales effort was launched, and the sales staff was strengthened by the addition of key personnel. Also, Cobb had an ability, which he used to the utmost, to develop a better spirit among employees. The long struggle of the depression years, of course, had discouraged them; but Cobb was able to rekindle their enthusiasm. After all, the business was in a sense part theirs, he pointed out to the men, and their jobs represented opportunities as well as responsibilities.[7]

Important, too, was the gradual improvement in the economy that came in the late 1930s, permitting an expansion in all lines of business. In fact, for the Ruralist Press the corner was turned in 1937. During the year ending August 31, the company was able to repay $38,000 of the RFC loan, and it resumed payment of dividends on its common stock.[8]

When it appeared that the company was on the road to recovery, Cobb resolved to reduce the firm's fixed obligations as soon as possible. Some of the preferred stock was in the hands of people "not wholly congenial" but more to the point the $84,000 par value issue drew 7 percent a year and constituted a burden on the company. Accordingly, with the permission of the RFC in the fall of 1938 Ruralist Press bought 162 shares at from $70 to $75 a share and canceled them. The process continued into the next decade. By February, 1943, the amount outstanding was $41,681. At that time, the directors voted to redeem the entire amount, paying $105 a share for it.[9]

Cobb's handling of the RFC loan similarly illustrated his acute sense of the cost and uses of borrowed money. In the late 1930s, his payments to the governmental agency consistently exceeded requirements, and by January, 1939, the debt was down to $75,000. At that time, in order to conserve funds for needed operating expenses and capital improvements and to take advantage of the 5 percent interest rate charged by the RFC, Cobb renegotiated the loan and arranged for its repayment in equal installments spread over five years. The loan was retired in November, 1943.[10]

In the early years, and to some degree throughout the period that he headed the Ruralist Press, Cobb's dividend policy was conservative. Repeatedly, he pointed out to his associates that a business such as theirs had to conserve its resources. To stay competitive, a printing firm was constantly faced with the necessity of spending large sums for new machinery and other improvements. Moreover, the nature of the business was such that huge inventories and substantial amounts of working capital were essential. Since in the main these funds had to be generated internally, Cobb contended that dividends had to be kept low. In line with that policy, from 1938 to 1947 the company paid only $6 or $7 a share per year. An exception came in 1940 when the directors voted a lump sum dividend of $25,000.[11]

By the late 1940s Cobb's dividend policies had antagonized some minority stockholders. By financing capital improvements largely out of net earnings and by maintaining dividends on "less than a token basis," they complained, Cobb was harming those who could not wait until some time in the future to receive a reasonable return. Majority interests and officers were doing well through salaries and bonuses, they contended, while they were left with dividends that amounted to roughly one-twentieth of the current net earnings or "actually only a small fraction of one percent of the high book value of the stock because of the great under capitalization of the company." In point of fact, Cobb's salary had been raised to $1,000 a month in 1940, and during the war period, the directors had regularly voted bonuses for officers and certain other employees; but even the malcontents agreed that management "has done a splendid job and has earned every cent paid" it. In an effort to placate these dissidents, Ruralist Press paid $10.00 a share in 1948 and 1949,[12] but Cobb concluded that perhaps the best solution might be found in eliminating the minority stockholders' interest in the company.

That goal was accomplished in an arrangement that was worked out in 1949. The company issued 6 percent, cumulative preferred stock with a par value of $100 a share and traded it for common stock held by minority interests on the basis of eight shares of preferred for one share of common. Up to one third of the common stock involved could be turned in for cash at $800 a share. All common stock thus obtained by the company was to be retired. The company had the right to call and redeem each year up to 20 percent of the total amount of preferred stock issued. Under this plan, 201 shares of common stock were turned in, some owners taking preferred stock and others cash. The end result was that common stock outstanding was reduced to 299 shares, all of it owned by Cobb or held by him as trustee. The Ruralist Press had become a family-owned firm.[13]

Cobb paid dividends on the new preferred stock no longer than necessary. Twenty percent of the issue was retired in 1949, and the last of the issue was called in January, 1954. During those years, dividends on the common stock were raised to $48.00 a year to make earnings on the common comparable to the dividends paid on the preferred.[14]

Other changes in the company's capital stock came in 1958 and 1965. In the earlier year in order to bring the company's capital stock into a more reasonable relationship to the value of the firm, the company issued enough stock to increase the total outstanding to

10,000 shares. Seven years later Ruralist Press declared a stock dividend of 30 percent, swelling the total stock outstanding to 13,000 shares.[15]

Meanwhile, Cobb had transferred a sizable portion of the Ruralist Press stock to other members of the family. In 1948 the first shares went to Cobb's wife, his two sons, and a daughter-in-law. By 1971 Cobb held in his own name 5,510 shares of the 13,000 outstanding, but he continued to serve as president of the company until its sale in 1971.[16]

Since printing establishments invest large sums in complex and costly machinery, the building and maintaining of a successful printing business demanded as much technical know-how as managerial ability. Cobb recognized from the outset that, if his firm were to prosper, he had to keep a close eye on technical processes in his plant and become thoroughly knowledgable concerning developments in technology in the printing industry as a whole. Fortunately, Cobb had a natural feel for mechanics, and he was able to play the dual role of manager and engineer.

One of Cobb's first tasks was to examine the existing machinery of the Ruralist Press and determine its adaptability to his long range plans. As he had suspected, there were serious problems. The bulk of the heavy equipment was not designed for large-scale, high-speed production. The flatbed presses were becoming increasingly obsolete and could not be fitted into Cobb's overall scheme. Moreover, the rotary magazine presses, the most important equipment in the plant at the time, had not been designed for the type of operation Cobb had in mind, and there was some doubt that they could be converted. Probably the only encouraging conclusion from Cobb's initial examination of the property was the fact that the press building and real estate holdings seemed adequate for the moment.

Cobb, of course, had known something of the mechanical problems he would face when he took control of the Ruralist Press, so he immediately went to work to put things in order. Cobb decided at an early date that the best opportunity for reasonable success lay in a continuation of large-scale telephone directory production. This goal became Cobb's guide for all decisions in operational procedure, particularly in the field of technology. All matters involving planning for the future were evaluated in accordance with that objective. For example, Cobb decided that the flatbed presses, largely two-color presses and capable of producing high quality but limited quantity work, would be retained for the present. However, as small contract business diminished, these presses would be replaced by high-speed, four-color presses which would increase production and cut labor costs.

The rotary presses represented too large an investment to abandon, given the conditions of the time and the fact that they had practically no resale value. Cobb decided that, with extensive modifications, the capacity necessary for rapid production could be achieved. To accomplish this end, it was necessary for Cobb largely to redesign the giant presses. The task required several months, but at length the presses were transformed into efficient machines that served the firm for many years.

An important part of Cobb's long-range plan was the evolution of a well-organized and efficient assembly line for the binding of directories. Every effort was made to improve and speed the flow through the system. New gluing techniques, a cooling process which more rapidly dried the glue, and an innovative use of saws rather than the traditional knives to trim book spines were among the new procedures which kept pushing production figures upward. Cobb's objective was to make the assembly process as simple, natural, and fast as possible.

The operational procedures at the Ruralist Press eventually became what Cobb had dictated, one of logic and order. White and yellow page orders were received by the service and order department which coordinated and channeled them to various composition departments. Once composition was completed both white and yellow pages were photographed, and the photographic negatives were used to produce plastic plates for the actual printing. After printing, the "signatures" or folios, usually twelve to seventy-five pages, were collated, bound, and shipped to the customer.

The assembly procedure revealed some of the inherent advantages and disadvantages of directory manufacture. Yellow pages were a major source of income for telephone companies, but because of the complexity of their composition they were the most expensive part of the printing contract. They were also the most difficult to produce because of the combination of art work and custom printing involved. White pages could be handled quite rapidly by the use of a linotype system of semi-permanent files of individual names, addresses, and telephone numbers maintained on lead slugs. Changes and additions could be inserted easily into a master slug file. Appropriate slugs were assembled in page forms which were then photographed. These negatives were converted to printing plates and printed in the normal way.

Although the white pages could be printed in a rapid and efficient manner, the resulting lead files presented a storage problem. This problem was one of the factors which ultimately led Cobb to establish subsidiary printing plants at points outside Atlanta to handle white page production up to the point of platemaking. These subsidiary plants maintained the lead files in current form for their respective areas and were responsible for furnishing the Atlanta plant with galley proofs. These galleys, or scotch prints, were shipped to Atlanta where the central camera converted them into printing plates.[17]

During the almost thirty-four years that Cobb headed the Ruralist Press, the firm did many types of commercial printing, but increasingly its business came to be concentrated with a few large customers. As an example of an earlier type of work, in 1937 it printed a tabloid for a local paper in Pikeville, Kentucky, and a couple of years later it produced a rotogravure brochure for the Greenbrier Hotel in White Sulphur Springs, West Virginia. That item won an award for excellence for its printer.[18] The firm also printed rotogravure catalogs for the Hastings Seed Company in batches of 100,000 copies or more. Other customers included nursery concerns in Tennessee and real estate developers in Florida. Until the summer of 1940 the Ruralist Press printed the *American Cotton Journal*, the voice of the American Cotton Cooperatives Association. Its monthly issues consisted of 200,000 copies.[19]

For years the Ruralist Press had large contracts with the Coca-Cola Company and with the Salvation Army. For the latter organization Cobb's firm printed the *War Cry*, a weekly that circulated throughout the Army's southern territory. For example, in 1938

Ruralist Press had a contract providing for the printing of fifty-two issues with a minimum of thirty thousand copies per issue at a cost of $787.50 per issue. In 1940 a new five-year contract called for the same output, but the price had increased to $803 an issue. Almost twenty years later, the Ruralist Press was still printing the *War Cry* as well as the Salvation Army's *El Grito*, a publication used in the missionary work of the organization in Mexico and elsewhere.[20]

For Coca-Cola the Ruralist Press produced a wide variety of advertising, promotional, and record-keeping items that were used by bottlers and retailers throughout the nation. Included were a cooler catalog, a booklet entitled "Every Job Needs the Pause that Refreshes," and a folder that emphasized that "Soft Drink Sales Help Gasoline Business." In addition, the company produced a multitude of salesmen's manuals, redemption cards, window strip advertisements, and other kinds of promotional materials. Many of the football programs in the Southeast carrying Coca-Cola advertisements came from the Ruralist Press. Cobb's plant also printed Coca-Cola dispenser tickets that were used at the World's Fair in 1939. For years the Ruralist Press printed *The Red Barrel*, a house publication of the Coca-Cola Company that went to bottlers all over the world.[21] Some of the materials produced by the Ruralist Press were "the best that we have had . . . so far," according to a Coca-Cola Company official.[22] But as the printing of telephone directories grew in importance to the Ruralist Press, business with the soft drink firm declined in volume.

Over the years of Cobb's direction and ownership of the Ruralist Press, the firm's biggest customer by far was the Western Electric Company, which in addition to its other functions served as the purchasing agent for the Bell telephone system. The old Southern Ruralist Company had begun to print telephone directories in the 1920s, and the business increased sharply in both volume and relative importance as the years passed. In the late 1930s, the Ruralist Press produced telephone directories for Southern Bell for the states of Florida, Georgia, the Carolinas, and Alabama; thirty-five years later the company was performing essentially the same service, except that in 1970 Alabama was shifted to South Central Bell. In 1937 the telephone business generated for the Ruralist Press approximately 30 percent of its total gross sales, but by the 1960s almost 90 percent of all revenues came from the manufacture of directories.[23] In the early years, at least, Ruralist Press printed some additional publications of the telephone company. In 1940, for example, it produced for the Southern Bell Telephone and Telegraph Company its monthly *Southern Telephone News*, a house organ.[24]

In many ways, the printing of telephone books was a unique business, offering both advantages and disadvantages to a firm engaged in it. On the surface, the near monopoly in telephone service enjoyed by the Bell system would suggest a buyer's market, but reality belied the appearance. While the number of firms with the highly specialized equipment and technical knowledge necessary to produce directories was limited, there was keen competition between them, and all contracts were let on the basis of competitive bids. Negotiations between the Western Electric Company and the printing firm were often quite extended. Resulting contracts were long term arrangements, since both parties recognized that the printer had to have reasonable assurances in order to invest in the necessary but highly specialized and expensive machinery. On the other hand, with a contract in effect the printing company had substantial protection against at least short-run fluctuations in the economy, and it could expect a continuous growth in the volume of business, tied as it was to increasing population, improved living standards of the people, and economic growth.[25]

In these areas, the Ruralist Press enjoyed an especially favorable geographic position, and its fortunes followed closely the rapid growth in the southeastern part of the nation that occurred after World War II. As late as 1947 there were only one million telephones in Florida, Georgia, and the Carolinas, but by 1971 the number had jumped to seven million. Over that span of years, in fact, Cobb figured that annual growth had averaged close to 10 percent a year.[26]

To handle more effectively and promptly its growing volume of business, the Ruralist Press in the 1950s and later established a number of subsidiaries and satellite plants. To some degree these new firms represented attempts to move into new technological fields and to diversify the interests of the parent company. Most important was

Florida Printers, Inc., a wholly owned subsidiary established in Miami in 1955 to service the Bell system in that state. The very rapid growth of population there, combined with the need to have a firm incorporated in the state to give more prompt service, induced the Ruralist Press to take that step. Later, Florida Ruralist Press was created at Jacksonville. For essentially the same reasons Cobb incorporated in North Carolina in 1959 the Carolina Ruralist Press, Inc., and built a new plant at Charlotte. This company and Florida Printers acquired in 1968 Superior Type, Inc., a firm that had been established in Atlanta in 1954. It produced linotype and monotype compositions for printing and publishing companies and reproduction proofs and advertising copies for circulation media and for offset printers throughout the Southeast. It also had a capability in computerized typesetting.

Other subsidiaries included Bluff Street Corporation, a firm which was part owner of two apartment complexes in Atlanta and sole owner of Books, Inc. The latter company had been established in 1966 to engage in commercial printing in Birmingham, Alabama. The United States Air Force Training Command was its principal customer. The Ruralist Press also organized Videotype, Inc., a separate corporation established in Atlanta to supply the parent concern and to market advanced techniques of photographic composition. Videotype was charged with the task of technical research for both the telephone company and the Ruralist Press. Cobb's firm also owned the Smart Advertising Company of Smyrna, Georgia. Acquired in the late 1960s, it prepared the advertising copy that went into telephone directories.[27]

The financial record of the Ruralist Press and its subsidiaries must have been pleasing to the owners. In 1936–1937, the year before Cobb took active control of the company, the Ruralist Press had assets valued at $528,000. Its net sales amounted to $565,000, operating profit was $69,000, and net income $46,000. By 1969–1970 assets of the firm and its subsidiaries had grown to $6.7 million. Net sales were $12.3 million, operating profit $1.2 million, and net income $720,000.[28] During the 1940s, when Cobb was making every effort to conserve resources in order to pay its debts and build up the firm, dividends on common stock aggregated only $59,500. But in the 1950s the company paid out a total of $520,525, and in the 1960s the figure was $401,390.[29]

Despite the solid growth of the firm and the generally satisfactory earnings that it generated for its owners, on June 24, 1971, Cobb sold the Ruralist Press to J. P. Stevens and Company. That concern, an extensive textile manufacturer headquartered in New York with many plants in the southeastern states and abroad, was in the process of diversifying its activities, a common practice in American business in the 1950s and 1960s. The Ruralist Press's record of earnings and its potential for future growth made it an attractive target for men interested in diversification; thus the existence of the Ruralist Press as a family-owned firm came to an end.[30]

While the motives of the purchaser were clear and easily understood, those of the seller were more complex. Cobb had a deep, personal attachment to a firm which he had built over a period of thirty-four years into perhaps the most modern printing establishment for the production of telephone directories in the world. But more pressing considerations now entered the picture. Conceivably, Cobb was deeply concerned for the future of the company. The increasing complexities of doing business in the later decades of the twentieth century, with heavy tax burdens and growing interference by governments, distressed him. The problems of operating a concern in the heart of one of America's great cities, especially in view of modern racial relations and social pressures, were always on his mind. It was certain to him that in the not far distant future the owners of the Ruralist Press would have to move the major plant from its existing site in downtown Atlanta to open country beyond that city's suburbs, a tremendous undertaking that would require the expenditure of huge amounts of money, energy, and time.

But while Cobb was fully aware of the challenges such problems presented, he gave no indication that he doubted the ability of the family-owned Ruralist Press to master them, and his decision to sell the property rested on other considerations. For years Cobb had wanted to make substantial contributions to certain institutions to which he felt he owed much. The sale of the Ruralist Press to a company that promised to maintain its integrity over the years permitted the fulfillment of that goal. Accordingly, in the summer of 1971, at the age of eighty-seven, Cobb became "unemployed" for the first time since 1904 when he had appeared at the gates of Mississippi Agricultural and Mechanical College.[31]

One of the most enjoyable aspects of Cobb's life after 1937 was additional time that he was able to devote to his family. Cobb had married Ora May "Byrdie" Ball in Buena Vista, Mississippi, on December 23, 1910. Byrdie was a quiet and attractive woman who enjoyed a wide circle of friends and who devoted most of her time to her husband and children. The first child born to the Cobbs was Cully Alton, Jr., born on October 3, 1916, while the family was living in Starkville. Their second child, David Alexander, was born in Atlanta on March 8, 1924. Eight years later, on October 15, 1932, Byrdie Cobb died of cancer, leaving her husband with two school-age children.

Cully Cobb married again on August 24, 1934, in Bethesda, Maryland, to Lois P. Dowdle. Like Cobb, Miss Dowdle was a graduate of a land-grant college, the University of Georgia. She had been a pioneer in girls' club work, ultimately becoming state leader in Georgia. She had served terms as president of the Association of Southern Agricultural Workers and of the Georgia Home Economics Association. She had been woman's editor on the staffs of both the *Southern Ruralist* and the *Progressive Farmer*. At the time of her marriage, Miss Dowdle was chief executive of the Institute of American Fats and Oils, an organization headquartered at Washington. Her training and professional experience enabled Lois Cobb to become involved directly in Cobb's career. Consequently, in addition to her responsibilities as mother to the Cobb boys and homemaker, Mrs. Cobb kept herself informed concerning her husband's business interests and took an active part in reaching decisions concerning the management of the Ruralist Press.

Education had been a difficult but rewarding experience for Cobb, so he devoted a great deal of attention to the education of his sons. Specifically, he told them to seek the best training available in their particular areas of interest. Cully, Jr., the elder son, chose a medical career and trained at George Washington University and Harvard Medical School. A neurosurgeon, Cully, Jr., eventually

Wedding portrait, Cully A. Cobb with his bride, the former Lois P. Dowdle, August 24, 1934.

joined the staff at Vanderbilt University. David followed his father into printing. A veteran of naval service in World War II, he received a degree in business management from the University of North Carolina and a degree in printing engineering from Carnegie Tech. Later, he joined the Ruralist Press and in time rose to be vice-president of the firm.[32]

Cobb found after 1937 that he could not make such a dramatic shift in careers and abandon completely his interest in agriculture. Agriculture and agriculture-related areas had dominated his life to that point and could not easily be forgotten. Accordingly, Cobb kept abreast of the farm situation and often appeared before civic and professional groups as a speaker on agricultural matters. He prided himself on being well versed on current agricultural issues and maintained an extensive correspondence with congressional leaders concerning agricultural problems.[33] He also continued his interest in club work and served as an agricultural advisor to several civic groups.

Numerous tributes to Cobb's active role in agriculture came during his last months in Washington and after he left the Agricultural Adjustment Administration. In 1937 Clemson College (now Clemson University), the land-grant institution of South Carolina, bestowed upon him the honorary degree of doctor of science in agriculture. A quarter of a century later, Cobb was inducted into the Agricultural Hall of Fame, an organization existing to honor men with outstanding accomplishments in American agriculture and to preserve some aspects of the nation's agricultural heritage. Subsequently, Cobb was elected to the group's board of directors, and, typically, he became a financial supporter of the organization. In 1968, on the thirty-fifth anniversary of the signing of the Agricultural Adjustment Act, Cobb was one of several who were invited to Washington to receive from President Lyndon B. Johnson certificates of recognition commemorating their role in the implementation of that pioneer legislation.[34]

Since Cobb now had some leisure for the first time in his life, he decided to put his farming ideas into practice. He had purchased a home with an 85-acre farm near Decatur, Georgia, and proceeded to make a profitable operation of it. Concentrating on grain crops and sheep in the beginning, he later shifted to quality turkey production. In his farm operations, Cobb practiced what he had long encouraged others to do; he sought the advice of the land-grant colleges and their extension personnel, using their expertise to supplement his own management decisions.[35] Later, much of the farm was converted into a residential subdivision and sold, but Cobb continued to reside at the "Briar Patch," the antebellum home on the property.

Cobb gave a large measure of his leisure time to religious and civic organizations. Certainly first on Cobb's list of priorities was the time and energy he devoted to the Druid Hills Baptist Church in Atlanta, Georgia. A sincere and dedicated Christian, Cobb served his church as a deacon and Sunday School teacher for many years. Because of his rural background and his long association with farm organizations and farmers' meetings, Cobb found civic involvement to be a particularly rewarding experience. In fact, he prided himself on taking part in community activities. He was a member of the

The "Briarpatch," Cobb's antebellum home near Atlanta, Georgia.

Rotary Club, the Chamber of Commerce of Atlanta, and the U.S. Chamber of Commerce.[36] Cobb was usually not content merely to keep his name on the membership rolls by paying his dues; he often led the way in directing the groups' efforts toward worthy causes.

As a printer, Cobb developed his interest in professional organizations in this field in much the same manner as he had during his years as an agricultural leader. He served in many positions of responsibility with the local trade associations, including the Atlanta Graphic Arts, Inc., the Atlanta Master Printers Club, and the Georgia Printers Club, of which he served as president and director. He was a member of the Printing Industry of America and served as a member of the Board of Directors and as president of that group's Union Employees Section. During World War II Cobb was a member of the Printing Industry Commission of the War Production Board. In 1952 he was inducted into the Ash Khan Crew, the prestigious social organization for executives of the Printing Industry of America.[37]

Cully Cobb was always conscious of his background and of what he termed the good fortune that contributed to his rise to prominence, both in agriculture and in the business world. He felt that much of his success was due to opportunities provided him, and he felt that he was obligated to make similar opportunities available to others. Consequently, throughout his career, Cobb made efforts to encourage in a tangible way those people whom he felt showed promise and desire. His assistance was sometimes limited to a letter of introduction or a personal recommendation to his friends and associates, but in other cases he was a generous friend when he determined that a loan or an anonymous gift could be most beneficial.

Cobb's philanthropy began with a small donation to the YMCA building at Mississippi State University in 1910 and continued through his agricultural and business careers. His gifts were usually made to religious and educational organizations rather than directly to individuals. Among the benefactors of his donations of money, personal property, or real estate were Emory University; Southern Baptist Theological Seminary at Louisville, Kentucky; Methodist Children's Home in Decatur, Georgia; Lynnville Baptist Church, Lynnville, Tennessee; and several others.[38]

Cobb and H. H. Williamson, pioneers in agricultural extension, recounting their experiences in 1970.

The chief recipient of Cobb's philanthropy was his alma mater, Mississippi State University. Cobb was a steady contributor to that school after he graduated, and his gifts ranged from an extensive collection of woodworking tools to the erection of a historical shaft at the site of one of the nation's first irrigation experiments in a humid region. He provided funds for scholarships, contributed to building funds, and played a major role in the development of the school's Patrons of Excellence program. Cobb's largest gift was an endowment fund to finance the Cobb Institute of Archaeology and to erect a building to house the institute. The institute was established in 1971 to undertake archaeological work in the East, Near East, and Mediterranean areas and on the archaeological sites of the pre-Columbian Americans in the southeastern United States.[39]

While Cully Cobb's management of the Ruralist Press and his philanthropic and other activities after 1937 were certainly worthy of note, it is plain that his major contributions came during the twenty-nine years that he spent in pursuits related to agriculture. Not only were his accomplishments in that area substantial and far-reaching, but to a remarkable degree his career in agriculture reflected some of the most important themes in American agricultural history of the twentieth century.

In the first decades of the twentieth century, agricultural leaders were satisfied that the problems of the American farmer could be solved through the widespread use of better and more efficient methods and through increased production. Education of both adult farmers and rural youth was thought to be an essential step toward those goals. The land-grant colleges, with their experiment stations and extension activities, constituted the foundation upon which a structure of scientific agriculture was to be built. Agricultural high schools represented an early attempt to take agricultural science to farm boys and girls. Those institutions proved to be inadequate for the task at hand, and they were soon replaced by vocational training in the public schools. Far more significant, of course, was the corn clubs. From them came the modern 4-H movement and later came the Future Farmers of America. Agricultural journalism also played a major role in the crusade for better farming. Rural journalists were educators in their own right, and, while preaching the gospel of scientific agriculture, they were vigorous supporters of the agricultural colleges, county agents, and rural youth clubs.

The coming of the Great Depression, which found farmers with vast overproduction and no markets, precipitated a dramatic shift in the thinking of the nation's agricultural and industrial leaders. A decade of rural hardship that became more acute after the Crash of 1929 made it clear that increased production of itself held no final answer to the problems of the countryside. Instead, governmental control of output and assistance in marketing was now deemed necessary, and Franklin D. Roosevelt's New Deal inaugurated a novel departure in agricultural policy that represented a sharp break with the past.

Cobb's accomplishments in agriculture clearly reflected the background, training, and environment from which he came. To say that Cobb was a product of his time and place is inadequate. He was a child of the Tennessee hill country, born to poor but highly intelligent and religiously disciplined parents. He was endowed with an ambition and ability that could find no satisfactory fulfillment in his native Giles County. However, he was able to rise above his environment by combining the gifts of discipline and honesty gained from his parents with his own tenacity, drive, and willingness to work up to the limits of his ability. As a boy, and later as a college student, he discovered the value of friendships and the need at times to compromise on issues while holding steadfastly to basic principles. He also learned to accept that which he could not change and to seek practical, workable solutions within the system of which he was a part.

After graduating from Mississippi Agricultural and Mechanical College, a typical southern land-grant institution, Cobb joined a generation of agricultural teachers and extension personnel who approached their tasks with a missionary zeal. During his tenures at the agricultural high school in Chickasaw County and with the boys' clubs in Mississippi, Cobb never doubted that his work was a part of the most important development of the times. To be sure, some of the direct results expected of both the agricultural high school and the corn clubs were limited—the Buena Vista school did not survive and corn failed to become a major crop in the Magnolia State—but both were intimately related to Cobb's ultimate objective, the improvement of rural life.

During those early years of his career in agriculture, Cobb learned much that would be of use to him later. He found that the role of the innovator in the rural South was not an easy one. He encountered those unique characteristics of the rural mind that never fail to confound men from other backgrounds, and he faced the difficulties inherent in working with the masses in the countryside. Cobb proved to be an apt student; he learned how to establish rapport with farmers, sometimes by avoiding untouchable topics; how to organize large scale programs; and how to administer projects that involved people with little or no formal education. His experiences reinforced his faith in the ordinary southern farmer and undoubtedly strengthened his native conservatism by convincing him that change in the countryside could never come without the support, freely given, of the rural people themselves.

Cobb's service with the *Southern Ruralist* and later with the *Progressive Farmer* also proved to be a training ground. Those magazines were aimed at the small farmer of the South, the same type of rural dweller that Cobb had worked with in Mississippi; but because the papers covered the entire Cotton Belt Cobb's knowledge of southern agriculture was broadened and deepened. Meanwhile, his contacts with regional, national, and international leaders increased, and Cobb's reputation grew. Through involvement in the business management of the magazines, Cobb saw again the value of a course based on economic practicality rather than one resting upon unproven, if admirable, idealism.

Cully Cobb's career in agriculture was climaxed by his appointment as head of the Cotton Section of the Agricultural Adjustment Administration. His life before 1933 was in a very real sense a preparation for his four years in Washington. Certainly Cobb's performance there can be evaluated accurately only by an understanding of and appreciation for his background and earlier experiences. He was a conservative in a time and place which abounded with people whose New Deal ideologies were for the most part in opposition to his own. He was one of the best-informed men in the country on cotton but being a product of the South his fitness for any place in the New Deal program was suspect to many in Washington, especially to liberal reformers. Cobb was by virtue of his experience a practical man, preferring always to reject unproven perfection for worthwhile results. This, too, set him apart from some of his associates in Washington. At the same time, Cobb was perhaps unduly sensitive to criticism by those whom he believed to be uninformed or misguided. Yet, he found these criticisms of enormous value in helping him perform his tasks. A fair and honest man, Cobb expected as much from both his Washington colleagues and from the men toward whom the cotton program was directed. This, in fact, may have been Cobb's major limitation.

Certainly Cobb was a successful administrator. Throughout much of his adult life he had managed schools, rural clubs, and farm papers. With the AAA, Cobb was given the Herculean task of administering one of the most complex and controversial programs in American history. It was a project that required the coordinated efforts of thousands of field agents dealing with millions of farmers, many of whom were traditionally hostile to governmental interference and largely ignorant of the economics involved. Here Cobb met his greatest challenge and undoubtedly made his greatest single contribution to agriculture. Despite vigorous criticism of his work by some contemporaries and by historians later, it is abundantly clear that Cobb's Cotton Section performed the basic task for which it was established. Given the conditions of the time, practical and reasonable men could expect no more.

## NOTES TO CHAPTER IX

1. H. G. Hastings to Clarence Poe, July 7, 1930, Ruralist Press, Inc., Minutes, Ruralist Press Papers (Mississippi State University Library).

2. Cobb interviews; Ruralist Press, Minutes, January 30, March 18–19, July 11, 1935, March 19, June 19, 1936, Ruralist Press Papers.

3. Ruralist Press, Inc., Minutes, June 20, August 7, 10, 1936; W. H. James and Associates to Cobb, September 21, 1937; unidentified author to B. C. Stafford, January 7, 1939, Ruralist Press Papers.

4. Cobb interviews; Charles D. Hurt, Jr., Memo, March 2, 1972; Cobb, Statement of Assets, March 17, 1927, Ruralist Press Papers. Until 1965 stock in the Ruralist Press consisted of fractional shares to three or four places. In this account, holdings have been rounded off to the nearest whole number.

5. Charles D. Hurt, Jr., Memo, March 2, 1972; Cobb to H. W. Brown, January 6, 1937; Ruralist Press, Inc., Minutes, January 19, August 2, 1937; W. J. Davis to Ruralist Press, October 14, 1940, Ruralist Press Papers.

6. W. H. James and Associates to Cobb, September 21, 1937, Ruralist Press Papers.

7. Cobb interviews.

8. W. H. James and Associates to Cobb, September 21, 1937; Ruralist Press, Inc., Minutes, August 2, 1937, Ruralist Press Papers.

9. C. A. Cobb to Scott Candler, August 18, October 6, 1938; W. S. Jones to Cobb, October 21, 1938; Cobb to B. C. Stafford, November 4, 1938; Cobb to M. E. Everett, September 24, 1940; Ruralist Press, Inc., Minutes, January 25, 1943, Ruralist Press Papers.

10. C. A. Cobb to Scott Candler, August 18, 1938, January 11, 1939; B. C. Stafford to Cobb, February 20, 1939; C. B. Turner to W. H. James, September 5, 1940, Ruralist Press Papers.

11. Ruralist Press, Inc., Minutes, appropriate years, Ruralist Press Papers.

12. Ruralist Press, Inc., Minutes, October 17, 1947, June 30, 1948, June 9, 1949; W. J. Davis to Ruralist Press, October 14, 1940, Ruralist Press Papers.

13. Ruralist Press, Inc., Minutes, July 27, 1949, Ruralist Press Papers.

14. Ruralist Press, Inc., Minutes, December 8, 1949, June 22, November 14, 1950, June 27, November 30, 1951, March 26, October 30, 1952, June 11, October 26, 1953, Ruralist Press Papers.

15. Ruralist Press, Inc., Minutes, November 5, 1958, November 26, 1965, Ruralist Press Papers.

16. Ruralist Press, Inc., Minutes, October 25, 1948, March 3, 1971, Ruralist Press Papers.

17. The authors' knowledge of printing technology was supplemented by interviews with Cully Cobb and James W. Crosby of Mississippi State University's

Central Duplicating Department and by a tour of the Ruralist Press plant in Atlanta, Georgia. See figure 2.

18. Cobb to B. C. Stafford, October 22, 1937; Cobb to W. C. Arnold, July 14, 1939, Ruralist Press Papers.

19. Cobb interviews; Wingate Jackson, Memo, February 17, 1938; Jackson to Stanley Andrews, August 13, 1940, Ruralist Press Papers.

20. Vincent Cunningham to Cobb, May 24, 1938; Robert Young to Vincent Cunningham, June 21, 1939; Lillian Hansen to Cobb, August 13, 1957, Ruralist Press Papers.

21. Miscellaneous items in Ruralist Press Papers.

22. Price Gilbert to Harrison Jones, April 21, 1939, Ruralist Press Papers.

23. Cobb interviews; Ruralist Press, Inc., Minutes, August 31, 1970; P. L. Bridges to E. H. Highlander, January 19, 1938, Ruralist Press Papers.

24. Chester E. Martin to S. B. Hungerford, February 21, 1940, Ruralist Press Papers.

25. H. L. Fassett to Wingate Jackson, July 21, 1939; Ruralist Press, Inc., Minutes, August 31, 1970, Ruralist Press Papers.

26. Atlanta *Constitution*, February 11, 1971, p. 12d; Cobb to R. V. Scott, October 6, 1972, enclosing presentation prepared for J. P. Stevens Company, Cobb Papers.

27. Cobb to R. V. Scott, October 6, 1972, enclosing presentation prepared for J. P. Stevens and Company; Charles D. Hurt to Cobb, October 6, 1972, Cobb Papers.

28. W. H. James and Associates to Cobb, September 21, 1937, Ruralist Press Papers; Charles D. Hurt to Cobb, October 6, 1972, Cobb Papers. The fiscal year for the Ruralist Press was September 1–August 31.

29. Ruralist Press, Inc., Minutes, various dates, Ruralist Press Papers.

30. Charles D. Hurt, Jr., Memo, March 2, 1972, Cobb Papers; *Moody's Industrial Manual*, 1972, p. 2752; New York *Times*, June 18, 1971, p. 53.

31. Ruralist Press, Inc., Minutes, November 16, 1967, April 7, 1969, December 16, 1969, Ruralist Press Papers; Cobb to R. V. Scott, October 6, 1972, enclosing presentation prepared for J. P. Stevens and Company, Cobb Papers.

32. *Cobbs of Tennessee*, 62–77; Clarence Poe to Lois P. Dowdle, August 25, 1933; Charles N. Shepardson to Lois Cobb, November 12, 1952, and assorted news clippings and publications of the American Institute of Fats and Oils, Lois Dowdle Cobb Papers (Mississippi State University Library).

33. Cobb and Senator Richard Russell of Georgia were friends of many years and corresponded on a regular basis. Richard Russell letters, Ruralist Press Papers.

34. J. H. Longwell to Cobb, January 30, 1963, Ruralist Press Papers; *Cobbs of Tennessee*, 68.

35. Cobb to D. W. Watkins, September 22, 1939; Cobb to L. R. Neal, October 2, 1939; Cobb to Ralph Davis, October 3, 1940; Cobb to T. M. Thomas, January 11, 1955, Ruralist Press Papers.

36. *Cobbs of Tennessee*, 69.

37. Cobb to J. R. Brackett, February 1, 1950; Printing Industry of America, Executive Letter, November 6, 1950; Cobb to B. J. Taymans, May 11, 1956; Cobb to Gerald W. Walsh, July 2, 1956; International Printing Pressmen and Assistants' Union of North America, Convention Calendar, Philadelphia, Pa., September 27, 1956; J. R. Brackett to Cobb, February 20, 1952, Ruralist Press Papers.

38. *Cobbs of Tennessee*, 70.

39. Jackson *Clarion-Ledger*, July 11, 1971.

# Bibliography

PRIMARY SOURCES

MANUSCRIPTS

Agricultural Stabilization and Conservation Service Records. Central Correspondence Files, 1933–1947. Record Group 145. National Archives, Washington.

Agricultural Stabilization and Conservation Service Records. Production Control Program, 1933–1940. Record Group 145. National Archives, Washington.

[Baker, Gladys]. Discussion with Wayne Darrow, June 22, 1964. Typescript in United States Department of Agriculture Library, Washington.

Bureau of Plant Industry Records. National Archives, Washington.

C. A. Cobb Papers. Mississippi State University Library, Mississippi State, Mississippi.

Lois P. Dowdle Cobb Papers. Mississippi State University Library, Mississippi State, Mississippi.

Darrow, Wayne. Farm March–1935. Typescript in United States Department of Agriculture Library, Washington.

A. W. Garner Papers. Mississippi State University Library, Mississippi State, Mississippi.

John C. Hardy Papers. Mississippi State University Library, Mississippi State, Mississippi.

Perry G. Holden Memoirs. Michigan State University Library, East Lansing, Michigan.

W. H. Magruder Papers. Mississippi State University Library, Mississippi State, Mississippi.

Mississippi Agricultural and Mechanical College. Minutes of the Board of Trustees. Mississippi State University Library, Mississippi State, Mississippi.

Mississippi Extension Service Records. Mississippi State University Library, Mississippi State, Mississippi.

Mississippi State University Alumni Association Files. Alumni Office, Mississippi State, Mississippi.

Mississippi State University, Extension Service. Annual Narrative and Statistical Reports. National Archives, Washington. Copy in Mississippi State University Library, Mississippi State, Mississippi.

Robert R. Moton Papers. Hollis Burke Frissell Library, Tuskegee, Alabama.
Nils A. Olsen Papers. Iowa State University Library, Ames, Iowa.
President's Correspondence. Mississippi State University Library, Mississippi State, Mississippi.
Franklin D. Roosevelt Papers. Franklin D. Roosevelt Library, Hyde Park, New York.
Ruralist Press, Inc., Papers. Mississippi State University Library, Mississippi State, Mississippi.
Secretary of Agriculture Records. Case Files of the Office of the Solicitor, Record Group 16. National Archives, Washington.
James E. Tanner Papers. Mississippi State University Library, Mississippi State, Mississippi.
Rexford G. Tugwell Papers. Franklin D. Roosevelt Library, Hyde Park, New York.
Henry A. Wallace Papers. University of Iowa Library, Iowa City, Iowa.

CULLY A. COBB, SELECTED PUBLICATIONS

"The Agricultural Adjustment Act in Its Application to Cotton." Association of Southern Agricultural Workers, *Proceedings*, 1933–1935. N.p., n.d. Pp. 183–87.
"This Agricultural Adjustment Act as Applied to Cotton." *The Cotton and Cotton Oil News*. Vol. 35 (April 7, 1934), 3–5.
"Application of the Agricultural Adjustment Act to the Cotton Cooperative." American Institute of Cooperation, *American Cooperation*, 1933. Washington, 1934. Pp. 68–72.
"Boys' Corn Clubs." Mississippi Teachers' Association, *Proceedings*, 1911. Jackson, n.d. Pp. 145–47.
"Boys' Clubs—What They Can and Do Accomplish." Agricultural Extension Committee of the National Implement and Vehicle Association, *Agricultural Extension*. Chicago, 1916. Pp. 72–78.
"The Contribution of the Press to Agriculture," Texas Agricultural Extension Service, *Silver Anniversary: Cooperative Demonstration Work, 1903–1928*. College Station, n.d. Pp. 24–30.
"Cooperation and Stability." *American Cotton Grower*, Vol. 3 (August, 1937), 24–25.
"The Coordination of State and Federal Efforts in the Development of a Land-Utilization Program." National Conference on Land Utilization, *Proceedings, November 19–21, 1931*. Washington, 1932. Pp. 103–106.
"The Cotton Adjustment Program." *Extension Service Review*, Vol. 4 (September, 1935), 67–68.
"Cotton and the AAA Program." *American Cotton Grower*, Vol. 2 (November, 1936), 6–7.
"Cotton in the Nation's Cropping Program." Association of Southern Agricultural Workers, *Proceedings*, 1933–1935. N.p., n.d. Pp. 380–84.
"Cotton Production Adjustment for 1934—What It Proposes to Accomplish." *Extension Service Review*, Vol. 4 (December, 1935), 115–16.
"Economic Position of the Cotton Ginner." *The Cotton and Cotton Oil*

*News*, Vol. 35 (April 7, 1934), 9.

"The Future Promise of Farm Life." *Journal of Home Economics*, Vol. 24 (November, 1932), 974–75.

"Relations between Farm Papers and Cooperative Papers." American Institute of Cooperation, *American Cooperation*, 1929. Washington, 1930. Pp. 257–59.

"The South's Farm Tenancy Problem, an Address before the Conference of Rural Ministers, State College, Mississippi, June 26, 1936." United States Agricultural Adjustment Administration, *Southern Region Series*, Item 1. Washington, 1936.

"What One Southern County Agricultural High School Has Done and Is Doing." Conference for Education in the South, *Proceedings*, 1910. Washington, n.d. Pp. 64–69.

"Where Farming Is Taught in Every Public School." *Forbes*, Vol. 15 (January, 1925), 464–66.

"The World Situation with Regard to Cotton." Association of Southern Agricultural Workers, *Proceedings*, 1932. N.p., n.d. Pp. 6–9.

With Others. "Report of Resolutions Committee." Association of Southern Agricultural Workers, *Proceedings*, 1927. N.p., n.d. Pp. 12–13.

GOVERNMENT DOCUMENTS

"The Agricultural Outlook for the Southern States, 1930–1931." U. S. Department of Agriculture, *Miscellaneous Publication* 102. Washington, 1930.

American Association of Farmers' Institute Workers. *Proceedings*, 1907. Washington, 1908.

Benson, O. H. and Gertrude L. Warren. "Organization and Results of Boys' and Girls' Club Work, 1918." United States Department of Agriculture, *Circular* 66. Washington, 1920.

Crosby, Dick J. "Agriculture in the Public High Schools." United States Department of Agriculture, *Yearbook*, 1912. Washington, 1913. Pp. 471–82.

Davis, Chester C. "The Development of Agricultural Policy since the End of the World War." United States Department of Agriculture, *Yearbook of Agriculture*, 1940. Washington, 1940. Pp. 297–326.

Davis, Kary C. "County Schools of Agriculture in Wisconsin." United States Office of Experiment Stations, *Annual Report*, 1904. Washington, 1905. Pp. 677–86.

Dickins, Dorothy. "Agricultural High School Dormitories of Mississippi." Mississippi Agricultural Experiment Station, *Bulletin* 293. A and M College, 1931.

Evans, J. A. "Recollections of Extension History." North Carolina Extension Service, *Circular* 224. Raleigh, 1938.

Farrell, George E. "Boys' and Girls' 4–H Club Work under the Smith-Lever Act, 1914–1924." United States Department of Agriculture, *Miscellaneous Circular* 85. Washington, 1926.

*First Annual Livestock Show, November 24–25, 1922.* A and M College, n.d.

Gray, L. C. "National Conference Recommends Program of Study and

Action." United States Department of Agriculture, *Yearbook of Agriculture*, 1932. Washington, 1933. Pp. 460–62.

Hill, I. W. and C. L. Chambers. "Boys' Agricultural Club Work in the Southern States." United States Department of Agriculture, *Department Circular* 38. Washington, 1919.

*Historical Statistics of the United States, 1789–1945*. Washington, 1949.

Howe, F. W. "Boys' and Girls' Agricultural Clubs." United States Department of Agriculture, *Farmers' Bulletin* 385. Washington, 1910.

Johnson, A. A. "County Schools of Agriculture and Domestic Economy in Wisconsin." United States Office of Experiment Stations, *Bulletin* 242. Washington, 1911.

Knapp, Bradford. "Results of Demonstration Work in Boys' and Girls' Clubs in 1912." United States Bureau of Plant Industry, *Publication* 865. Washington, 1913.

―――― and O. B. Martin. "Boys' Demonstration Work: The Corn Clubs." United States Bureau of Plant Industry, *Publication* 644. Washington, 1912.

――――. "Results of Boys' Demonstration Work in Corn Clubs in 1911." U. S. Bureau of Plant Industry, *Publication* 741. Washington, 1912.

Lamon, Harry M. "The Organization of Boys' and Girls' Poultry Clubs." United States Department of Agriculture, *Farmers' Bulletin* 562. (Washington, 1913.

Lloyd, William A. "County Agricultural Agent Work under the Smith-Lever Act, 1914–1924." United States Department of Agriculture, *Miscellaneous Circular* 59. Washington, 1925.

Martin, O. B. "A Decade of Negro Extension Work, 1914–1924." United States Department of Agriculture, *Miscellaneous Circular* 72. Washington, 1926.

Mercier, William B. "Extension Work among Negroes." United States Department of Agriculture, *Circular* 190. Washington, 1921.

――――. "Status and Results of Extension Work in the Southern States, 1903–1921." United States Department of Agriculture, *Department Circular* 248. Washington, 1922.

Mississippi Agricultural Experiment Station. *Bulletin* 120. Agricultural College, 1908.

Mississippi Agricultural and Mechanical College. *Catalogue*, 1909–1920. Nashville, n.d.

――――. *Biennial Report*, 1906–1921. Nashville, 1906–1921.

――――. *Bulletin*, 1904–1905. Agricultural College, 1905.

――――. *College Reveille*, 1908. N.p., n.d.

*Mississippi Boys' Corn Club Congress*. N.p., n.d.

Mississippi Extension Work in Agriculture and Home Economics. *Annual Report*, 1916, 1918–1919. N.p., n.d.

Mississippi, *Laws*. 1908–1916.

Mississippi State Superintendent of Public Education. *Biennial Report*, 1901–1967. Nashville, 1904–.

Mississippi Survey Commission. *Public Education in Mississippi: A Report*. Jackson, 1926.

National Conference on Land Utilization. *Proceedings, November 19–21, 1931.* Washington, 1932.

"Regulations and Suggestions Concerning County Agricultural High Schools in Mississippi." Mississippi State Board of Education, *Bulletin* 12. Jackson, 1919.

"Rockefeller Foundation." U. S. Senate *Document* 538. 63rd Cong., 2nd Sess., 1914.

Smith, C. B. "Boys' and Girls' 4-H Club Work." U.S. Department of Agriculture, *Miscellaneous Circular* 77. Washington, 1926.

Smith, C. Beaman and K. H. Atwood. "The Relation of Agricultural Extension Agencies to Farm Practices." U.S. Bureau of Plant Industry, *Circular* 117. Washington, 1913.

Strauss, Frederick and Louis H. Bean. "Gross Farm Income and Indices of Farm Production and Prices in the United States 1869–1937." U.S. Department of Agriculture, *Technical Bulletin* 703. Washington, 1940.

Texas Agricultural Extension Service. *Four Who Won.* N.p., n.d.

Tramel, Thomas E. and David W. Parvin. "Prices Received and Paid by Mississippi Farmers and Index of Seasonal Variations in Farm Prices, 1910–1955." Mississippi Agricultural Experiment Station, *Bulletin* 535. State College, 1955.

True, Alfred C. *A History of Agricultural Education in the United States, 1785–1925.* Washington, 1929.

———. *A History of Agricultural Extension Work in the United States, 1785–1923.* Washington, 1928.

——— and Dick J. Crosby. "The American System of Agricultural Education." U.S. Office of Experiment Stations, *Circular* 106. Washington, 1911.

U.S. Agricultural Adjustment Administration. *Report,* 1933–1935, 1937–1938. Washington, 1936, 1939.

U.S. Department of Agriculture. *Agricultural Statistics,* 1938. Washington, 1938.

———. *Annual Report,* 1914–1920. Washington, 1914–1920.

———. *Cooperative Extension Work in Agriculture and Home Economics,* 1917–1920. Washington, 1919–1922.

———. Form No. Cotton 1, *Cotton Contract,* 1934–1935.

———. *Report on Agricultural Experiment Stations and Cooperative Agricultural Extension Work in the United States,* 1915–1917. Washington, 1916–1919.

———. *Yearbook,* 1915, 1931, 1933, 1940, 1964. Washington, 1916, 1931, 1933, 1940, 1964.

U.S. Office of Experiment Stations, *Annual Report,* 1909, 1911 (Washington, 1910, 1912).

U.S. *Thirteen Census: Population; Agriculture.*

"A Vacation Course in Junior Farm Mechanics." Mississippi Agricultural Extension Department, *Extension Circular* 24. Agricultural College, 1919.

Ward, W. F. "Boys' Pig Clubs," U.S. Department of Agriculture, *Farmers' Bulletin* 566. Washington, 1913.

"The World Cotton Situation With Outlook for 1931–1932." U.S. Department of Agriculture, *Miscellaneous Publication* 104. Washington, 1930.

BOOKS AND ARTICLES

Association of Agricultural Colleges and Experiment Stations. *Proceedings*, 1911–1912. Burlington, Vt., 1912.

N. W. *Ayer and Son's American Newspaper Annual and Directory*, 1916, 1929. Philadelphia, 1916, 1929.

Blum, John M., ed. *From the Morgenthau Diaries*. 3 vols. Boston, 1959–1967.

Conference for Education in the South. *Proceedings*, 1913–1914. Washington, n.d.

Crosby, Dick J. "Agriculture in High Schools." *Southern Educational Review*. Vol. 4 (February–March, 1907), 37–43.

————. "The Place of the Agricultural High School in the System of Public Education." National Education Association, *Journal*, 1910. Winona, Minn., 1910. Pp. 1103–1107.

————. "Special Agricultural High Schools." National Education Association, *Journal*, 1909. Winona, Minn., 1909. Pp. 974–76.

Davenport, Eugene. "Industrial Education: A Phase of the Problem of Universal Education." National Education Association, *Journal*, 1909. Winona, Minn., 1909. Pp. 277–88.

Duncan, Clyde H. *Straight Furrows: A Story of 4–H Club Work*. Albuquerque, 1954.

Eisenhower, Dwight D. *At Ease, Stories I Tell to Friends*. Garden City, N.Y., 1967.

General Education Board. *General Education Board: An Account of Its Activities, 1902–1914*. New York, 1915.

Harrill, L. R. *Memories of 4–H*. Raleigh, 1967.

International Live Stock Exposition. *Review and Album*, 1922. N.p., n.d.

Kiern, Nellie. *Paper Read before the Teachers' Club of the Industrial Institute and College, October 9, 1908*. Columbus, n.d.

Knapp, Seaman A. "How Can the Masses Be Induced to Adopt a Better System of Agriculture?" Conference for Education in the South, *Proceedings*, 1910. Washington, n.d. Pp. 253–58.

Martin, Oscar B. "Boys' and Girls' Clubs." Conference for Education in the South, *Proceedings*, 1912. Washington, n.d. Pp. 206–15.

————. "Boys' and Girls' Demonstration Work in the Southern States." Conference for Education in the South, *Proceedings*, 1914. Washington, 1914. Pp. 57–62.

————. *The Demonstration Work: Dr. Knapp's Contribution to Civilization*. San Antonia, 1941.

Mississippi Teachers' Association, *Proceedings*, 1912. Gulfport, n.d.

*Moody's Industrial Manual*, 1972.

Noble, Stuart G. "The Agricultural High School in Mississippi." *Mississippi School Journal*, Vol. 15 (January, 1911), 1–6.

————. "The Alabama System of Agricultural High Schools." *Educational Exchange*, Vol. 26 (January, 1911), 10–13.

————. "The Curriculum of the Agricultural High School." *Mississippi School Journal*, Vol. 15 (March, 1911), 7–11.

————. "Shall We Have a Secondary School of Agriculture?" *Mississippi School Journal*, Vol. 15 (December, 1910), 8–11.

Nourse, Edwin G., Joseph S. Davis, and John D. Black. *Three Years of the Agricultural Adjustment Administration*. Washington, 1937.

*Official and Statistical Register of the State of Mississippi*, 1912. Nashville, 1912.

Poe, Clarence. *My First Eighty Years*. Chapel Hill, 1963.

*RUS: A Biographical Register of Rural Leadership in the United States and Canada*, 1920–1930. Ithaca, 1920–1930.

Reynolds, J. H. "Agricultural High Schools." Southern Educational Association, *Journal*, 1908. Chattanooga, n.d. Pp. 515–25.

Richards, Henry I. *Cotton and the AAA*. Washington, 1936.

————. *Cotton under the Agricultural Adjustment Act: Developments up to July 1934*. Washington, 1934.

Schaub, I. O. "Boys' Corn Clubs." University of Virginia, *Rural Life Conference*, 1910. Charlottesville, 1910. Pp. 287–88.

Soule, A. M. "The Work of the Agricultural High School in the Scheme of State Education." Southern Educational Association, *Journal*, 1907. Chattanooga, n.d. Pp. 181–91.

Southern Cattlemen's Association. *Fifteenth Annual Meeting*, January 10–12, 1927. N.p., n.d.

Swing, R. G. "Purge at the AAA." *Nation*, Vol. 140 (February 20, 1935), 216–17.

Thomas, Norman. *The Plight of the Sharecroppers*. New York, 1934.

Tugwell, Rexford G. "The Place of Government in a National Land Program." *Journal of Farm Economics*, Vol. 16 (January, 1934), 55–69.

Watkins, D. W. "The Southern Agricultural Outlook Conference." *Journal of Farm Economics*, Vol. 13 (January, 1931), 160–62.

Wilson, William L. "Southeast Seeks Representation on Federal Farm Board." *Manufacturers Record*, Vol. 100 (July 30, 1931), 30–31.

FARM JOURNALS AND MISCELLANEOUS NEWSPAPERS

*Agricultural and Industrial Bulletin* (Kansas City, Mo.).
*Agricultural Development Bulletin* (St. Louis).
*Amory* (Miss.) *Advertiser*.
*The Bulletin* (Jackson, Miss.).
*College Reflector* (Agricultural College, Miss.).
*The* (Atlanta) *Constitution*.
*Country Gentleman* (Philadelphia).
*Hinds County Gazette* (Jackson, Miss.).
*Hoard's Dairyman* (Fort Atkison, Wisc.).
*Houston* (Miss.) *Advocate*.
*Houston* (Miss.) *Post*.
*Jackson* (Miss.) *Daily Clarion-Ledger*.
*Jackson* (Miss.) *Daily News*.

*Louisiana Club and Extension News* (Baton Rouge).
*Magnolia Farmer* (Agricultural College, Miss.).
*Manufacturers Record* (Baltimore).
*The Mary Hardin-Baylor College Belles* (Belton, Texas).
Memphis *Commercial Appeal.*
Memphis *Press-Scimitar.*
*Mississippi A. and M. Alumnus* (Agricultural College).
*Mississippi Agricultural Student* (Agricultural College).
*Mississippi Club Boy* (Agricultural College).
*Mississippi Educational Advance* (Jackson).
*Mississippi School Journal* (Jackson).
New York *Times.*
*Ohio Farmer* (Cleveland).
*Okolona* (Miss.) *Messenger.*
*The Outlook* (New York).
*Printers' Ink* (New York).
*Progressive Farmer* (Raleigh, N.C. and elsewhere).
*Progressive Farmer and Southern Farm Gazette* (Starkville, Miss).
*Progressive Farmer and Southern Ruralist* (Raleigh, N.C. and elsewhere).
*Rural America* (New York).
*Southern Educational Review* (Chattanooga).
*Southern Farm Gazette* (Starkville, Miss.).
*Southern Farm Magazine* (Baltimore).
*Southern Reporter* (St. Paul).
*Southern Ruralist* (Atlanta).
Starkville *East Mississippi Times.*
*Starkville* (Miss.) *News.*
*Tupelo* (Miss.) *Journal.*
*U.S. News and World Report* (Washington)
*Wallaces' Farmer* (Des Moines)
Washington *Evening Star*
Washington *Post*

INTERVIEWS

W. B. Camp
C. A. Cobb. Typescripts of some interviews with Cobb are available at
    Mississippi State University Library, Mississippi State, Mississippi, and at
    the University of California Library, Berkeley, California.
Lois Dowdle Cobb
Victor Christgau
J. W. Crosby
Harold McGeorge
Guy H. Palmes
H. H. Williamson

# SECONDARY MATERIALS

BOOKS AND ARTICLES

Atkinson, James R. "A History of Chickasaw County, Mississippi, to the Civil War." *Northeast Mississippi Historical Journal*, Vol. 2 (December, 1968), 3–68.

Bailey, Joseph C. *Seaman A. Knapp: Schoolmaster of American Agriculture.* New York, 1945.

Baker, Gladys L. " 'And to Act for the Secretary': Paul H. Appleby and the Department of Agriculture, 1935–1940." *Agricultural History*, Vol. 45 (October, 1971), 235–58.

Bayard, E. S. "The Farm Paper—A Vital Educational Force." *American Fertilizer*, Vol. 71 (July 6, 1929), 48, 51–52.

Benedict, David. *A General History of the Baptist Denomination in America.* 2 vols. Boston, 1813.

Benedict, Murray R. *Farm Policies of the United States, 1790–1950.* Washington, 1953.

Bettersworth, John K. *People's College: A History of Mississippi State.* Tuscaloosa, 1953.

Broom, Knox M. *History of Mississippi Public Junior Colleges, 1928–1953.* N.p., 1954.

Butler, Eugene, Dr. Tait Butler: Veterinarian, Editor and Publisher, and Agricultural Leader. Typed manuscript in Mississippi State University Library, Mississippi State, Mississippi.

Cash, W. J. *The Mind of the South.* New York, 1941.

Christianson, J. O. "A Folk School for Farmers." *Hoard's Dairyman*, Vol. 84 (August 25, 1939), 456, 469.

*Class of 1908.* Atlanta, 1963.

*The Cobbs of Tennessee, Descendants of John Cobb of Cobbs Court, County Kent, England, 1325–1968.* Atlanta, 1968.

Conkin, Paul K. *Tomorrow a New World: The New Deal Community Program.* Ithaca, 1959.

Conrad, David E. *The Forgotten Farmers: The Story of Sharecroppers in the New Deal.* Urbana, 1965.

Epsilon Sigma Phi. *The Spirit and Philosophy of Extension Work.* Washington, 1952.

Evans, James F. PRAIRIE FARMER *and WLS: The Burridge D. Butler Years.* Urbana, 1969.

Fite, Gilbert C. *George N. Peek and the Fight for Farm Parity.* Norman, 1954.

Folmsbee, Stanley J., Robert E. Corlew, and Enoch L. Mitchell. *Tennessee, a Short History.* Knoxville, 1969.

Fosdick, Raymond B. *Adventure in Giving: The Story of the General Education Board.* New York, 1962.

Fusfeld, Daniel R. *The Economic Thought of Franklin D. Roosevelt and the Origins of the New Deal.* New York, 1956.

Gleason, John P. "The Attitude of the Business Community toward Agriculture during the McNary-Haugen Period." *Agricultural History*, Vol. 32 (April, 1958), 127–38.

Grubbs, Donald R. *Cry from the Cotton: The Southern Tenant Farmers' Union and the New Deal.* Chapel Hill, 1971.

———. "Gardner Jackson, That 'Socialist' Tenant Farmers' Union, and the New Deal." *Agricultural History*, Vol. 42 (April, 1968), 125–37.

Hale, Harrison. *University of Arkansas, 1871–1948.* Fayetteville, 1948.

Hassell, Cushing B. *History of the Church of God, from the Creation to A.D. 1885.* Middleton, New York, 1886.

Hilbun, Ben. *William Flowers Hand: The Life and Philosophy of a Mississippi Scientist and Educator.* State College, Mississippi, 1952.

Holley, Donald. "The Negro in the New Deal Resettlement Program." *Agricultural History*, Vol. 45 (July, 1971), 179–93.

Houck, U. G. *The Bureau of Animal Industry of the United States Department of Agriculture.* Washington, 1924.

*Houston Times-Post, History of Chickasaw County, Mississippi.* Houston, Miss., 1936.

Hubbard, Preston J. *Origins of the TVA: The Muscle Shoals Controversy, 1920–1932.* Nashville, 1961.

Johnson, William R. "National Farm Organizations and the Reshaping of Agricultural Policy in 1932." *Agricultural History*, Vol. 37 (January, 1963), 35–42.

Jones, C. Clyde. "The Burlington Railroad and Agricultural Policy in the 1920's." *Agricultural History*, Vol. 31 (October, 1957), 67–74.

Kirkendall, Richard S. "Howard Tolley and Agricultural Planning in the 1930's." *Agricultural History*, Vol. 39 (January, 1965), 25–33.

———. "L. C. Gray and the Supply of Agricultural Land." *Agricultural History*, Vol. 37 (October, 1963), 206–14.

———. *Social Scientists and Farm Politics in the Age of Roosevelt.* Columbia, 1966.

Leuchtenburg, William E. *Franklin D. Roosevelt and the New Deal, 1932–1940.* New York, 1963.

Lord, Russell. *The Wallaces of Iowa.* Boston, 1947.

McCallum, James. *A Brief Sketch of the Settlement and Early History of Giles County, Tennessee.* Pulaski, Tennessee, 1876.

Manchester, Harland. "The Farm Magazines." *Scribner's*, Vol. 104 (October, 1938), 25–29, 58–59.

Mitchell, Broadus. *Depression Decade: From New Era through New Deal.* New York, 1947.

Moley, Raymond. *The First New Deal.* New York, 1966.

Noblin, Stuart. *Leonidas LaFayette Polk: Agrarian Crusader.* Chapel Hill, 1949.

Percy, William A. *Lanterns on the Levee.* New York, 1941.

Perkins, Van L. "The AAA and the Politics of Agriculture: Agricultural Policy Formulation in the Fall of 1933." *Agricultural History*, Vol. 39 (October, 1965), 220–29.

———. *Crisis in Agriculture: The Agricultural Adjustment Administration and the New Deal, 1933.* Berkeley and Los Angeles, 1969.

Peterson, Theodore. *Magazines in the Twentieth Century*. Urbana, 1956.
Powell, Fred W. *The Bureau of Plant Industry, Activities and Organization*. Baltimore, 1927.
Rauch, Basil. *The History of the New Deal, 1933–1938*. New York, 1944.
Reck, Franklin M. *The 4-H Story: A History of 4-H Club Work*. Ames, 1951.
Rowley, William D. "M. L. Wilson: 'Believer' in the Domestic Allotment." *Agricultural History*, Vol. 43 (April, 1969), 277–87.
————. *M. L. Wilson and the Campaign for the Domestic Allotment*. Lincoln, 1970.
Saloutos, Theodore. *Farm Movements in the South, 1865–1933*. Berkeley and Los Angeles, 1960.
Schapsmeier, Edward L. and Frederick H. Schapsmeier. "Henry A. Wallace: Agrarian Idealist or Agricultural Realist?" *Agricultural History*, Vol. 41 (April, 1967), 127–137.
————. *Henry A. Wallace of Iowa: The Agrarian Years, 1910–1940*. Ames, 1968.
Schlesinger, Arthur M., Jr. *The Coming of the New Deal*. Boston, 1959.
Scott, Roy V. *The Reluctant Farmer: The Rise of Agricultural Extension to 1914*. Urbana, 1970.
Sillars, Malcolm O. "Henry A. Wallace's Editorials on Agricultural Discontent, 1921–1928." *Agricultural History*, Vol. 26 (October, 1952), 132–40.
Slay, Ronald J. *The Development of the Teaching of Agriculture in Mississippi*. New York, 1928.
Slichter, Almy G. "Franklin D. Roosevelt's Farm Policy as Governor of New York State, 1928–1932." *Agricultural History*, Vol. 33 (October, 1959), 167–76.
Smith, Mapheus. "Circulation of Farm Magazines." *School and Society*. Vol. 46 (September 11, 1937), 350–52.
Socolofsky, Homer E. *Arthur Capper: Publisher, Politician, and Philanthropist*. Lawrence, 1962.
————. "The Development of the Capper Farm Press." *Agricultural History*, Vol. 31 (October, 1957), 34–43.
Sternsher, Bernard. *Rexford Tugwell and the New Deal*. New Brunswick, 1964.
Tindall, George B. *The Emergence of the New South, 1913–1945*. Baton Rouge, 1967.
Venkataramani, M. S. "Norman Thomas, Arkansas Sharecroppers, and the Roosevelt Agricultural Policies, 1933–1937." *Mississippi Valley Historical Review*, Vol. 47 (September, 1960), 225–46.
Wengert, Norman. "Antecedents of TVA: The Legislative History of Muscle Shoals." *Agricultural History*, Vol. 26 (October, 1952), 141–47.
Williamson, Frederick W. *Origin and Growth of Agricultural Extension in Louisiana, 1860–1948*. Baton Rouge, 1951.
Winters, Donald L. *Henry Cantrell Wallace as Secretary of Agriculture, 1921–1924*. Urbana, 1970.

Wyer, Malcolm G. "Agricultural Periodicals for a Public Library." *Library Journal*, Vol. 53 (October 15, 1928), 850–52.

THESES

Beck, Oscar A., Jr. "The Agricultural Press and Southern Rural Development, 1900–1940." Ph.D. thesis, George Peabody College, 1952.
Pope, George J. "Agricultural Extension in Mississippi prior to 1914." M.A. thesis, Mississippi State University, 1963.
Robson, George L., Jr. "The Farmers' Union in Mississippi." M.A. thesis, Mississippi State University, 1963.
Wilson, Allen D. "Agricultural Periodicals in the United States." M.A. thesis, University of Illinois, 1930.

# Index

Abt, John, 222
Advertisers: in *Southern Ruralist*, 142
Agricultural Act of 1933: passed, 198, 207; declared unconstitutional, 235
Agricultural Adjustment Act of 1938, 237
Agricultural Adjustment Administration: established, 207; organization of, 207–209; cotton payments under, 213, 216, 219; criticism of, 216, 222–223; cotton plow-up first test of, 218; conflict in, 220–221, 223–229; purge in, 229–231; farmers' march supports programs of, 235; mentioned 3, 204, 243, 263
Agricultural credit: Cobb's views on, 160–161
Agricultural education: in 1908, 36; in public high schools, 37; role of, 261
Agricultural experiment stations: Cobb's views on, 158
Agricultural extension work: reorganization under Smith-Lever Act, 87–88; expenditures for, 89; Cobb's views on, 157–158
Agricultural Hall of Fame, 257
Agricultural high schools: in various states, 38–39; in Mississippi, 39, 44–45, 53; problems of, 53–55; disappearance of, 55–56; contributions of, 56, 261
Agricultural High School Act: of 1908, 42–43; of 1910, 43
Agricultural Marketing Act of 1929, 126, 185, 191, 207
Agricultural outlook conferences, 187, 196–197

Agricultural problems: Cobb's views on, 188–189, 193–194, 204
Agricultural Publishing Company, 121
Agricultural short courses, 39, 52, 93
Amberson, William R., 227
American Agricultural Editors' Association, 171, 179, 180–182
*American Cotton Journal*, 250
*American Cotton Planter*, 119
*American Farmer*, 119
American Institute of Cooperation, 174–175
American Land and Irrigation Company, 74
American Railway Development Association, 173, 187, 197
American Society of Agricultural Engineers, 197
Appleby, Paul: and conflict in the AAA, 228–229
Archaeology: Cobb Institute of, 260
Ash Khan Crew, 259
Ashley, Roy: club work of, 112–113
Association of Land-Grant Colleges and Universities, 126, 197
Association of Southern Agricultural Workers, 197, 255, 275–276
Atlanta Chamber of Commerce, 176, 259
Austin, Alex, 10

Baby beef clubs, 99–101
Bailey, Liberty Hyde, 37
Bankhead Cotton Control Act, 219
Bayard, E. S., 196
Beeson, Bennie, 75

ganization under, 235; Cobb and ad-
ministration of, 235–236; results of,
236–237
South: Cobb and future of, 150–151; im-
pact of Great Depression upon, 206
*Southern Agriculturist*: history of, 121;
circulation of, 121, 144; ceases publication, 146
Southern Bell Telephone and Telegraph
Company, 251, 252
Southern Cattlemen's Association, 173
*Southern Cultivator*: history of, 121
circulation of, 121, 144; mentioned, 119
*Southern Farm Gazette*: merges with
*Progressive Farmer*, 122; mentioned,
35n, 172
*Southern Planter*: history of, 121; circulation of, 121, 144
*Southern Ruralist*: Cobb named editor,
118, 124; circulation of, 121, 142, 144,
171; history of, 122, 124; editorial staff
of, 129–133; nature of, 133–140; and
contests, 136–137; introduces readers
to good literature and to masterpieces
of art, 139; gets new quarters, 139–140;
subscribers, 140; territory covered,
140; absorbs *Modern Farming*, 141; advertising policy of, 141–142; impact of
Great Depression upon, 145; merges
with *Progressive Farmer*, 146; mentioned, 90, 210, 243, 244, 255, 262
Southern Ruralist Company: publishes
*Southern Ruralist*, 122; ceases to exist,
243; prints telephone directories, 251
*Southern Telephone News*, 252
Southern Tenant Farmers' Union: and
Norcross case, 225; Cobb's view of,
227; complaints of, 231
Spillman, William J.: and agricultural
extension, 87–88; and domestic allot-
ment plan, 194
Spinks, Peter E., 91, 95
Staple Cotton Cooperative Association:
praised by Cobb, 159
Steadman, Alfred D., 208
Stephens, Hubert D., 190
Stockbridge, Horace E.: edits *Southern
Ruralist*, 122, 124
*Successful Farming*, 168
Sumners, Hatton W., 196
Superior Type, Inc., 253
Swaim, John, 107

Sweet potato clubs, 102

Taft, William H., 75
Tannenbaum, Frank, 229
Tariff policy: and McNary-Haugen
bills, 127; Cobb's views on, 161, 188,
189, 190; mentioned, 126, 128
Taxation: Cobb's views on, 161
Telephone directories: printing of, 248–
254
Tenants and tenancy: in Chickasaw
County, 47; nature of, 206; problems
of dealing with, 206; basis of friction
within AAA, 223; Cobb's views on,
223–224; accusations of unfair treat-
ment of, 224; and Paragraph 7, 224–
225; on Norcross plantation, 225, 227;
Landlord-Tenant Relations Unit
created to hear complaints of, 232
Tennessee Valley Authority, 164
Thomas, J. T., 94
Thornton, Duke, 15
Tolley, Howard R.: and land use con-
ference, 186; supports Cobb, 197; re-
places Davis, 235; Cobb's relations
with, 236
Transportation: Cobb's views on, 158–
159
Tri-State Fair, 76–77, 178
True, Alfred C., 87
Tugwell, Rexford G.: considered for
Secretary of Agriculture, 194; on ex-
tension service personnel, 211; and
Cobb, 221–222; mentioned, 208
Turner, Jack, 179
Tuskegee Institute, 193
Tyronza, Arkansas, 225–228

*Union Agriculturist and Western Prai-
rie Farmer*, 119
U. S. Air Force Training Command, 253
U. S. Bureau of Agricultural Economics
208
U. S. Bureau of Animal Industry, 91, 97
U. S. Bureau of Markets: supported by
Cobb, 159
U. S. Bureau of Plant Industry, 66
U. S. Chamber of Commerce, 186, 259
U. S. Department of Agriculture: and
agricultural high schools, 40–41, 54;
and the improvement of southern
agriculture, 60; and early corn clubs,